P9-CLB-558

R E A D I N G
W R I T I N G

READING
WRITING

ESSAY STRATEGIES FOR CANADIAN STUDENTS

GERI DASGUPTA AND JON REDFERN
Centennial College

Nelson Canada

I(T)P An International Thomson Publishing Company

Toronto • Albany • Bonn • Boston • Cincinnati • Detroit • London • Madrid • Melbourne
Mexico City • New York • Pacific Grove • Paris • San Francisco • Singapore • Tokyo • Washington

I⊤P™
International Thomson Publishing
The ITP logo is a trademark under licence

© Nelson Canada
A division of Thomson Canada Limited, 1995

Published in 1995 by
Nelson Canada
A division of Thomson Canada Limited
1120 Birchmount Road
Scarborough, Ontario M1K 5G4

All rights reserved. No part of this work covered by copyrights hereon may be reproduced or used in any form or by any means—graphic, electronic or mechanical, including photocopying, recording, taping or information storage and retrieval systems—without prior written permission of the publisher.

To show your appreciation for the time and effort that the authors and publisher have invested in this book, please choose **not** to photocopy it. Choose instead to add it to your own personal library. The investment will be well worth it.

Every effort has been made to trace ownership of all copyrighted material and to secure permission from copyright holders. In the event of any question arising as to the use of any material, we will be pleased to make the necessary corrections in future printings.

Cover and interior design: Kevin Connolly

Canadian Cataloguing in Publication Data
Dasgupta, Geri, 1949–
   Reading writing : essay strategies for Canadian students

Includes index.
ISBN 0-17-604870-7

1. English language – Rhetoric. 2. Essay.
I. Redfern, Jon, 1946–   . II. Title

PE1408.D37 1994   808'.0427   C94-932434-5

Acquisitions Editor	Andrew Livingston
Production Editor	Bob Kohlmeier
Developmental Editor	Joanne Scattolon
Art Director	Liz Harasymczuk
Composition Analyst	Zenaida Diores
Input Operators	Elaine Andrews and Michelle Volk
Senior Production Coordinator	Sheryl Emery

Printed and bound in Canada
1 2 3 4 (BG) 99 98 97 96

Contents

Unit Four

Unit Five

Unit Six

Appendix A

Appendix B

Preface

The title of this book—*Reading Writing*—indicates its double approach to communication. We believe reading and writing are mutually dependent. Reading improves one's ability to recognize and create rhetorical structures, to build vocabulary, to enrich comprehension, and thus to develop personal style and fluency in writing. Writing encourages one to develop one's ideas and to communicate them effectively to an audience.

The book begins by concentrating on reading skills—skimming, scanning, reading from context—and their use in constructing writing strategies. When we chose rhetorical models, we divided them into two categories: informative and affective discourse. We admit that such a division can be interpreted as an arbitrary distinction, because informative writing ultimately attempts to affect readers whereas affective writing seeks to educate. In addition, descriptive and narrative prose (as separate from fiction) is often a component or subcategory of other rhetorical modes, and argument and persuasion subsume all other rhetorical modes. For these reasons, we separated narration, description, and argumentation/persuasion from the more clearly delineated expository patterns of organization, such as classification and cause and effect, found in Unit Four.

Unit Six, on the research paper, shows how composing the research essay uses reading *for* writing. Our reading selections were based on three criteria: brevity, depth, and student interest; all selections have been used in classroom teaching.

Appendix A offers an editorial checklist for essays. It covers grammar and mechanics and should be used along with the suggestions for revisions of essay writing found in Unit Three. The additional readings (Appendix B) have no follow-up exercises, leaving teachers and students free to utilize them as they wish. We have often included these readings as parts of unit studies or as subjects for seminar discussions and oral reports.

Acknowledgments

We wish to thank all of our students for their inspiration. We'd also like to acknowledge the patience and generosity of our teaching colleagues, in particular Diane Fagel, Carole Short, Wendy Struthers, David O'Rourke, Gary Lipshutz, and Tom Hartley. Special thanks to Jack David for guidance and excellent advice. We are grateful also for the comments and suggestions on the manuscript that were provided by several of our peers: Cynthia Brouse, George Brown College; Harriet Duer, Dawson College; John F. Green, Durham College; John Lucas, Dawson College; Roger Mann, Mohawk College; Elaine R. Mullen, Mount Royal College; Karen Pancer, Humber College; and Pat Rogin, Durham College. Finally, a word of thanks to Olive Koyama for her copy edit and to Sarah Robertson and Bob Kohlmeier for their help in proofreading and checking formatted pages.

Unit One

Reading the Writing:
Skimming, Scanning, Reading from Context

Canadian and American: Is There a Difference?

By Mayra Perea

Introductory paragraph:
A comparison of U.S.A. &
Canada introduced.

Thesis statement: limited
subject + key ideas:
  1) Environment
  2) Economy
  3) Social issues

Topic sentence for key
idea #1.

1st body paragraph with
supporting details that
explain the topic
sentence.

Supporting details for key
idea #1.

Good transition to next
key idea.

Back in my country, people would refer to Canadians as Americans. I always thought that was wrong. "But they are all the same," people would say, even when I pointed out they were mistaken. Having lived in both Canada and the U.S., I felt there were differences, even though at first glance the two countries seemed very much alike. Had I known, as I do now, the results of *Maclean's* "Decima Two-Nations Poll," I would have been able to argue with something objective and not just a feeling. The poll showed there are fundamental differences in how Canadians and Americans view and react to a broad range of topics, such as the environment, the economy, and social issues.

For Canadians, the most important problem is the environment. The Americans rank it much lower as an issue of concern. Canadians have confidence in the air and water quality of their country and are willing to sacrifice personal comfort and convenience to benefit all citizens. The *Maclean's* poll shows, for example, that fifty percent of Canadians feel that driving an automobile should, and can be, restricted further to reduce congestion, as opposed to only thirty-four percent of Americans willing to do the same. The poll also indicates that Canadians would prefer to shut down a major company that pollutes, regardless of the loss of jobs, while the Americans would be less inclined to do so. In general the poll shows that in comparison to Canadians, the Americans put materialistic considerations first, favouring the economy over the environment.

Economically, the U.S. is a world leader that doesn't depend on international trade as much as Canada does, which means that Americans have a

1

Supporting details for
key idea #2.

Topic sentence for key
idea #2. Notice that you
can place this sentence
mid-paragraph.

Topic sentence for key
idea #3.

A good transition from
one key idea to the next
is achieved by compar-
ing the two major
sources of anxiety.

This key idea is divided
into two paragraphs
because the writer has
more supporting details
to emphasize her point.

Summary of discussion.

Restatement of thesis.

Personal views.

relatively stable economic base. In spite of its status as the world's largest debtor nation, the U.S. feels secure. When global inflation rises, the Americans tend to be less preoccupied by their economic situation than Canadians are. Although the U.S. is not immune to economic hardships, Canada seems to suffer more anxiety over its economy caused in part by a combination of the current recession, the free trade agreement, the GST, and the ever-increasing national debt.

American anxiety is most evident, as the poll shows, in areas where the U.S. is weakest and most troubled. The biggest of these concerns social issues. Social services in America are notoriously underfunded, underdeveloped, and in need of improvement. By comparison, Canada is regarded as a model for social services seen in its superb medicare system. In the U.S., each state has its own version of a private medicare system that is often expensive, restrictive, and in some cases inadequate. Canada's medicare system, on the other hand, is a national government policy offering free and uniformly efficient access to basic health care.

As social problems in the U.S. grow and seem to be untreatable, fear of the future in that country mounts. One problem area of great concern is the increasing abuse of drugs and alcohol. This abuse affects all facets of American society, from the economy to politics, from life in big cities to life in small towns. The *Maclean's* poll clearly shows that such issues are very much on Americans' minds, and in fact rank number one as their most difficult problem. Canadians, in comparison, seem relatively untouched by the same anxiety although they are aware such social issues are a growing aspect of Canadian life.

It is evident, then, that Canadians are conscious of and value highly facets of society that are not as much appreciated by Americans. Conversely, Americans worry about things Canadians view as less important. Americans and Canadians may look alike, sometimes talk alike, and even share the same continent, but they see the world through very different eyes. The environment, the economy and social issues are just three indications of how they are not the same. The *Maclean's* poll reaffirms what I've felt for a long time: Canadians and Americans are truly different.

•

Discussion

Mayra Perea, a student at Centennial College, wrote the above essay in her first-year English course. The poll referred to in her essay was first published in the Canadian magazine *Maclean's*.

"Canadian and American: Is There a Difference?" is an example of a comparison-and-contrast essay. Based on your reading of the essay and the comments in its margins, write a definition of each of the following:

1. an introductory paragraph _____ .
2. a thesis statement _____ .
3. a topic sentence _____ .
4. a body paragraph _____ .
5. a transition _____ .
6. a supporting detail _____ .

Knowing these terms can help you as a reader to understand how information in an essay may be organized. Mayra Perea used reasons and examples to present her observations on Canada and the United States. Reasons explain why an idea is true, while examples illustrate an idea with specific details. Mayra also compared and contrasted her subjects by pointing out how they were alike and how they were different. Other patterns of information that writers use can include classification or process analysis—formats that will be covered later on in this textbook.

Good writing depends on careful reading. One of the best ways to learn how to write effective essays like Mayra Perea's is to read what other writers have written. Careful reading helps you develop vocabulary, introduces you to sentence style, and makes formats such as comparison and contrast familiar. There are *kinds* of reading, each with its own useful purpose. Three kinds are outlined below.

Skimming

Skimming means reading a text rapidly in order to get a general understanding of its content. It can be used to introduce yourself to the style of a piece of writing, to its format and its key ideas. Skimming is also very useful as a technique for reviewing familiar material.

Skimming begins with reading the title of a piece of writing (such as the title of Mayra Perea's essay or that of a textbook chapter). A title gives a general idea of a piece's content or states one important aspect of the author's point of view. In Mayra Perea's case the title poses a question that the essay answers. Once you've read the title, run your eyes quickly over the paragraphs in order to find any subtitles or headings (these are printed like titles, above the text) that may further indicate the scope of a piece's content. Following this read-through, the next step to skimming entails a deliberately slower reading of all the sentences in both the introductory and concluding paragraphs. By reading only those specific paragraphs, you can locate the **thesis statement**, if there is one (some essays imply rather than state a thesis statement), and get a summary of important ideas and supporting facts that are frequently gathered in a final paragraph.

Finally, to complete your skimming, read the topic sentences of each of the **body paragraphs** as they state the key ideas. Skimming should be a fast process, a speedy reading or "overview" reading of content, for you want only a glance at the more obvious features of a piece of writing, a partial understanding of the shape and extent of its content.

Skim the following essay. It is written by the American writer Kurt Vonnegut, the author of such novels as *Slaughterhouse-Five*, *Jailbird*, and *Cat's Cradle*.

How to Write with Style

By Kurt Vonnegut

Newspaper reporters and technical writers are trained to reveal almost nothing about themselves in their writings. This makes them freaks in the world of writers, since almost all of the other ink-stained wretches in that world reveal a lot about themselves to readers. We call these revelations, accidental and intentional, elements of style.

These revelations tell us as readers what sort of person it is with whom we are spending time. Does the writer sound ignorant or informed, stupid or bright, crooked or honest, humorless or playful—? And on and on.

Why should you examine your writing style with the idea of improving it? Do so as a mark of respect for your readers, whatever you're writing. If you scribble your thoughts any which way, your readers will surely feel that you care nothing about them. They will mark you down as an egomaniac or a chowderhead—or, worse, they will stop reading you.

The most damning revelation you can make about yourself is that you do not know what is interesting and what is not. Don't you yourself like or dislike writers mainly for what they choose to show you or make you think about? Did you ever admire an empty-headed writer for his or her mastery of the language? No.

So your own winning style must begin with ideas in your head.

1. Find a subject you care about

Find a subject you care about and which you in your heart feel others should care about. It is this genuine caring, and not your games with language, which will be the most compelling and seductive element in your style.

I am not urging you to write a novel, by the way—although I would not be sorry if you wrote one, provided you genuinely cared about something. A petition to the mayor about a pothole in front of your house or a love letter to the girl next door will do.

2. Do not ramble, though

I won't ramble on about that.

3. Keep it simple

As for your use of language: Remember that two great masters of language, William Shakespeare and James Joyce, wrote sentences which were almost childlike when their subjects were most profound. "To be or not to be?" asks Shakespeare's Hamlet. The longest word is three letters long. Joyce, when he was frisky, could put together a sentence as intricate and as glittering as a necklace for Cleopatra, but my favorite sentence in his short story "Eveline" is this one: "She was tired." At that point in the story, no other words could break the heart of a reader as those three words do.

Simplicity of language is not only reputable, but perhaps even sacred. The Bible opens with a sentence well within the writing skills of a lively fourteen-year-old: "In the beginning God created the heaven and the earth."

4. Have the guts to cut

It may be that you, too, are capable of making necklaces for Cleopatra, so to speak. But your eloquence should be the servant of the ideas in your head. Your rule might be this: If a sentence, no matter how excellent, does not illuminate your subject in some new and useful way, scratch it out.

5. Sound like yourself

The writing style which is most natural for you is bound to echo the speech you heard when a child. English was the novelist Joseph Conrad's third language, and much that seems piquant in his use of English was no doubt colored by his first language, which was Polish. And lucky indeed is the writer who has grown up in Ireland, for the English spoken there is so amusing and musical. I myself grew up in Indianapolis, where common speech sounds like a band saw cutting galvanized tin, and employs a vocabulary as unornamental as a monkey wrench.

In some of the more remote hollows of Appalachia, children still grow up hearing songs and locutions of Elizabethan times. Yes, and many Americans grow up hearing a language other than English, or an English dialect a majority of Americans cannot understand.

All these varieties of speech are beautiful, just as the varieties of butterflies are beautiful. No matter what your first language, you should treasure it all your life. If it happens not to be standard English, and if it shows itself when you write standard English, the result is usually delightful, like a very pretty girl with one eye that is green and one that is blue.

I myself find that I trust my own writing most, and others seem to trust it most, too, when I sound most like a person from Indianapolis, which is what I am. What alternatives do I have? The one most vehemently recommended by teachers has no doubt been pressed on you, as well: to write like cultivated Englishmen of a century or more ago.

6. Say what you mean to say

I used to be exasperated by such teachers, but am no more. I understand now that all those antique essays and stories with which I was to compare my own work were not magnificent for their datedness or foreignness, but for saying precisely what their authors meant them to say. My teachers wished me to write accurately, always selecting the most effective words, and relating the words to one another unambiguously, rigidly, like parts of a machine. The teachers did not want to turn me into an Englishman after all. They hoped that I would become understandable—and therefore understood. And there went my dream of doing with words what Pablo Picasso did with paint or what any number of jazz idols did with music. If I broke all the rules of punctuation, had words mean whatever I wanted them to mean, and strung them together higgledy-piggledy, I would simply not be understood. So you, too, had better avoid Picasso-style or jazz-style writing, if you have something worth saying and wish to be understood.

Readers want our pages to look very much like pages they have seen before. Why? This is because they themselves have a tough job to do, and they need all the help they can get from us.

7. Pity the readers

They have to identify thousands of little marks on paper, and make sense of them immediately. They have to *read,* an art so difficult that most people don't really master it even after having studied it all through grade school and high school—twelve long years.

So this discussion must finally acknowledge that our stylistic options as writers are neither numerous nor glamorous, since our readers are bound to be such imperfect artists. Our audience requires us to be sympathetic and patient teachers, ever willing to simplify and clarify—whereas we would rather soar high above the crowd, singing like nightingales.

That is the bad news. The good news is that we Americans are governed under a unique Constitution, which allows us to write whatever we please without fear of punishment. So the most meaningful aspect of our styles, which is what we choose to write about, is utterly unlimited.

8. For really detailed advice

For a discussion of literary style in a narrower sense, in a more technical sense, I commend to your attention *The Elements of Style,* by William Strunk, Jr., and E.B. White (Macmillan, 1979). E.B. White is, of course, one of the most admirable literary stylists this country has so far produced.

You should realize, too, that no one would care how well or badly Mr. White expressed himself, if he did not have perfectly enchanting things to say.

•

How much of Vonnegut's essay were you able to grasp by skimming? Test yourself by answering the following questions. Do not reread the essay before you start.

1. List the main pieces of advice on writing well that Vonnegut gives.
2. Why, according to Vonnegut, should we try to improve our writing style?
3. Write a sentence of your own (using your own words) stating what Vonnegut's essay is about.

Now, reread the essay. Go more slowly than when you were skimming. Notice how Vonnegut included numbered subheadings (e.g., 2. Do not ramble, though; 3. Keep it simple) and how they served as topic sentences for his body paragraphs. Notice, too, how he uses examples and definitions and how, like Mayra Perea, he states his personal views. You may also find names and references that will need some research (who was Cleopatra, for instance, or Picasso?). Looking up new words and references is more a function of close reading than of skimming.

Making skimming a regular part of your reading of *any* piece of writing will increase your reading efficiency and prepare you for the close reading or in-depth reading that careful readers must develop.

Scanning

Scanning, like skimming, is selective reading, but unlike skimming it is a much slower activity. It is a deliberate searching for a detail or fact, and its purpose is to locate a specified item of information. For instance, how do you use the telephone book? You do not sit down for an hour to study its names and numbers. Instead, like most people, you run your eyes over the columns on the pages to find one single name or number. Scanning is like reading the telephone book.

Scanning begins with the "something" you must locate. You know what you want, you just have to find it. As a reading skill, scanning is useful for finding a key fact or name while doing research or looking up a quick reference. It is also helpful in studying when you need to locate a formula in a textbook chapter or look up a specific name in an essay. To help make scanning a more efficient reading exercise, it is helpful to ask yourself how the material you are reading is organized. Are you searching through a list, like the telephone directory, or an essay, a report, a series of step-by-step instructions, a manual? Understanding the structure of a piece of information can save time in your search.

Reports, for instance, often list statistics in a separate section. If you were looking for a specified number or percentage, it would help you to know where the statistics are placed. Often the thesis statement in a long essay will define the sections of information to be discussed. Again, if you needed to locate a man's name or a description of an event, knowing how the essay is set up would help you to locate faster the data you are looking for.

To try your hand at scanning, go back to Kurt Vonnegut's essay in this chapter and locate the following:

1. James Joyce
2. With how many words does James Joyce "break the heart of the reader"?
3. When should a writer cut out a sentence in a piece of writing?
4. What should your attitude be toward your readers? Why?

Reading from Context

Reading from context is a third useful reading skill. When you were skimming Vonnegut's essay, did you notice a number of difficult words? Did you see any new words? You may have done so quite often, but like most readers you read on, because you gained the general meaning of the content without actually knowing the exact definition of those particular words. Careful readers can guess or give a temporary meaning to new or difficult words as they read because the other words nearby supply enough information to make the ideas reasonably clear. In doing this, careful readers are *reading from context*.

In one way, reading from context is a kind of single-word skimming. You grasp a general meaning from a quick guess. Nevertheless, it is important that new words be properly defined. You will need to consult a dictionary. Once you have identified new or difficult words, you must go and look up their meaning. Here, reading from context can guide you as to which meaning in the dictionary is the correct one. Many words in English have more than one meaning. The author who has written the piece you are reading has chosen his words carefully, so you must be sure the context of his ideas helps you find the correct meaning of the word in the dictionary.

You will face a more difficult task in reading from context when you come across an **idiomatic expression**. Such groups of words cannot be read (or defined) literally—that is, just as they are written down on the page. Consequently, the meaning of an idiom must be understood from the context.

To test your ability to read from context, look at some of the idiomatic expressions Kurt Vonnegut uses. Once you have read over these expressions in the context of their sentences, try to explain the meaning of each in your own words.

1. If you scribble your thoughts *any which way*, your readers will surely feel that you care nothing about them.
2. They will *mark you down* as an egomaniac or a chowderhead—or, worse, they will stop reading you.
3. I won't *ramble on* about that.
4. At that point in the story, no other words could *break the heart* of a reader as those three words do.
5. *Have the guts* to cut.
6. It may be that you, too, are capable of making necklaces for Cleopatra, *so to speak*.
7. English was the novelist Joseph Conrad's third language, and much that seems piquant in his use of English was no doubt *colored by* his first language, which was Polish.
8. The one most vehemently recommended by teachers has no doubt *been pressed on you*, as well.
9. Our audience requires us to be sympathetic and patient teachers, ever willing to simplify and clarify—whereas we would rather *soar high above the crowd*, singing like nightingales.
10. A love letter to the girl next door *will do*.

In the following brief summary of the Vonnegut essay, write in the missing words. Try not to use the same words the author wrote; instead, use **synonyms**— words that are different but convey the same meaning.

Kurt Vonnegut provides eight _____ to improve your writing style so that readers will not only _____ but also _____ you. First, find a _____ that you _____, but keep your discussion short. Make your language _____ and direct and be willing to _____ unnecessary words. Try to write so that you sound natural; however, you must follow the rules of _____ English to communicate effectively. A good writer is aware of the _____ readers often have. For more _____ advice, Vonnegut suggests consulting *The Elements of Style*.

Comprehension

Answer each question in your own words. According to Kurt Vonnegut:

1. How should you choose the subject you write about?
2. What kind of language should you use when you write?
3. What is the best way to say what you mean?
4. What approach to your readers should you take?
5. Why is it important to edit your work?

Analysis

1. Find some examples of Vonnegut's sense of humour. What is the effect of his humour on the reader?
2. Find some examples of references Vonnegut makes to other writers. In what ways are these references supposed to influence the reader?
3. Who is the intended reader of this essay? How can you tell?
4. In what ways does the order of Vonnegut's suggestions help a writer write more effectively? Could the order be changed? Why or why not?

Discussion

Did you notice how much a good writer like Vonnegut considers his readers? He presents his ideas with detailed examples, references, and definitions. As readers, we also learn about Vonnegut's approach to writing through his sense of humour, which both delights and instructs. Learning biographical information about Vonnegut would be another way of discovering how he, as a writer, thinks and reacts. Searching out background facts of this kind is an important facet of careful reading. Finding out about a writer through research helps readers understand not only a writer's bias but also his values and his way of looking at the world.

Does the fact that you know Vonnegut is a famous and respected novelist (both humour and science fiction) affect your attitude toward the advice he gives in his essay? His argument can stand alone, since it is logical and well expressed, but are you more apt to believe him than you would an unknown professional? Famous people are often experts in their chosen fields. The reputation of such a person has a wide-reaching influence. When this essay first appeared, it was as an advertisement sponsored by a paper company that claimed in a sidebar to "believe in the power of the printed word." The ad was accompanied by Vonnegut's signature and by a number of whimsical photographs of the author. How might the presence of these visual elements affect the reader's impression of the text?

Language and Vocabulary

What I Have Lived For

By Bertrand Russell

Three passions, simple but overwhelmingly strong, have governed my life: the longing for love, the search for knowledge, and unbearable pity for the suffering of mankind. These passions, like great winds, have blown me hither and thither, in a wayward course, over a deep ocean of anguish, reaching to the very verge of despair.

I have sought love, first, because it brings ecstasy—ecstasy so great that I would often have sacrificed all the rest of life for a few hours of this joy. I have sought it, next, because it relieves loneliness—that terrible loneliness in which one shivering consciousness looks over the rim of the world into the cold unfathomable lifeless abyss. I have sought it, finally, because in the union of love I have seen, in a mystic miniature, the prefiguring vision of the heaven that saints and poets have imagined. This is what I sought, and though it might seem too good for human life, this is what—at last—I have found.

With equal passion I have sought knowledge. I have wished to understand the hearts of men. I have wished to know why the stars shine. And I have tried to apprehend the Pythagorean power by which number holds sway above the flux. A little of this, but not much, I have achieved.

Love and knowledge, so far as they were possible, led upward toward the heavens. But always pity brought me back to earth. Echoes of cries of pain reverberate in my heart. Children in famine, victims tortured by oppressors, helpless old people a hated burden to their sons, and the whole world of loneliness, poverty, and pain make a mockery of what human life should be. I long to alleviate the evil, but I cannot, and I too suffer.

This has been my life. I have found it worth living, and would gladly live it again if the chance were offered me.

•

Simply looking up words in the dictionary cannot always convey the full meaning of language as poetic as that found in this essay by Bertrand Russell, an English philosopher and mathematician. The power of Russell's last sentence in paragraph one arises from his use of a **metaphor,** a literary device that compares one thing to another. Russell compares the force and motivation of his passions to the winds of an ocean blowing a ship. Like a ship, Russell was occasionally pushed to an extreme, an emotional edge: five hundred years ago on the Atlantic sailors believed that storms could push them and their boats off the edge of the known world.

Read over the following selection of quotations from Russell's essay and try to rephrase them in more ordinary language:

- "[O]ne shivering consciousness looks over the rim of the world into the cold unfathomable lifeless abyss."
- "Love and knowledge, so far as they were possible, led upward toward the heavens."
- "Echoes of cries of pain reverberate in my heart."

Russell's remarkable vocabulary astonishes most readers because his simple words are made to express deep feelings and complex ideas. He wrote the essay to address readers with a similar philosophical background, yet a person not familiar with his background could readily grasp his profound thoughts.

Read these quotations from Russell's essay and answer the questions that follow each.

1. "Three passions ... have governed my life." What part of speech is *passion*? What is the adjective form of the word? Write a sentence using the adjective form.

2. One of Russell's governing passions is his "unbearable pity for the suffering of mankind." *Pity* here is used as a noun, but it can also be a verb and it has adjective forms. Write two sentences using *pity* as a verb and an adjective.

3. The author's passions have pushed him "to the very verge of despair." Use *despair* as a verb in a sentence.

4. "[L]ove ... brings ecstasy." What is the adjective form of *ecstasy*? Is there a verb form for *ecstasy*?

5. Love gives Russell a consciousness of relationships. The verb form of *consciousness* is *to be conscious of*. Use this verb form in a sentence.

6. "[I]n the union of love I have seen, in mystic miniature, the prefiguring vision of the heaven that saints and poets have imagined." Write a sentence using the word *miniature* as an adjective.

7. Russell tried to apprehend mathematics, the power of numbers, spoken of by the philosopher Pythagoras. There is a noun form for *apprehend*. Write a sentence using it as a noun. There is also an adjective form. Use it in a sentence.

8. *Reverberate* is used as a verb by Russell. Change it to a noun form and write the noun in a sentence.

9. Pain makes a mockery of human life. Use the verb form of *mockery* in a sentence. What is the adjective form of *mockery*? What is a synonym for *mockery*?

10. "I long to alleviate the evil." Here, *alleviate* is a verb. Use the noun form in a sentence. What is a synonym of *alleviate*? Use it in a sentence.

11. Write in the missing words but do not use the same ones in the Russell essay. Instead, find synonyms.

Three _____ that have _____ Bertrand Russell are the _____ for love and _____ and the resulting _____ for all life. The desire for _____ brings him much _____ and gives him a sense of his own special place in the world. The ____ for _____ helps him _____ the physical universe and human beings. Finally, _____ allows him to care deeply for _____. His _____ to achieve this adds to his own suffering.

Discussion

What lifts Russell's writing above the average is the power and intensity of his imagery, some of which you studied in the vocabulary section of this chapter. Russell was an English philosopher who became famous for his writings on mathematics and physics in the first 60 years of the 20th century. In his later life, he devoted his time to world peace and often spoke at conferences and rallies for the elimination of nuclear weapons and the greater distribution of food to starving nations. His interest in both science and human affairs affected his writing style, for he wished to communicate with as many people as possible through a direct use of everyday language rather than through the heightened formal style more often favoured by scientists and academics. In fact, he became famous for his ability to relate complex ideas in a simple but eloquent manner. "What I Have Lived For" is a part of his autobiography, a book that influenced many people to take a more active part in world affairs.

Comprehension

1. What is the thesis statement of Russell's essay? Could you rewrite it using different words?
2. What reasons does Russell give for pity's bringing him back to earth?
3. Who was Pythagoras? Why is he important to Russell?
4. How does the concluding paragraph relate to Russell's thesis statement?
5. What three reasons does Russell give for seeking love?

Analysis

1. What does Russell mean by his title, "What I Have Lived For"?
2. For Russell, in what way is pity different from love and knowledge?
3. What do you think Russell means when he claims he was driven to the *verge of despair* by his passions?

Writing Suggestions

1. What has made your life worth living? Start by identifying the three most important things in your life and then, using reasons and examples, show readers in a paragraph why *one* of them is important.
2. Would you, like Russell, choose to live your life again? Why or why not? Explain your answer, using reasons and references to actual experiences in your life.

3. Compare your life as you have chosen to live it with the life of someone else you know well. How are you alike in your values, your passions, and your fears? Write this in the form of a letter to a best friend.

4. Discuss in what ways Russell's essay has influenced your thoughts about your own life. Write this either as a paragraph or as a letter to one of your parents. Be sure to keep in mind the expectations of your reader.

Unit Two

"Brevity is the soul of wit." (Shakespeare)

Writing from Readings:

Summary, Paraphrase

Summary

A **summary** is a shortened version of another piece of writing. It is reworded by the writer, who follows the same order of information as the author. An essay or a textbook chapter can be summarized. In business and government, long reports are frequently written in summary form.

Writing a summary begins by identifying the author's focus. Skim the article and locate the *thesis statement*. Follow this by identifying the *key ideas*, which are usually found in the topic sentences of the paragraphs. Reading through a second time, you can study the supporting details and choose the ones that best illustrate the key ideas.

Begin the actual writing of the summary with a single sentence that states the author's name, the title of the essay, and a shortened reworded form of the thesis statement. (In a textbook chapter, the thesis or focus is often contained in the title or a short statement of intent introducing the chapter.) Continue your summary by locating the topic sentences of the main paragraphs. Always follow the pattern of information and development found in the original piece. A summary does not comment upon or redesign information. It is a technique to condense but not to refashion an author's work.

Summary writing can be time-consuming. You may need to rewrite often, changing unclear phrases, correcting verb tenses, combining sentences, and revising paragraphs.

Read the following. It is an essay about language by Barry Chodirker, written for an audience of business people in the journal *Canadian Secretary*. Be sure to prepare yourself for summary writing by first skimming to get an overview of Chodirker's content.

What We Write Reveals How We Think

By Barry Chodirker

1   Nothing impresses me more about language than its ability to reveal who we are. Relentlessly, it tells people how we look at ourselves and at the world, exposing our values, assumptions and too often our frailties.

2   Much of language's revealing nature is rooted in *connotation,* that is, the feelings, emotions, attitudes, judgements associated with or generated by the words we use. Effective communication is often a matter of how carefully we control connotations. There's quite a difference between "strategically withdrawing" from a battlefield and "hastily retreating" from it. It depends, of course, on whose side you're on, and who is doing the running!

3   Throughout Rick Hansen's incredible odyssey, I was struck by his language. It repeatedly urged us to reconsider how we should look at Rick and others like him. Most of us, I hope, have come a long way from "crippled" with its harshly negative and stereotypical connotations. Too many of us, however, are probably still stuck on "handicapped" or "disabled," nicer words but still words which emphasize what *can't* be done. The Hansen experience, on the other hand, introduced us to a wonderful phrase. He spoke throughout of the "physically challenged." The phrase itself challenged us to look differently at people in wheelchairs, dared us to confront our worn-out attitudes.

4   Connotation, then, isn't so much a matter of *what* you're looking at. It's a matter of *how* you're looking. In that sense, it can also work against us, revealing what we perhaps did not intend to reveal but which was unmistakable.

5   Take the word "fired" for example. It has a remarkable precision and clarity about it. It is surely the only word to use when baseball managers are sent packing! Saying, however, that someone was "relieved of his duties" or "separated out of the organization" sacrifices much of that precision. Moreover, there is at least the hint that the person doing the talking can't quite accept things for what they are. Referring to prisons as "correctional facilities" is to make believe about what goes on in prison. Business people who insist on calling budget cuts "advance downward adjustments" are probably ducking responsibility. I have actually seen death referred to by medical practitioners as "terminal living" or "negative patient care outcome." I begin to worry about people who write or talk that way.

6   We are what we say. Our language is our signature. Even more importantly, we are responsible for our words just as if we had invented them ourselves and patented their meanings. For millions of people, this language lesson was graphically illustrated not long ago on nationwide television. We watched in amazement as Al Campanis, then a senior vice-president with the Los Angeles Dodgers, appeared on Ted Koppel's *Nightline,* ironically to help celebrate the 40th

anniversary of Jackie Robinson's breaking the color bar. It was soon clear that Mr. Campanis would pause only to change feet. Much of what he said, in "tribute" to Jackie betrayed instead the most sterile prejudices. When he finally noted that most blacks lacked the "necessities" for management positions in baseball, his fate was sealed. Public furor erupted. He would resign, in disgrace, the very next day.

7   Al Campanis had been a sad sight. Obviously, much of what he said wasn't precisely what he meant. In part he was victimized by his own inarticulateness. As I listened to him, I sympathized, but realized at the same time that he should have known better. He should have had the skills to handle the situation. Not having them cost him a career.

•

Once you've skimmed Chodirker's essay, read it once more, slowly, and notice the following:

Chodirker uses a variety of examples ranging from war to business to baseball.

In paragraph 3, Chodirker writes about Rick Hansen, a Canadian athlete who made a remarkable journey around the world in his wheelchair. Hansen did this to demonstrate the ability of those whom many people call *disabled*. The author refers to Hansen to show how words like *disabled* do not fairly or accurately describe a man of Hansen's courage and physical strength.

The thesis statement is located in the title. The author defines a key term—connotation—referring to our "feelings, emotions, attitudes, judgements associated with or generated by the words we use."

Summary Exercises

1. Write a sentence with Chodirker's name, the title of the essay, and his thesis statement. Do not copy his thesis exactly, but rewrite it in your own words.
2. Write out Chodirker's first two paragraphs, basing your shortened version on his topic sentences and *one* key supporting detail from each paragraph.
3. Summarize one of the examples Chodirker uses. For instance, note the examples that refer to business, medicine, and baseball.
4. Summarize in *one* paragraph the final half of Chodirker's essay, starting from his paragraph four.
5. Practise your summary skills by taking any short passage from a magazine or newspaper and rewriting it in a shorter form. Or choose a chapter from one of your program textbooks, skim the chapter, note its focus, and then summarize its key ideas following the same order of information used by the textbook's author.

Paraphrase

Sometimes students feel confused when asked to rewrite a piece of prose in their own words. Should one simply "translate" the words of the original by using a dictionary? Can a writer use the same words as the author but rearrange them in a different manner? Writing in your own words may include both those tasks, but you must remember that rewriting, or **paraphrasing**, means changing the wording as much as possible without changing the original meaning.

Here is a quotation from Chodirker's essay:

"Even more importantly, we are responsible for our words just as if we had invented them ourselves... ."

A paraphrase of this quotation might look as follows:

"Significantly, we must account for what we say as though we made up our language on our own... ."

Or:

"We must be very aware of the words we choose and their effect, for we are as responsible for them as if we'd made them up... ."

To paraphrase effectively:
1. Have a clear understanding of the passage you must rewrite. Look up new or difficult words in the dictionary. Words often have multiple meanings, and the right choice of definition is needed to reword the passage correctly.
2. Find appropriate synonyms for the main subject and verb of each sentence in order to keep the central meaning of the author. Other words, such as adjectives and some nouns, can often be deleted or reworded.

Slang

English can be both formal and informal. Formal English is used in business, education, and government. It more often follows the strict rules of grammar and has an elevated, exact vocabulary.

The most informal level of language is slang. Slang frequently changes the dictionary definitions of words and originates within a specific social group: teenagers, for example, invent slang as a kind of private language separate from their parents'. Slang is used only in speech, unless you are writing a chatty letter to a personal friend. In some instances, slang is used in journalism articles to add liveliness to the writing, particularly when the articles talk about such things as movies or rock music. The problem with slang is that it quickly loses its meaning and vitality. The following article by Terry E. Johnson points this out.

Slang: Language That's Out of Date

By Terry E. Johnson

Dave and Isobel Rosen considered themselves reasonably knowledgeable of contemporary slang until they ran into an old friend about a year and a half ago.

"We talked with him for about 15 minutes, and I only understood about three words he said," recalls Dave Rosen, a 30-year-old South Philadelphian. "And the guy's only about a half a year younger than I am.

"He told me that a friend of ours 'cracked up in a Z.' I thought he meant the guy overdosed on drugs. But I found out later that the guy was driving a Z car and got into an accident."

The problem is not that the Rosens are so out of touch with members of their own generation that they need an interpreter. The difficulty is that North American slang is so prolific and so ephemeral that it is almost impossible for anybody except the most astute students of the language to keep up with it.

"Slang is always going to be out of date," says Connie Eble, a University of North Carolina linguist who has written several articles on the subject. "By the time you and I (middle-aged adults) know about it, it's passé. When we know about it, that means it has left its control group and is into the mainstream."

The most widely accepted definition of slang is that it is those old or newly created words used consciously for a witty or satirical affect, says Stewart Flexner, a co-editor of the *Dictionary of American Slang,* currently considered the definitive book on the subject.

Thurayya Barry, 13, has never read the *Dictionary of American Slang,* but she can tell you that "decent" is the most frequently used slang word at St. Barbara's school in West Philadelphia, where she is in Grade 8.

"It means something really nice," she says. "Anything you like you would say it's decent. Like, if you saw a good movie, you would say it's decent."

Like decent, "awesome" is an old, established word with plenty of tradition behind it, but still it has been transformed into a slang word. While it once meant to inspire awe, "awesome" is now used vaguely to describe anything ranging from the beautiful to the grotesque.

"We can be watching the same thing on television and see something we both really like and I'll say it's 'baaad-to-the-bone' and my daughter will say that it's 'awesome,'" says Frank Morris, 42, of Philadelphia. Daughter Debbi is 14.

"I'd say my daughter's favorite word is "awesome"; my daughter thinks everything is 'awesome,'" says Morris, who still favors his 1960s vocabulary.

In the 1960s it was common to hear something good described as "bad," "neat" or "far out." And, primarily among those who identified with liberal social attitudes and various protest movements, almost everything important or profound was "deep," "real deep" or "heavy … very, very heavy."

While many words, including "bad" and "cool," have remained part of the slang vocabulary, the lengthy list of new entries includes "thorough," "fly," "kickin' it," "homey or home-boy" and "fresh."

For Jamie Cook, 19, getting dressed up is more than merely changing the clothes he wears to his job selling vegetables at a Philadelphia market. When Cook dresses up, he gets "thorough." "Say, for example, I had on a leather suit," says Cook. "I would be thorough."

Cook also says dressing up could be called getting "fly," "ragged" or "sharp."

"Doing it to death," a popular 1960s phrase that meant doing something to the point of excess, has been replaced in the 1980s by "kickin' it," which means doing something consistently or intensely. "If I were just doing something a lot I would be kickin' it," said Cook.

At school or on the subway, Philadelphia teenagers use the slang word "fresh" to describe something that is new or different. "Fresh" has already been used in the lyrics of several popular records, including Rockmaster Scott and Dynamic Three's hit *Request Line,* in which a teenager calls a disc jockey and asks to "hear something fresh from the request line."

In an age when many distinctions are blurred, slang tends to highlight differences that range from generational to cultural to geographic. Detroit's "What's up, doe?" and Philadelphia's "What's up, homey?" might both be inquiring as to the state of things, but in Detroit, the "doe" is a dog, or exploited person, while in Philadelphia the "homey" is someone from the neighborhood.

The use of slang is often a ritualistic method of expressing a person's eagerness to become part of a group or opposition to it. It can be derogatory. It can reveal as well as conceal secrets.

Eble says slang is sometimes used because it is not polite and represents rebellion against the status quo. In other words, it reflects general social and economic trends. In the 1830s, for example, "workie" was a popular slang word for members of a political party with a strong labor following.

"Slang has certain secretive characteristics about it," says Eble. "Its use is a way of including and excluding. Slang also has the ability to polarize. It is very much peer group-controlled and is used as a means of maintaining solidarity. Those groups that use it the most are those that need to feel solidarity and are not in a position of power."

John Lighter says that slang—not to be confused with black dialect—is prevalent among "minorities, blacks and anybody who has lived in the inner city at any time. But it all depends on your perspective. In some cases, what is slang for one person is not necessarily slang for another. Part of the fun and appeal of using slang is that you know what it means, but people outside your group don't know what it means."

In its more mainstream role, slang gives language the ability to change and adapt to new concepts and technological advances, says Lighter, who teaches linguistics at the University of Texas at Austin.

"The computer revolution, the atomic age and all the new trends in American life help create new words," says Lighter. Technology has given us such phrases as "space cadet" (a person who is out of touch with reality), "giving static" (causing trouble) and "overexposure" (the act of being in the public eye too long), among countless others.

"When there are new attitudes expressed by young people, very frequently those attitudes crystallize around a new sense of an old word or sometimes a new word," Lighter says. "The expression 'cool' is a good example of that."

The word "cool," according to the *Dictionary of American Slang,* is associated with the cool or progressive jazz movement of the 1950s.

The cool attitude became popular among Beat poets and writers of the 1940s and '50s as a result of their association with black jazz musicians, poet Allen Ginsberg says. "We were the first group of power writers to incorporate black slang and musical slang into our everyday speech," he said.

•

This article was written in 1985, and makes the point that slang expressions go out of date. Paraphrase the following slang expressions by writing them first in formal language and then in more current slang:

   a. workie
   b. It's bad to the bone.
   c. far out and real deep

What do the following slang expressions mean?
   a. off the wall
   b. It's the pits!
   c. foxy
   d. going down slow

Comprehension

   1. Explain each of the following expressions:
        out of date

> getting dressed up
> something fresh
> to run into an old friend

2. What three key ideas are in the thesis statement (paragraph 4)?
3. Johnson gives a lot of reasons for the use of slang. What are they?

Analysis

1. Johnson begins the article with an anecdote (a story used as an illustration) about Dave and Isobel Rosen. What is its purpose?
2. Why do you think Johnson quotes so many average Americans in his essay?
3. Given Johnson's examples, why do you think slang would be popular with teenagers?

Summary

Summarize the article by Johnson. Write out your first sentence with Johnson's name, the title of his essay, and his thesis statement from paragraph four, reworded. Make your summary approximately 250 words.

Paraphrase and Definition

How ambitious are you? Keeping in mind Barry Chodirker's advice about the careful use of language, how would you define ambition?

Joseph Epstein, who wrote the following essay, claims that when you define ambition "you instantly reveal a great deal about yourself."

The Virtues of Ambition

By Joseph Epstein

1   It may seem an exaggeration to say that ambition is the linchpin of society, holding many of its disparate elements together, but it is not an exaggeration by much. Remove ambition and the essential elements of society seem to fly apart. Ambition, as opposed to mere fantasizing about desires, implies work and discipline to achieve goals, personal and social, of a kind society cannot survive without. Ambition is intimately connected with family, for men and women not only work partly for their families; husbands and wives are often ambitious for

each other, but harbor some of their most ardent ambitions for their children. Yet to have a family nowadays—with birth control readily available, and inflation a good economic argument against having children—is nearly an expression of ambition in itself. Finally, though ambition was once the domain chiefly of monarchs and aristocrats, it has, in more recent times, increasingly become the domain of the middle classes. Ambition and futurity—a sense of building for tomorrow—are inextricable. Working, saving, planning—these, the daily aspects of ambition—have always been the distinguishing marks of a rising middle class. The attack against ambition is not incidentally an attack on the middle class and what it stands for. Like it or not, the middle class has done much of society's work in America; and it, the middle class, has from the beginning run on ambition.

2   It is not difficult to imagine a world shorn of ambition. It would probably be a kinder world: without demands, without abrasions, without disappointments. People would have time for reflection. Such work as they did would not be for themselves but for the collectivity. Competition would never enter in. Conflict would be eliminated, tension become a thing of the past. The stress of creation would be at an end. Art would no longer be troubling, but purely celebratory in its functions. The family would become superfluous as a social unit, with all its former power for bringing about neurosis drained away. Longevity would be increased, for fewer people would die of heart attack or stroke caused by tumultuous endeavor. Anxiety would be extinct. Time would stretch on and on, with ambition long departed from the human heart.

3   Ah, how unrelievedly boring life would be!

4   There is a strong view that holds that success is a myth, and ambition therefore a sham. Does this mean that success does not really exist? That achievement is at bottom empty? That the efforts of men and women are of no significance alongside the force of movements and events? Now not all success, obviously, is worth esteeming, nor all ambition worth cultivating. Which are and which are not is something one soon enough learns on one's own. But even the most cynical secretly admit that success exists; that achievement counts for a great deal; and that the true myth is that the actions of men and women are useless. To believe otherwise is to take on a point of view that is likely to be deranging. It is, in its implications, to remove all motive for competence, interest in attainment, and regard for posterity.

5   We do not choose to be born. We do not choose our parents. We do not choose our historical epoch, the country of our birth or the immediate circumstances of our upbringing. We do not, most of us, choose to die; nor do we choose the time or conditions of our death. But within all this realm of choicelessness, we do choose how we shall live: courageously or in cowardice, honorably or dishonorably, with purpose or in drift. We decide what is important and what is trivial in life. We decide that what makes us significant is either what we do or what we refuse to do. But no matter how indifferent the universe may be

to our choices and decisions, these choices and decisions are ours to make. We decide. We choose. And as we decide and choose, so are our lives formed. In the end, forming our own destiny is what ambition is about.

•

Vocabulary

1. Write your own formal definition of ambition as an introduction to a college-level essay on the topic.
2. Write an informal definition (you may use current slang) of ambition for an oral presentation in the classroom.
3. Are there other words you know of and could look up in a thesaurus that mean the same or almost the same as ambition?

Paraphrase

1. "[A]mbition is the linchpin of society, holding many of its disparate elements together."
2. "[A]mbition implies work and discipline to achieve goals."
3. "[H]usbands and wives ... harbor some of their most ardent ambitions for their children."
4. Using slang, paraphrase: "[A]mbition ... has, in more recent times, increasingly become the domain of the middle classes."

Comprehension

1. In paragraph one, Epstein gives a number of examples to prove that ambition keeps society functioning. What are they?
2. In paragraph two, Epstein imagines what life would be like without ambition. Why does he then say "how unrelievedly boring life would be without ambition"?
3. What do "success is a myth" and "ambition is a sham" mean? How does Epstein argue against the meaning of these two phrases in paragraph four?
4. Epstein indicates that we choose few things in life. What are we able to choose?

Analysis

1. Do you agree with Epstein that "ambition is the linchpin of society"? Write a paragraph explaining why you do or do not agree. Use your own examples.
2. What do you think Epstein means in his concluding sentence?
3. Epstein talks about society and the individual. What does he think the relationship between them is? Do you agree or disagree? Explain your viewpoint in a short paragraph.

Summary

Summarize Epstein's article in 100–150 words. Remember to start your summary with a sentence stating the author's full name, the title, and a reworded thesis statement.

Writing Suggestions

1. All of the essays in this chapter have dealt with language in some way. Can you think of an occasion when your use of English created a difficult situation for you? Write a well-organized paragraph discussing this occasion. Use examples and reasons.
2. What are the effects in someone's life of being overly ambitious? Are they negative or positive effects? Using examples, write a paragraph that discusses either the positive or the negative effects.
3. Write a short formal paragraph stating your thoughts on your current career choice or on your current experiences in college. Afterward, write out the same information in a more informal manner (as if you were writing a letter to your best friend) using slang.

Unit Three

"True ease in writing comes from art, not chance." (Alexander Pope)

Organized Writing:

Composing an Essay

Learning to write a five-paragraph essay is essential, because it enables you to select, order, and present information in a clear and logical fashion. Furthermore, the format of the five-paragraph essay can be adapted to all types of writing tasks ranging from the business letter to the research report and the project proposal. The steps you should take are as follows.

Brainstorm

First of all, an essay must have a **subject**, one idea worth writing about. For instance, a five-paragraph student essay may be about finding a job, describing a scientific procedure, or discussing why a war began. Sometimes you are not given a subject, so how do you come up with one? One way is to choose a topic you are interested in and know something about. To generate ideas and details you then **brainstorm**, which means thinking freely about ideas at random but recording only those related to your chosen subject. Set yourself a firm time frame—say, a maximum of ten minutes—and list everything you can think of. If you can't seem to put anything worthwhile down on paper, search for another topic. When you believe your subject has inspired you to produce plentiful material, you can move to the next step.

Question

Often student writers take on a subject that is too broad and therefore unmanageable. Their subject has so many angles to cover, it offers too much information to discuss in five paragraphs. With many details and ideas to choose from, student writers frequently find writing an essay a frustrating experience. It is necessary to narrow down or focus a subject.

The way to focus your subject is to ask questions: *who? what? when? where? why? how?*

These questions help you to sort out your ideas and details. For example, take the subject of driving, something of interest to many of us. There is much you could say about the costs of driving, the hazards, the joys, the frustrations. Asking questions such as the following may help you decide exactly what your essay on driving will be about:

Who drives? What makes an effective driver? When should a person learn to drive? Where is the best place to drive? Where is the best place to learn to drive? Why drive at all? Why do people drive as they do? How can one improve driving methods? How does one learn to drive a car well?

How you answer any one of these questions will depend on what you know and how many facts you can come up with to arrange in a five-paragraph format. You may find that one question will be enough to activate your imagination. However, once you have questioned and found what you consider to be satisfactory answers, which of the ideas and details can you use best to write the actual essay?

Select

Selecting your best ideas and details depends on two criteria:

1. A subject that you know will interest your readers.
2. A subject that you know will interest you as the writer.

A subject that interests you often falls into shape on its own. You must keep in mind, however, that the subject must be a worthwhile one for you as well as your readers.

You must make sure it is valid:

1. Are there enough supporting details?
2. Are the details separate and unique?
3. Can the details be verified with reasons and examples?

This step can be difficult and must be thought through with care. Try labelling your details and ideas, sorting them into groups, to see if you have a sufficient number to write into paragraphs. Check to see that you haven't repeated yourself. Once you've completed checking, you can begin to organize your selection for your readers.

Organize

Readers appreciate clarity. As a writer, you must choose and order your details in a way that best suits the subject of your essay. There are four basic ways to arrange information:

1. *Climactic order.* Arrange your details from the least important to the most important. Save the most difficult, complex, or convincing ideas for the last.
2. *Chronological order.* Present details in a series of steps or events, following a logical time sequence.
3. *Logical order.* Show how one idea leads to another, or how one idea causes another to occur.
4. *Equivalent order.* Arrange details in any order, as each one is of equal importance.

Outline

An outline is a working plan for your essay. You can write it in point form or draw a diagram. Its purpose is to give you a preliminary overview of the scope of your essay. It helps you to "see" the essay's structure and to define your audience. Write out your selected ideas and details in a brief format. You may use titles, abbreviated in point form, as in this model outline based on Bertrand Russell's essay in Unit One.

SUBJECT: *What has made my own life worth living*

AUDIENCE: *the general reader*

PATTERN—KEY IDEAS:

1. *Love—need for, reasons why*

2. *Knowledge—desire for, reasons why*

3. *Pity—recognition of, reasons why*

4. *Conclusion*

Notice how few specific details were included. The outline serves only as a foundation upon which you can build up details in a first draft. For a longer essay, such as the research paper, a fuller outline may be required. See Unit Six for two more model outlines.

Write the Thesis Statement

A **thesis statement** tells your readers what your essay is about. It acts as a brief guide to what will follow.

A thesis statement is written most often in a single sentence stating the focused subject of the essay and its key ideas in the order to be discussed.

A thesis statement is valuable in two ways: it helps the writer remain aware of the organization of his or her details, and it guides readers by letting them know from the start exactly what the essay is about.

A thesis statement must be simple, direct, and clear; its key ideas should be written in a grammatically parallel structure.

A thesis statement should not be vague or misleading. It should avoid stating the obvious. It must state precisely what the essay will discuss in supporting details.

Let us look at how one student writer used these steps to compose a five-paragraph essay on driving. After he had decided to talk about driving, he asked himself these questions:

- How do we learn to drive?
- How did I become an effective driver?
- What are examples of effective driving?

By asking these questions and coming up with a series of responses, student writer Marcelo Olenewa wrote down the following focused subject:

"I learned to become an effective driver."

Exploring the idea of effective driving, Olenewa eventually developed his thesis statement:

"Effective driving involves the mastery of vehicle management, interaction with the driving environment, and recognition of the need for courtesy."

Notice how Olenewa has three key ideas to write about:

- mastery of vehicle management
- interaction with the driving environment
- recognition of the need for courtesy.

These three key ideas have been written in parallel grammatical structure. Each idea is written as a noun phrase.

Each key idea is explained later in the essay, in a paragraph of its own. Before you begin to write your essay, you must make sure you have enough details that really explain each of the key ideas. You must also make sure that supporting details are not repeated, for repetition will give your readers the impression that you don't really know enough about your subject.

Effective Driving

By Marcelo Olenewa

When I was growing up, I had an absolute trust in my parents' driving ability. This trust was often translated by my prolonged day-dreams while my mother or father slalomed through the congested city streets; they were in absolute control. The first time I drove my parents' car fear overcame me. I did not own the same sense of confidence I had in my parents' ability to manage the four-wheeled weapon I was now piloting. However, with practice, I learned to be confident. I learned to become an effective driver. Effective driving involves the mastery of vehicle management, interaction with the driving environment, and courtesy.

When I became a member of the driver's licence club, my choices were to take the bus or to learn how to drive a car with a manual transmission. Since I had been taking the bus for too many years already, the latter seemed like a better choice. After watching my friends drive manual transmission for years, I felt like a seasoned professional; however, all thoughts of my reasoned mastery of this form of driving quickly dissipated when I was told to put the car in first gear and roll away. First, the car began bucking like a wild stallion (due to the fact that I let the clutch out too fast); then forgetting that I was supposed to be the driver of the car, I tried to squeeze myself into the passenger seat. My poor father was not impressed. After all, I told him I could manage a manual transmission car with the greatest of ease. I eventually learned to master the fundamentals of driving a car with a manual transmission, everything from up-shifting to down-shifting, speeding up to slowing down; actual vehicle management became second nature to me. This, however, was only a part of the driving experience. Now I had to put my driving abilities to the test. It was time to move from empty parking lots to the open road.

Interacting with the driving environment seemed daunting at first but became easier with practice. The perspective of the pedestrian is quite different from that of the driver in terms of having to negotiate the road with other cars around you and, sometimes, ominous weather. Rain, sleet, and snow often spell chaos to many drivers and I was no different. It frightened me. In times of poor weather, extra caution needs to be exercised. I learned quickly not to follow too close, to signal my intentions to change lanes well in advance, and to begin slowing down a good distance from where I wanted to stop the car. What strikes me as crucial is how much I have to be aware of the position of my car in relation to other cars. This reminds me of the time I was on a slight incline and my car began to roll backwards, almost into a Rolls-Royce. After that incident I make sure always to check for other cars before making any sort of move. Interaction with the environment, however, goes beyond just being aware of traffic lights and weather; courtesy is the aspect of driving that is not taught in the classroom but is taught on the road.

Regardless of how a driver has mastered his vehicle and regardless of the skill with which he negotiates driving with other vehicles, effective driving has a philosophical dimension to it that transcends mechanical aptitude: courtesy. I learned that I must abide by the notion that driving is a privilege, not a right, and that every privilege has a responsibility that has to do with respect for the laws that lend to making road conditions as safe as possible for all drivers. Driving is more than mechanical skill. Driving is common sense (something most of us seem to lack when driving a car). How often have I been frustrated by the person who insists on being a road hog and not letting me change lanes? A lesson in the etiquette of driving was taught to me in a most horrifying incident. I was in the express lanes and wanted to merge onto the collector lanes and this other car knowingly blocked the lane and I almost ended up as part of the guardrail.

There needs to be a greater appreciation for the skill required to be an effective driver. This skill is acquired only through many years of experience on the road. However, there are basic guidelines that can be followed. It is important to master the fundamentals—that is what makes an effective driver. The key is to be familiar with the car you are operating, be attentive while on the road, and always be kind to other drivers. My experiences throughout the years have allowed me to gain a true appreciation for what my parents were doing in the car while I was chasing rainbows or flying to the moon. Now I am the one who slaloms through the congested streets of the city.

•

Write the Paragraphs

A **paragraph** is a series of related sentences that develop or explain one key idea. For this reason, the standard paragraph has a **topic sentence** and a **body.**

The topic sentence states *what* the key idea of the paragraph will be and indicates *how* and *why* the paragraph will develop.

The body is made up of supporting details. Each detail explains an aspect of the key idea (by using an example, say, or giving a reason). Details must be separate and unique, and they must explain what the topic sentence tells readers. The scope and variety of the supporting details develop the key idea. Because the topic sentence controls the paragraph body by indicating its content, it is most important to write one that is clear.

I learned to drive manual transmission.

This sentence appears to have a topic (manual transmission); however, while it states what a paragraph could be about, it doesn't direct the development of the supporting details by stating how and why. It could not be an effective topic sentence because it gives no direction for paragraph development.

Look at this potential topic sentence:

I began to drive on the roads.

Again, while we as readers know what the paragraph will be about, this sentence gives no indication as to why and how the topic will be developed.

Both of these examples of potential topic sentences simply state facts. Statements of fact do not require explanation. To become topic sentences in a paragraph, they have to be improved and give a paragraph a direction to follow. Notice the following revisions:

Learning to drive manual transmission was harder than I had thought it would be. (what and how and why)

When I began to drive on the roads, I found myself in a dangerous environment. (what and how and why)

Now, these revised sentences both have clear topics and a direction for development.

In the first body paragraph of Marcelo Olenewa's essay, the topic sentence appears after two opening sentences:

After watching my friends drive manual transmission for years I felt like a seasoned professional; however, all thoughts of my reasoned mastery of this form of driving quickly dissipated when I was told to put the car in first gear and roll away.

This topic sentence presents Marcelo's first key idea: mastery of vehicle management. It also leads readers to expect supporting details that will show how difficult learning to drive a car with manual transmission was.

In the paragraph that follows this topic sentence, Olenewa makes references to such varied details as a wild stallion, his father's reaction, and methods of changing gears.

First, the car began bucking like a wild stallion (due to the fact that I let the clutch out too fast); then forgetting that I was supposed to be the driver of the car, I tried to squeeze myself into the passenger seat. My poor father was not impressed. After all, I told him I could manage a manual transmission car with the greatest of ease. I eventually learned to master the fundamentals of driving a car with a manual transmission, everything from up-shifting to down-shifting, speeding up to slowing down; actual vehicle management became second nature to me. This, however, was only a part of the driving experience. Now I had to put my driving abilities to the test. It was time to move from empty parking lots to the open road.

Are Olenewa's supporting details relevant and logical? How many separate and unique supporting details does he include?

Now, let's look at his second topic sentence.

Interacting with the driving environment seemed daunting at first but became easier with practice.

What sort of supporting details do you expect? Examples here might show how scary driving on the road can be initially. When you read his second paragraph, notice how Marcelo Olenewa finishes up the paragraph and how many supporting details he uses to develop his topic. His details range from the weather to an anecdote about a Rolls-Royce.

In his third topic sentence, Olenewa introduces courtesy, the third key idea of the thesis statement.

Regardless of how a driver has mastered his vehicle and regardless of the skill with which he negotiates driving with other vehicles, effective driving has a philosophical dimension to it that transcends mechanical aptitude: courtesy.

Readers expect this paragraph to give examples of courteous or discourteous driving. They also expect the paragraph to show that a driver's attitude is an important component of effective driving. Does Olenewa actually do this?

I learned that I must abide by the notion that driving is a privilege, not a right, and that every privilege has a responsibility that has to do with respect for the laws that lend to making road conditions as safe as possible for all drivers. Driving is more than mechanical skill. Driving is common sense (something most of us seem to lack when driving a car). How often have I been frustrated by a person who insists on being a road hog and not letting me change lanes? A lesson in the etiquette of driving was taught to me in a most horrifying inci-

dent. I was in the express lanes and wanted to merge onto the collector lanes and this other car knowingly blocked the lane and I almost ended up as part of the guardrail.

Remember, the paragraph is a *single unit of thought*. It must have a clear beginning—in a topic sentence stating what, how, and why—and it must lead readers logically through a series of related, pertinent ideas and details that develop the topic sentence. Each *supporting detail* must be separate and unique, adding information or complementing other details that *expand* and *develop* the topic sentence. A paragraph that develops a single unit of thought must be complete and must end with a logical *conclusion*, a final detail or a summary of previous details or a *transition* statement leading toward the next paragraph. Paragraphs in an essay are linked to one other with *transitions* and their pertinence to the thesis statement.

To develop separate and unique details, you must select and question each one you have chosen to include to make sure it is pertinent. To develop a paragraph in a varied manner, you must use such devices as *examples, definitions, comparison, statistics, analogies, summary,* and *facts*. Unit Four of this text offers a number of paragraph-writing strategies that define specific writing methods. In particular, look at the section on the essay of example, where we discuss typical student problems in paragraph development and suggest solutions.

The final phase of writing the five-paragraph essay is actually the beginning: readers need an introduction.

Introduction

The **introduction** is a paragraph, or in some cases a couple of sentences, that presents a general view of the subject of the essay. The introduction offers a preview of the focused subject leading to the thesis statement. The main purpose of an introduction is to catch readers' attention and interest. There are several ways of doing this: by telling an anecdote, by revealing a list of questions, by relating a startling fact, to name just three. These techniques are used to attract readers and lead them, by reference, to the thesis statement and the essay itself. The introduction should not use details that belong in the essay's later paragraphs. The information used in the opening sentences should be separate and general in content.

Marcelo Olenewa starts his essay by relating his feelings about his parents' driving ability, which leads readers toward his thesis statement. By writing about his general feelings in this section of the essay, he has given readers a chance to relate to his subject and his point of view. Readers can relate to Olenewa's personal feelings. Thus, Olenewa has caught his readers' attention.

Conclusion

The **conclusion** of an essay is essential. Readers need to have an ending that is not abrupt or disruptive. The conclusion commonly provides a short summary of the essay's key ideas, stated in different words. Often the thesis statement is presented in different terms, to reinforce the writer's focus on the subject. Writers use the conclusion to provide a closing to their discussion; however, they frequently add a statement to inspire readers to explore the subject further. As well, a conclusion can present one final detail or idea (both of which relate directly to the thesis statement) that may stimulate readers to think beyond the scope of the essay, or to reflect on it in a slightly different way. Compare the way Olenewa concludes his essay with the way Bertrand Russell concludes *his*.

Unity and Coherence

Just as the essay has to present a single focused subject, each paragraph must do the same. In each of Olenewa's paragraphs the rules of **unity** and **coherence** were observed. When a paragraph has unity, all the sentences relate in content directly to the topic sentence. No sentence should contain an idea beyond the range introduced by the topic sentence. When a writer wanders "off topic" (adding unrelated information), the paragraph lacks unity. To achieve unity, a writer must check each detail and idea, making sure it relates, discusses, and refers to the topic sentence.

One method for checking is to start with the paragraph's final sentence and read each sentence before it back to the topic sentence, asking yourself if the details relate. *Coherence* means making sentences "stick together." Sentences should lead smoothly from one to the other. **Transitions** are used for this purpose. Paragraphs in an essay should flow from one to the other as well, so connecting words and phrases or "pointing" words help readers move forward. To help you understand transitions, unity, and coherence, read first the list of transition words and phrases and then explore the exercises that follow.

Using Transitional Words and Phrases

1. **Adding a Point**

and	a second point	furthermore
also	besides	next
or	again	further
moreover	another	likewise

| too | as well as | in addition |
| by comparison | in the same way | |

2. **Showing Connections in Time**

before	next	when
previously	immediately	thereafter
formerly	lately	once
soon	eventually	then
now	in the future	ultimately
subsequently	presently	meanwhile
at this time	at present	nowadays
simultaneously	after	afterward

3. **Emphasizing a Point**

above all	in fact	especially
certainly	to be sure	chiefly
in particular	without doubt	to repeat
doubtless	unquestionably	indeed
primarily	obviously	undoubtedly
of course	truly	for sure

4. **Showing Similarity**

in like manner	in the same way	similarly
like	in comparison	likewise
also	to compare	

5. **Showing Difference**

but	nevertheless	yet
however	on the contrary	otherwise
on the other hand	despite	in contrast
unlike	contrary to	still
instead	although	whereas
conversely	nonetheless	in spite of

6. **Introducing Examples or Details**

for example	for instance	namely
as you can see	for one thing	in fact
in particular	to illustrate	that is

7. **Restating a Point**

in other words	to put it another way	that is
in effect	that is to say	similarly
in short		

8. **Showing Cause and Effect**

as	then	accordingly
because	therefore	hence
as a result	for	thus
consequently	for that reason	since
it follows that	so	thereby

9. **Indicating Chronology or Sequence**

first (second, …)	next	also
in the first place	then	

10. **Concluding**

in brief	as a result	therefore
to sum up	on the whole	thus
consequently	to conclude	accordingly
finally	as we have seen	briefly

Coherence in Paragraph Writing

The following sentences are adapted from an essay on the subject of *Unwritten Laws Which Rule Our Lives* by the author Bob Greene. All *linking* words and *transition* words have been removed to illustrate how disjointed the paragraphs would be without any variation in sentence structure and punctuation.

After reading the disconnected sentences, you will read two more coherent versions of the same passage. We have written the passage in two different ways to demonstrate the variations that are available to you, as a writer, when you are writing your own paragraphs. Which version do you prefer?

Last week I was sitting in a restaurant with my husband.
A steady hum of conversation hung over the room.
The man sitting next to me started shouting at the top of his voice.
His face was red.
He yelled at the woman sitting opposite him for about 15 seconds.
In the crowded restaurant it seemed like an hour.
All other conversation in the room stopped.
He must have realized this.
As abruptly as he had started, he stopped.
He lowered his voice.
He finished whatever it was he had to say.
He spoke in a tone the rest of us could not hear.

It was startling.
This was precisely because it almost never happens.
There are no laws against such an outburst.
With the pressure of our modern world you would almost expect to run
    into such a thing on a regular basis.
You don't.
I had never thought about it before.
As a matter of fact it was the first time I had witnessed such a
    demonstration.
I have eaten many meals in restaurants.
I have never seen a person start screaming at the top of his lungs.

When you are eating among other people, you do not raise your voice.
This is just an example of the unwritten rules we live by.
I have been thinking about it.
These rules probably govern our lives on a more absolute basis than
    the ones we could find if we looked in the lawbooks.

There would be chaos without them.
Society is disintegrating in the 1990s.
For some reason we still obey these rules.

Version A
Last week I was eating dinner in a restaurant with my husband; a steady hum
of conversation hung over the room. Suddenly, the man sitting next to me
started shouting at the top of his voice. His face was reddened, and he yelled
at the woman sitting opposite him for about 15 seconds. In the crowded
restaurant, it seemed like an hour. All other conversation in the room
stopped, and everyone looked at the man. He must have realized this, because
as abruptly as he had started, he stopped; he lowered his voice and finished
whatever it was he had to say in a tone the rest of us could not hear.

It was startling precisely because it almost never happens, there are no
laws against such an outburst, and with the pressures of our modern world
you would almost expect to run into such a thing on a regular basis. But you
don't; as a matter of fact, when I thought about it, I realized that it was the
first time in my life I had witnessed such a demonstration. In all the meals I
have had in all the restaurants, I had never seen a person start screaming at
the top of his lungs.

When you are eating among other people, you do not raise your voice; it
is just an example of the unwritten rules we live by. When you consider it,
you recognize that these rules probably govern our lives on a more absolute
basis than the ones you could find if you looked in the lawbooks. The
customs that govern us are what make a civilization; there would be chaos

without them, and yet for some reason—even in the disintegrating society of the 1990s—we obey them.

Version B

Last week while I was sitting in a restaurant with my husband, a steady hum of conversation hung over the room. Abruptly, the man sitting next to me started shouting at the top of his voice; his face was red. He yelled at the woman sitting opposite him for about 15 seconds, although in the crowded restaurant it seemed like an hour. He must have realized this, for as abruptly as he had started he stopped. Lowering his voice, he finished whatever it was he had to say in a tone the rest of us could not hear.

It was startling precisely because it almost never happens, yet there are no laws against such an outburst. With the pressures of our modern world, you would almost expect to run into such a thing on a regular basis, but you don't. As a matter of fact, when I thought about it, I realized that it was the first time in my life I had witnessed such a demonstration. Even though I have eaten many meals in restaurants, I had never seen a person start screaming at the top of his lungs.

When you are eating among other people, you do not raise your voice. This is just an example of the unwritten rules we live by. When I think about it, these rules probably govern our lives on a more absolute basis than the ones you could find if you looked in the lawbooks; there would be chaos without them. Oddly, even though society is disintegrating in the 1990s, for some reason we still obey these rules.

Assignment

Rewrite the following passage of disconnected sentences into more coherent paragraphs. Vary your sentence structure using **complex sentences** (an independent clause plus a subordinate clause) as well as **compound sentences** (two independent clauses joined by coordinate conjunctions).

1.   In restaurants and coffee shops, people pay their cheques.
This is a simple enough concept.
Yet it would be remarkably easy to wander away from a meal without paying at the end.
In these difficult economic times, you might expect that to become a common form of cheating.
It doesn't happen very often.
Whatever the unwritten rules of human conduct are, people automatically pay for their meals.
They would no sooner walk out on a cheque than start screaming.

2. Rest rooms are marked "Men" and "Women."
Often there are long lines at one or another of them.
Males wait to enter their own washrooms.
Women enter theirs.
This is an era of sexual equality.
You would expect impatient people to violate this rule on occasion.
There are private stalls inside.
It would be less inconvenient to use them than to wait.
It just isn't done.
People obey these signs.

3. I know a man.
When he pulls his car up to a parking meter, he will put change in the meter.
He does this even if there is time left on it.
He regards this as the right thing to do.
He says he is not doing it just to extend the time remaining.
Even if there is sufficient time on the meter to cover whichever task he has to
    perform at the location, he will pay his own way.
He believes that you are supposed to purchase your own time.
The fellow before him purchased only his.

Revise Your Essay

Once you've written a draft or two of your essay, you need to read it over carefully one last time before you hand it in. **Revision** is the final step in composing an essay.

To revise means to rewrite, clarify, and polish. **Revision** includes restructuring sentences, moving them around in your paragraphs if clarity is to be achieved, checking facts, adding and deleting information. Revision is difficult because most writers are protective of their writing and feel it is complete in itself simply because it exists on the page.

How do you revise an essay effectively?

There are many methods, but here are a few suggestions:

1. Write your essay in final draft, leave it for a day or two, then reread it. Ask yourself: Have I written what I truly *wanted* to write? You may or may not be able to be objective. Have a friend read your essay out loud to you and *listen* to your own words. Do they make sense? Read your essay aloud to yourself, pretending it was written by a colleague. Is it clear?
2. You should read your essay at least twice in the revision stage. Read from the conclusion back to the thesis. Does it hold together as a coherent collection of data? Does the thesis relate to the body paragraphs? If you find

your essay lacks coherence or clarity, you will have to rewrite, rephrase sentences, or change or add facts.

3. Once you feel that the facts and the format are sufficiently polished, check the grammar, mechanics, and spelling. This can be done by referring to your dictionary or the spell-check on your computer. You can also read over the points in the Editorial Checklist found in Appendix A of this textbook.

So far in this chapter you've read an essay of example written according to the format of the five-paragraph essay. This next essay, by J.B. Priestley, is a classification essay with a three-part thesis statement. In its structure, it follows the format discussed above, but Priestley changes the format—lengthening it—to suit his needs.

Priestley writes about ideology, ideas or beliefs that influence our behaviour, which he calls "isms." He divides or classifies political ideology into three distinct types. Notice that each type is stated in the thesis statement and that each is then discussed in a series of paragraphs. Also, there are more than five paragraphs in this essay, but Priestley does not go off topic: his examples and reasons explain only the three main points of his thesis statement.

Wrong Ism

By J.B. Priestley

1   There are three isms that we ought to consider very carefully—regionalism, nationalism, internationalism. Of these three the one there is most fuss about, the one that starts men shouting and marching and shooting, the one that seems to have all the depth and thrust and fire, is of course nationalism. Nine people out of ten, I fancy, would say that of this trio it is the one that really counts, the big boss. Regionalism and internationalism, they would add, are comparatively small, shadowy, rather cranky. And I believe all this to be quite wrong. Like many another big boss, nationalism is largely bogus. It is like a bunch of flowers made of plastics.

2   The real flowers belong to regionalism. The mass of people everywhere may never have used the term. They are probably regionalists without knowing it. Because they have been brought up in a certain part of the world, they have formed perhaps quite unconsciously a deep attachment to its landscape and speech, its traditional customs, its food and drink, its songs and jokes. (There are of course always the rebels, often intellectuals and writers, but they are not the mass of people.) They are rooted in their region. Indeed, without this attachment a man can have no roots.

3   So much of people's lives, from earliest childhood onwards, is deeply inter-
twined with the common life of the region, they cannot help feeling strongly
about it. A threat to it is a knife pointing at the heart. How can life ever be the
same if bullying strangers come to change everything? The form and colour, the
very taste and smell of dear familiar things will be different, alien, life-destroying.
It would be better to die fighting. And it is precisely this, the nourishing life of
the region, for which common men have so often fought and died.

4   This attachment to the region exists on a level far deeper than that of any
political hocus-pocus. When a man says "my country" with real feeling, he is
thinking about his region, all that has made up his life, and not about that political entity, the nation. There can be some confusion here simply because some
countries are so small—and ours is one of them—and so old, again like ours,
that much of what is national is also regional. Down the centuries, the nation,
itself, so comparatively small, has been able to attach to itself the feeling really
created by the region. (Even so there is something left over, as most people in
Yorkshire or Devon, for example, would tell you.) This probably explains the fer-
vent patriotism developed early in small countries. The English were announcing that they were English in the Middle Ages, before nationalism had arrived
elsewhere.

5   If we deduct from nationalism all that it has borrowed or stolen from regionalism, what remains is mostly rubbish. The nation, as distinct from the region,
is largely the creation of power-men and political manipulators. Almost all
nationalist movements are led by ambitious frustrated men determined to hold
office. I am not blaming them. I would do the same if I were in their place
and wanted power so badly. But nearly always they make use of the rich warm
regional feeling, the emotional dynamo of the movement, while being almost
untouched by it themselves. This is because they are not as a rule deeply loyal
to any region themselves. Ambition and a love of power can eat like acid into the
tissues of regional loyalty. It is hard, if not impossible, to retain a natural piety
and yet be forever playing both ends against the middle.

6   Being itself a power structure, devised by men of power, the nation tends to
think and act in terms of power. What would benefit the real life of the region,
where men, women and children actually live, is soon sacrificed for the power
and prestige of the nation. (And the personal vanity of presidents and ministers
themselves, which historians too often disregard.) Among the new nations of our
time innumerable peasants and labourers must have found themselves being cut
down from five square meals a week to three in order to provide unnecessary air-
lines, military forces that can only be used against them and nobody else, great
conference halls and official yachts and the rest. The last traces of imperialism
and colonialism may have to be removed from Asia and Africa, where men can
no longer endure being condemned to a permanent inferiority by the colour of
their skins; but even so, the modern world, the real world of our time, does not
want and would be far better without more and more nations, busy creating for

themselves the very paraphernalia that western Europe is now trying to abolish. You are compelled to answer more questions when trying to spend half a day in Cambodia than you are now travelling from the Hook of Holland to Syracuse.

7   This brings me to internationalism. I dislike this term, which I use only to complete the isms. It suggests financiers and dubious promoters living nowhere but in luxury hotels; a shallow world of entrepreneurs and impresarios. (Was it Sacha Guitry who said that impresarios were men who spoke many languages but all with a foreign accent?) The internationalism I have in mind here is best described as world civilisation. It is life considered on a global scale. Most of our communications and transport already exist on this high wide level. So do many other things from medicine to meteorology. Our astronomers and physicists (except where they have allowed themselves to be hush-hushed) work here. The UN special agencies, about which we hear far too little, have contributed more and more to this world civilisation. All the arts, when they are arts and not chunks of nationalist propaganda, naturally take their place in it. And it grows, widens, deepens, in spite of the fact that for every dollar, ruble, pound or franc spent in explaining and praising it, a thousand are spent by the nations explaining and praising themselves.

8   This world civilisation and regionalism can get along together, especially if we keep ourselves sharply aware of their quite different but equally important values and rewards. A man can make his contribution to world civilisation and yet remain strongly regional in feeling: I know several men of this sort. There is of course the danger—it is with us now—of the global style flattening out the regional, taking local form, colour, flavour, away forever, disinheriting future generations, threatening them with sensuous poverty and a huge boredom. But to understand and appreciate regionalism is to be on guard against this danger. And we must therefore make a clear distinction between regionalism and nationalism.

9   It is nationalism that tries to check the growth of world civilisation. And nationalism, when taken on a global scale, is more aggressive and demanding now than it has ever been before. This in the giant powers is largely disguised by the endless fuss in public about rival ideologies, now a largely unreal quarrel. What is intensely real is the glaring nationalism. Even the desire to police the world is nationalistic in origin. (Only the world can police the world.) Moreover, the nation-states of today are for the most part far narrower in their outlook, far more inclined to allow prejudice against the foreigner to impoverish their own style of living, than the old imperial states were. It should be part of world civilisation that men with particular skills, perhaps the product of the very regionalism they are rebelling against, should be able to move easily from country to country, to exercise those skills, in anything from teaching the violin to running a new type of factory to managing an old hotel. But nationalism, especially of the newer sort, would rather see everything done badly than allow a few non-nationals to get to work. And people face a barrage of passports, visas,

immigration controls, labour permits; and in this respect are worse off than they were in 1900. But even so, in spite of all that nationalism can do—so long as it keeps its nuclear bombs to itself—the internationalism I have in mind, slowly creating a world civilisation, cannot be checked.

10   Nevertheless, we are still backing the wrong ism. Almost all our money goes on the middle one, nationalism, the rotten meat between the two healthy slices of bread. We need regionalism to give us roots and that very depth of feeling which nationalism unjustly and greedily claims for itself. We need internationalism to save the world and to broaden and heighten our civilisation. While regional man enriches the lives that international man is already working to keep secure and healthy, national man, drunk with power, demands our loyalty, money and applause, and poisons the very air with his dangerous nonsense.

•

Comprehension

1. Paraphrase in one or two sentences what Priestley means by:
   a. regionalism
   b. nationalism
   c. internationalism

2. Explain what is meant by each of the following words or expressions. You may use a dictionary but will have to rely on context to aid your choice of definition:
   a. big boss
   b. rather cranky
   c. they are rooted in their region
   d. hocus-pocus
   e. emotional dynamo
   f. to play both ends against the middle
   g. paraphernalia
   h. entrepreneurs and impresarios
   i. hush-hushed
   j. nationalist propaganda

3. Answer the following in full sentences:
   a. Why does Priestley compare nationalism to a bunch of plastic flowers?
   b. Priestley says that regionalism nourishes people. What examples prove this?
   c. Why does Priestley say nationalism is "mostly rubbish"?

d. Explain what Priestley means when he says: "You are compelled to answer more questions when trying to spend half a day in Cambodia than you are now travelling from the Hook of Holland to Syracuse."
   e. What is the relationship between the United Nations and Priestley's idea of "internationalism"?

Analysis

1. In the last sentence of paragraph eight, Priestley changes the form of his essay. In making a "clear distinction between regionalism and nationalism," he begins to compare these two "isms." Why does he do this? What is the argument he is making here?
2. Does this comparison change the focus or thesis of his essay, or can you find evidence in the introduction to show that he intended this comparison from the start?
3. How does he bring the idea of "internationalism" back into the essay discussion in paragraph nine?

Discussion

1. Priestley relates nationalism to a desire for power. Do you think he is right?
2. Given current events, do you think Priestley is right when he says: "Even the desire to police the world is nationalistic in origin"?
3. How optimistic are you about the political future of the world? How accurate do you think Priestley was in his analysis of political states given the world events now?

Writing Suggestions

Write a five-paragraph essay with a three-point thesis statement on one of the following topics. Make sure when you compose your thesis that you write in parallel form. That is, write each of the main points in the same format. If you choose to write each as a noun, make sure you use three nouns. Do not mix up nouns and phrases. Here is an example:

PARALLEL: *I have three delights in my life: movies, parties, and skiing.*

NOT PARALLEL: *I have three delights in my life: movies, parties, and going to the ski hill. (The last five words make up a phrase. To be parallel, they should be written as one word—the noun, skiing.)*

Essay Topics

1. What are three main concerns facing students graduating from colleges and universities in a recession?
2. In what important ways has television educated young people in the past ten years?
3. What are the three worst effects of racism on an individual?

This unit's final essay was written by the Canadian novelist and teacher Edward McCourt. He worked at a university on the prairies, in Saskatoon, Saskatchewan, and wrote a number of travel books, one of them about the north of Canada called *The Yukon and the Northwest*. He begins "The Little Things" with a personal definition of travel and states his point of view on his focused subject in a three-point thesis statement. The paragraphs use examples, definitions, and personal reminiscence to develop his key ideas.

The Little Things

By Edward McCourt

The pleasures of travel are rarely confined to scenery and contacts with people. Indeed I would go so far as to say that the chief pleasure of travel is the sum of little things that happen or are seen and heard along the way—little things that linger in the memory long after the impact of big things like a twenty-thousand-foot mountain or a meeting with a great man has weakened almost to extinction.

In Watson Lake, for instance, I came across a peculiar treasure—a brochure advertising the merits of a motel association in prose that belongs to the ages. Grading of the member units began with "excellent"—nothing lower—and progressed upwards through "exceptional" to "extraordinary". And the description of the attractions of one western member of the association is something I'm sure I will cherish all the days of my life: "Air conditioning and double sound-proof walls, plus a welcome as big as the surrounding Cariboo country—vast and rugged—and hospitality as western as any cowboy ballad ... Elizabethan decor ..." It seems superfluous to add that this motel rates "extraordinary".

And what of the attraction, indeed the awful fascination, of the word spoken but uncomprehended, the phrase snatched from a vagrant breeze, the sentence isolated from its fellows that brands itself upon the brain for no other reason than the sure knowledge that being in transit you will never know what went before or came after. Thus, strolling down the main street of Watson Lake I saw approaching me through the dust-haze the two mini-skirted Alaska-bound California girls in the company of a handsome white-haired elderly gentleman wearing a flaming red shirt. The girls had been our road companions for several days now and I bared my teeth in anticipation of a brisk exchange of social pleasantries, but they never so much as glanced my way. All their attention was fixed on the white-haired gentleman. "And then," I heard him say as we drew abreast, "I was bitten by a seal. At thirteen thousand feet."

And that was all. They went their way, the girls playing duplicate Desdemonas to the white-haired gentleman's Othello ("They loved me for the dangers I had pass'd"), and I went mine: they no doubt light-hearted, not a care in the world, and I with a phrase snatched out of a passing stranger's mouth that assured me many a sleepless tortured hour. How in God's name could a man be bitten by a seal at thirteen thousand feet? Of course there was Richthofen's World War I Flying Circus but I don't think any seals belonged.

The little things. Printed words. Spoken words. And tangible objects which in ordinary circumstances would not arouse the faintest curiosity but in the extraordinary circumstances under which I so often find them in the course of my wanderings serve to oppress me with the awful burden of the unsolved riddles of existence.

For instance, the false teeth.

We found them in a deserted cabin which stood on the bank of a nearly dry Klondike creek. They sat in the middle of the cabin floor and grinned up at us. They were surrounded by dust and debris and they posed the fearful question— *where was the rest of the man?* Was he the dust in which they sat? Had he, being a careful man not wishing to destroy an expensive set, removed the plates before putting the muzzle of the gun into his mouth and blowing his head off? I will never know.

The teeth are just one more addition to the sum of unanswered questions that hurried journeys pose. Like Ulysses, but for different reasons, I cannot rest from travel. Particularly around 4 a.m. when I'm home and in bed and a seal starts biting me with his false teeth.

•

Comprehension

1. Where is the thesis statement in McCourt's first paragraph? How are his topic sentences used to relate information to the thesis statement?
2. Do the paragraphs follow the format discussed in this chapter? How do they achieve unity and coherence? How are they different from the way Jeff Haas (Unit Four) organizes his information?
3. Who is Othello? What are "duplicate Desdemonas"? How does McCourt

explain his reference to these names?

4. In what way do the details in the conclusion relate to the introduction and thesis statement?

Analysis

1. Why is McCourt's thesis statement perfect for an essay of example?
2. In what ways is the brochure described in McCourt's second paragraph so unusual? What would be the more common language of such a brochure?
3. Why does McCourt describe the scene with the old man and the two girls in the miniskirts? How does it relate to his focused subject and his thesis statement?
4. Why do the "little things" oppress McCourt with "the awful burden of the unsolved riddles of existence"? (paragraph five)
5. Who was Ulysses and why does McCourt refer to him?

When a writer makes a reference to another piece of writing or an event, he or she is making an **allusion**. An allusion gives readers a chance to compare what they are reading with their own background knowledge. An allusion may also expand readers' ideas. McCourt alludes to two heroes from literature: Othello and Ulysses.

Writing Suggestions

Write a five-paragraph essay with a three-point thesis statement on one of the following:

1. the pleasures of travelling to an unknown place
2. the problems of travelling with a friend
3. the effects of staying in one place for too long
4. the results of learning about new people while travelling
5. the changes occurring in an individual after a great trip to a foreign city or country

Unit Four

"The pen is the tongue of the mind." (Cervantes)

Patterns in Reading and Writing:

Example, Process, Comparison/ Contrast, Analogy, Classification, Cause and Effect

The reading techniques you've practised so far in this textbook are the basis of all good reading. However, the ability to recognize and follow a writer's pattern of thought, the structure chosen by the writer to express ideas, will help you understand what you read more efficiently. This unit will help you recognize an author's organizational format, and offer rhetorical models to structure your own writing.

Remember, the purpose of any writing is to share information or ideas. Organizing your writing into distinct patterns enables you to express yourself more clearly and allows your readers to follow more easily.

Patterns of Organization

EXAMPLE: Explains through illustrations or specific instances

PROCESS: Illustrates how to do something or how something happened

COMPARISON/CONTRAST: Draws similarities and differences between two subjects

ANALOGY: Describes one subject in terms of another

CLASSIFICATION: Sorts subjects into categories based on an organizing principle

CAUSE AND EFFECT: Shows how subjects can be related through conditions and consequences

I. Essay of Example

An **example** is a verbal snapshot. An example, or set of examples, works like a photograph in a magazine or a diagram in a textbook. It helps readers see and feel and sometimes taste an idea. An example is an explanatory group of words (in one or more sentences) that makes an idea "come alive" by using concrete details.

The Common Stone

By Jeff Haas

Thesis statement

Introductory paragraph

1   <u>The common stone, despite its simplicity, has guided the design and use of many tools and institutions in technology, science and politics from ancestral times to the present</u>. The simple stone has actually provided us with many things, without which our modern complicated lives would not be possible.

Key example #1

2   Technology is tool making, and tools are a human construction used to make living easier. While the stone age hammer has been replaced by ones of steel, their general design does not differ. Basic similarities can be found amongst many tools. The stone chisel is much the same as its modern counterpart. But even though the stone chisel is inferior, it helped create the pyramids and the statues of Easter Island, feats which are still wondered at. While the stone drill, powered by a wooden bow, has been replaced in workshops by electric powered steel drills, it's not uncommon to find stone drills and cutters in the modern world. Diamond-studded drills are used to cut through rock to get at oil, the staple of modern technology.

Key example #2

Body paragraphs

3   Stone, while not normally considered a part of science, has actually played a major role in scientific development. Ancient humans, without knowing it, discovered many important scientific facts. They learned trajectories from throwing rocks and spears at animals. They learned kinetic energy from observing what the rock did to the target. They learned stress factors and gravity from standing too close to the edge of a cliff. Modern science has developed geology to study how the earth developed. Stones have taught us of the shifts in the magnetic poles, and where to look for oil and metals. Thus the simple stone with its aspects of metallurgy is not so simple after all.

Key example #3

4   The influence of the stone has shown itself in many odd places, such as politics. But was it not common to settle the first disputes by bashing in the head of the opposition? Since that time little has changed except the method of delivery and the composition of that which is delivered. Stone arrow-heads were in use in Europe long after the introduction of bronze or steel. This is because stone was sharper and cheaper; obsidian, for example, can be made into knives sharper than surgical steel. The common hand-thrown stone, settler of ancient disputes, has become the hand-grenade, settler of modern disputes. Where we once made catapults to hurl boulders at opponents' castles, we now make rockets and artillery to fire on the cities of our enemies. Thus the lowly stone has helped create our most frightening achievement: war.

5   <u>The common stone, still as simple as ever, continues in its service to
humankind in technology, science and politics</u>. In fact the stone has yet to leave
the arsenal. Its deployment can still be seen alongside modern weapons in
Korea, Ireland and the U.S.A. where it is being thrown at the police or any other
likely target.

•

Reading Strategy

Jeff Haas's essay, "The Common Stone," shows mastery of the five-paragraph
essay formula discussed in Unit Three. From the marginal notes accompanying
this essay, you can see that Haas begins with an *introductory paragraph,* the purpose of which is to introduce the subject of the essay while at the same time
catch the reader's attention. It is also written to state clearly the essay's *thesis
statement.*

In an **essay of example** the thesis statement is usually a single sentence that
consists of:

a. the focused subject to be discussed
b. the *key* examples, which illustrate the subject in the order they will be discussed
c. the writer's approach to the subject, which presents the essay's distinguishing point of view

Haas chose to introduce his essay directly with his thesis statement—the first
sentence of the essay. This statement can be broken down into a number of components:

• The *common stone* is the focused subject to be discussed
• *technology, science,* and *politics* are the three key examples placed in the
order Haas will discuss them in the body paragraphs.
• The words *despite its simplicity, has guided the design and use ... from
ancestral times to the present* link the focused subject to the key examples,
but they also tell readers what Haas's approach to the subject is—his particular point of view—on the uses of the humble stone. Readers can thus
expect the essay to develop a series of examples from past and present
illustrating the impact of the stone on our lives.

The sentence following Haas's thesis statement is transitional. It links the
sentences in the introductory paragraph to the first body paragraph by using
emphasis: it briefly points out the influence of the stone in modern times.

Jeff Haas wrote this essay when he was a student at Centennial College. He
wrote it in a first-year English composition course and followed the steps outlined
in this unit on writing the essay of example. As you read his essay again, notice
that Haas writes shorter paragraphs than Marcelo Olenewa (whose student essay

on driving is in Unit Three). Notice, too, that Haas's essay places the thesis statement right at the start, as the opening sentence to the reader. The general description of the subject—usually written as an introduction—follows the thesis statement as a transition sentence. Haas decided to reverse the order of his information for a reason: he wanted to make an unusual claim about the ordinary stone. By doing so, he allowed the essay to begin with a startling fact. Haas's thesis statement is complex in another way. Readers can expect not only a discussion on the use of the common stone in three areas (technology, science, politics) but also a comparison between the stone's use in the past and the present.

The next part of the essay format to notice in the diagram is the structure of the three body paragraphs. Each of the key examples stated in the thesis statement is discussed and developed in its own separate paragraph. Haas uses definition and a series of supplementary examples to illustrate each key example clearly stated in each paragraph's topic sentence.

The last paragraph is the concluding paragraph. Notice it begins with the same words as the thesis statement. As you read essays, notice how unity is created by the use of repetition or parallel structure. Haas repeats another device: the startling fact. His final words to his readers claim that the simple stone is still a part of modern guerilla warfare. This fact, witheld by Haas until the end of his essay, is used to reinforce his points of view and to secure his readers' interest in the subject of the essay.

Comprehension

1. Using paragraph two as a model, show how Jeff Haas compares examples from ancestral times to the present.
2. How does Haas explain the meaning of the following terms from paragraph three? (a) trajectories, (b) kinetic energy, (c) gravity?
3. How many separate supporting details are there in paragraph four?
4. How does Haas keep the comparison of the stone's uses in the past and present in his concluding paragraph?
5. In what other parts of the essay does Haas use repetition as a device? Haas uses the startling statement, definition, repetition, and comparison as devices. How many of each does he use with his examples? Does he use other techniques: analogy? cause and effect? If so, locate the examples that show these techniques.

Analysis

1. Why did Haas title his essay "The Common Stone"?
2. This essay received an A grade. Why?
3. Why is it important to Haas to discuss the past and the present in reference to the common stone? Does he have a particular reason behind his choice of examples?

When you as a student writer make a habit of careful reading, you will begin to notice how writers like Olenewa (essay in Unit Three) and Jeff Haas pattern information. Haas combined examples with comparison and other techniques to present his belief that the common stone is both humble and powerful, simple yet sophisticated.

Other writers you read in this text may employ many patterns to structure their ideas and facts, patterns such as classification or process analysis—two of the organizational structures to be discussed in this unit. Reading both student and professional writers can show you the value of learning basic techniques and applying them to your own compositions.

Writing Strategy

The first step in writing an essay is to make sure you have a focus and enough content to write about. In an essay of example, the content is the development of a series of illustrations.

Writing paragraphs using examples can be difficult for several reasons:

A. *You write the same example over and over.* This is a common error in paragraph development. You write a number of sentences believing that each contains a separate and unique example, but when you read over your work you discover all the examples are really just one, but each is written in different words. In such a case, once students have composed their topic sentence, they say the same thing repeatedly.

> *I find that writing exams is a terrifying experience. I get very nervous. My hands start to shake and I feel sweat breaking out on my forehead. I can't write because my hand is not steady. I feel uncomfortable because I'm feeling clammy and my face is damp. In fact, I'm jumpy and my hands just won't stay still as I try to write and I can't control the pen I'm holding.*

This paragraph *seems* to illustrate its topic sentence but it really doesn't develop the idea very far. Essentially, the student has used only two examples— shaky hands and a wet forehead—and reworded the two a number of times. Thus, the paragraph remains undeveloped. One way to overcome this problem is to isolate each sentence (as you reread your draft) and ask yourself if each contains a complete illustration. Then ask yourself if subsequent sentences introduce related but different illustrations that clearly pertain to the topic sentence. Does each sentence show the reader a new image each time? If not, go back, make a list, and revise.

B. *You write examples that illustrate something other than the main idea of the topic sentence.* When you write quickly, you may often go "off topic." That means you present examples that may or may not relate appropriately to the topic sentence. This problem may occur because you feel you need more information to fill out the paragraph and thus add material that doesn't belong.

My brother loves to argue. Any time our family sits down to dinner, Kevin is there ready to take on anyone who wants to discuss politics, money, you name it. Kevin loves a cause, either for or against, depending on what others decide to defend. He is an expert on graft and corruption in business and can set up an attack on corporation practices rivalling any lawyer. Kevin got his degree in law at university. He wanted to practise after he graduated, but wasn't able to find a position articling because the job market was full. Kevin can argue about the "lawyer" market, too. He loves to point out how big law firms send out calls for interviews even though they have no real positions to offer. Kevin can attack or defend almost any topic concerning the government or the way we spend our dollars.

Do readers need to know about Kevin's university days? Perhaps in another paragraph, with a different topic sentence, those facts would be pertinent. But in the paragraph above, his school history is "off topic." One way to deal with this excess information is to read your examples out of sequence. While you do this, ask yourself if each separate example relates or develops the topic sentence. If an illustration doesn't quite fit, remove it and save it for another part of the essay. In the paragraph above, cutting out the data on Kevin's school days would make the paragraph more focused and coherent. Remember, rejecting and revising information are essential parts of the writing process.

C. *The order of the examples is misleading.* Often you'll find as you write that you forget about arranging your examples so that a reader can follow your train of thought without getting confused. You discover that all your illustrations are pertinent and that you have remained "on topic," but, when you reread, there is something wrong with the unity or the flow of the paragraph. This impression may stem simply from erratic organization. Above all, readers want writers to be logical.

One of the most physically challenging activities I know is the sport of windsurfing. You need a board and a sail, of course, and you need a lot of confidence. You have to know how to stand on the board and lean into the wind. I find the worst part is the cold plunge. Before you start you need to get into shape by lifting weights and getting the biceps in form. Holding onto the mast in the wind is one of the hardest parts of windsurfing. Falling into cold water can take your breath away and may cause mild hypothermia, which can lead to exhaustion if you are out far from shore. Once you've gotten into shape, mainly with bicep curls and leg-strengthening bench-presses, the handling of the board is less of a hassle.

Where is this paragraph going? There are two sets of examples, but they are confusing and jumbled and mislead the reader as to what priorities need to be set. The writer needs to rearrange the examples into two separate sections, one following logically from the other. Both sets of illustrations develop the topic sentence, but, in their order as written above, they don't seem to relate. Try always to structure examples in a logical framework: from least important to most or from smallest to largest. Logical order shows a progression or a flow of development so that readers can understand what you wish to express.

The Thesis Statement

Writing a thesis statement for an essay of example is often done after you've focused your subject, compiled a list of examples, and written out your body paragraphs. Selecting examples and finding details can be time-consuming. You may know what you need to say, but you may have to write a draft of the essay first before you can decide on the final form of your thesis statement.

One sure method for determining the validity of your thesis statement in an essay using examples is to make sure you select clear key examples that

a. are comprehensive, so that other supporting examples can be used in the development of body paragraphs;
b. belong together and relate to each other, to illustrate the subject you've chosen to write about.

How can you tell if a key example is comprehensive, that it is broad enough in scope to be broken down into smaller examples? In the following demonstration, note how a simple series of ideas is tested with a number of questions.

THESIS STATEMENT: "A part-time job gives you money, self-confidence, and freedom."
SUBJECT: part-time job
LINK: gives
KEY EXAMPLES: money, self-confidence, freedom

How can you determine that *money* is comprehensive enough to be used as a key example? Ask yourself:

a. What does money buy?
b. Why is money earned in a part-time job a good thing?
c. How much money does a student earn in such a job?

Answers to these questions, written in detailed form, would provide supporting examples to develop your paragraph. If you have written an essay in draft form, apply the same questions, reading through your first paragraph to determine if the supporting examples can be related to a single key example.

Look at the word *freedom.* In the context of an essay about a part-time job, what supporting examples would expand upon the idea of freedom?

Supporting examples:

"A part-time job gives me the freedom to choose and buy the clothes I like, such as a leather vest or a long trench coat."

"With the money I earn from my job, I'm free to go on a holiday without my parents, if I choose!"

"Because I can now afford to pay rent, I have moved to my own place (a small apartment with its own kitchen) and can come and go when I want. I'm free to invite my friends over when I wish, at two in the morning or at six at night."

All three supporting examples relate to the key example, *freedom,* and thus would validate the use of the word in the thesis statement.

The Anecdote

Another writing technique you can use in an essay of example is the **anecdote.** This can be used as a supporting example in a paragraph, and could, in the right essay, make up an entire paragraph in itself. An anecdote is a short story or incident that illustrates a particular point about a person or an object. Banesh Hoffman, a British scientist and teacher, wrote an anecdote about his friend Albert Einstein, the mathematician and brilliant philosopher who stated the theory of relativity.

> *He was one of the greatest scientists the world has ever known, yet if I had to convey the essence of Albert Einstein in a single word, I would choose* simplicity. *Perhaps an anecdote will help. Once, caught in a downpour, he took off his hat and held it under his coat. Asked why, he explained, with admirable logic, that the rain would damage the hat, but his hair would be none the worse for its wetting. This knack for going instinctively to the heart of a matter was the secret of his major scientific discoveries. ...*

In "The Great Communicator," Margaret Atwood pays tribute to Northrop Frye on the occasion of his death. She uses a series of examples, often in the form of anecdotes, to demonstrate her thesis: Northrop Frye was "the great communicator."

The Great Communicator

By Margaret Atwood

1   I first encountered Northrop Frye where so many did: in a lecture room, at Victoria College in the University of Toronto, where he taught for five decades. It

was his famous "Bible" course, considered de rigueur for any serious literature student at the time. I don't know what I was expecting: thunder, perhaps, or a larger-than-life talking statue. What actually appeared was an unassuming, slightly plump and rumpled figure, with distracted hair and extremely sharp eyes behind Dickensian spectacles. This person placed one hand on the desk in front of him, took a step forward, took another step forward, took a step back, took another step back. While repeating this small dance pattern, he proceeded to speak, without benefit of notes or text, in pure, lucid, eloquent, funny and engaging prose, for the space of an hour. This was not a fluke. He did it every week.

2   Teaching was not something Northrop Frye engaged in as an unimportant and tedious academic duty. Despite his reputation as the foremost literary critic of his own and many another generation, both nationally and internationally, he always spoke of himself as an educator. He did not lock literature into an ivory tower; instead he emphasized its centrality to the development of a civilized and humane society. As a critic, he did not write for other critics, in an esoteric jargon only a few could comprehend; he wrote instead for the intelligent general reader. His early experiences as a divinity student and preacher stood him in good stead: pick up any of his books and what you will hear (not *see,* for he was enormously conscious of the oral and even the musical values of the word) is a personal voice, speaking to you directly. Because of its style, flexibility and formal elegance, its broad range and systematic structure, his literary criticism takes its place easily within the body of literature itself.

3   That sounds fairly intimidating, and a lot of people were intimidated by Frye. I suppose it's difficult not to be intimidated by someone so brilliant. But intimidation was not something Frye did on purpose. He didn't suffer fools gladly, it's true, and he could be devastatingly ironic when confronted with malicious or willed stupidity; but he was surprisingly gentle with youthful naivete and simple ignorance. In contrast to the image of austerity and superhuman power others projected on him, he could be quite impish. His students were often startled to find references to current pop songs, comic books or off-colour jokes injected dead-pan into an otherwise serious-minded lecture on *King Lear* or *Paradise Lost,* which probably intimidated them more: Was there anything this man hadn't read? Apparently not; but since one of his major themes was the way in which plots resemble other plots—whether they are found in fairy tales, epic poems or soap operas—there was nothing he refused to consider. He knew also that the way in which we understand ourselves is less through theory than through story. In the life of any individual, as in the lives of communities and nations, stories are primary.

4   So now I will tell a couple: because, when anyone dies one of the first things we do is tell stories about them. What to choose from? The apocryphal one about how he first came to Toronto by winning a speed-typing contest? (Actually, he didn't win; but he *was* a very swift typist.) The one about the adulating woman who said to him, "Oh, Dr. Frye, is there *anything* you don't know?" Norrie, gazing characteristically at his shoes, mumbled that he didn't really know very much about Japanese flower arranging and proceeded to deliver an informed page or two on the subject. Or, from M.T. Kelly, a writer friend with whom he discussed northern-exploration journals: "He came to my book-launch

at the Rivoli! Can you picture it? Queen Street West, with the black leather? The man was spiritually generous!"

5   Or the time we had him to dinner and something burnt in the kitchen and the fire alarm went off, waking our young daughter. She wandered downstairs and got into a conversation with Norrie. Despite his well-known social shyness, he had no difficulty talking with a six-year-old, and she herself was enchanted by him. That interlude, not the high-powered adult conversation that surrounds it, was the high point of the evening to him.

6   I think one of the sadnesses of his life was that he never had children. But there are many people, including some who never knew him personally, who will feel orphaned by his death.

•

Analysis

1. Notice how Atwood organizes her examples. She uses a chronological sequence:
   a. What is the first anecdote she tells? When did it happen and what clues assist you in determining this?
   b. What is the final anecdote she tells? When did it happen and what clues assist you in determining this?

2. In both the first and last anecdote in the essay, how does Atwood show that Frye was "the great communicator"? Based on these anecdotes, what qualities are essential to a great communicator, according to Atwood?

3. In both of these anecdotes, Atwood also presents Frye as an endearing human being. What examples achieve this effect?

4. In her second paragraph, Atwood stresses that Frye "always spoke of himself as an educator."
   a. How many examples of his role as educator does she present?
   b. What does Atwood identify as Frye's most powerful qualities as an educator?

5. In the third paragraph, Atwood concentrates on Frye's personality.
   a. How does she support her contention that Frye was brilliant as a communicator?
   b. What does she mean when she says "stories are primary?"

6. In the fourth paragraph, notice how well Atwood has established the transition from her third paragraph.
   a. What is the connection?
   b. What is the purpose of each of the anecdotes told in paragraph four?

7. Read Frye's essay "Don't You Think It's Time to Start Thinking?" in the Additional Readings section. Would you agree with Atwood that Frye was a great communicator?

Writing Suggestions

1. Northrop Frye had a profound influence on Margaret Atwood. Is there anyone in your life—a former teacher, a relative, a friend—who has affected you in a strong way? Write an essay celebrating that person's qualities. Use examples and anecdotes.
2. Write an essay of example about a simple object that has great significance. You might consider, as Jeff Haas did with the common stone, how greatly that simple object has affected your life.
3. What qualities do you think a great communicator should have? Actors, rock stars, and writers are all communicators. Choose one you know about and show what qualities have made this person effective as a communicator.
4. What lessons in good communication have you learned, or what experiences have you had in good communication? Discuss, using examples from your own life.

II. Essay of Process Analysis

Process analysis explains how something can be done, step-by-step, or how something happens. In the first case, readers can follow a process and achieve the same result (e.g., repeating a lab experiment). In the second, readers can understand a process but not repeat the actions (e.g., how World War II began).

All "how to" process analyses have the same purpose: to enable readers to follow a procedure, or a series of steps, to achieve a desired result. You are familiar with a variety of "how to" process analyses: recipes, manuals, lab experiments. You will also have read in magazines or seen on television "how to find a mate," "how to practise safe sex," "how to get into shape."

Read the following essay, "How to Use Less Communication."

How to Use Less Communication

By Stuart Johns

First-year composition courses serve no useful purpose. Being able to think and express oneself clearly on paper will never be an asset. Despite the *cri de coeur* from employers who list good communication skills as their #1 job requirement, learning to write clearly and correctly is redundant. Keep all of these ideas in mind as we tackle an essay of process analysis. Follow the steps given you and you will never master this means of communication: disregard the logical order of your content; refuse to think about the mechanics of your composition; and above all, show no consideration for your reader.

When you start to write a process analysis remember that this rhetorical mode is really a procedure with a beginning, middle and end. Don't you hate the obvious! Keep your reader in suspense; whatever you do, don't organize steps into a coherent sequence. After all, if a step is missed it really doesn't matter that much. For example, why bother with an introduction? Just leap straight in. If the reader is unsure about the subject or isn't interested enough to read on, that's not your problem. The order of any process isn't carved in stone any way, so why bother being organized? When you present the steps, assume the results are obvious and don't need to be described or explained in any way. Elaboration is boring. You can achieve confusion in your reader by jumping from one unconnected point to another. In addition, don't warn your reader of any upcoming step or resulting problem; clear signals are not the writer's concern. The reader will know better the next time! "Learn from your mistakes" is a great motto to live by.

While the reader will learn from mistakes, you have no responsibility for the mechanics of your composition. By that I mean you shouldn't worry about grammar at all. Just go with the flow! Checking spelling is a waste of time; who cares about using a dictionary anyway? If these errors add to your reader's frustration, don't worry! It doesn't reflect on you at all. In keeping with the disregard for organization of steps, supply no transition words. Smooth style is for teachers of English, not real people. In fact, even the use of paragraphs is entirely optional and you could write the whole process in one long surging paragraph. However you decide to present the process, make sure it has no names, no margins, no double spacing, no pagination. Let the reader figure all that out.

Letting the reader figure it out has been the key to this essay so far. Although I've discussed organization and mechanics, our discussion has always related to the reader. With this in mind, the final step in producing a totally useless piece of communication demands a lack of concern for your reader. Don't tell your reader any essential background details and omit any stages that are preliminary to the successful completion of the process you are discussing. Assume your reader knows the meaning of any special terms you might use. Explaining something you know to someone who doesn't already possess that knowledge is time-consuming and requires effort. Finally, an air of superiority will convince the reader you really know what you're talking about.

Following these suggestions will ensure that your reader has no necessary background information and makes no allowances for possible variations in the process. Being unaware of your reader's needs will alienate the reader completely if the confusion of the process and the sloppiness of the mechanics haven't already succeeded in this accomplishment. Above all, don't relate your process to any other similar process. This might add relevance to your analysis and that is a waste of your time. Follow the steps given you and you will achieve a complete failure in communication. You will prove that being able to think and express yourself clearly is not an asset you possess. You will have demonstrated that, for you, a first-year composition course serves no useful purpose.

•

Comprehension

1. What is the thesis statement in this essay? Identify the focused subject and its key ideas.
2. How does the thesis inform the reader that this is a "how to" process analysis?
3. How is this thesis linked to the opening ideas in the essay?
4. What attention-getting devices are used in the introduction?
5. Because this is a process analysis, each key idea in the thesis is actually a stage or sequence in the process. Each stage is composed of a series of related steps. List the separate steps in each stage.
6. The opening sentence of each body paragraph states a key idea/key stage. It also gives readers a link with the previous paragraph. What is each link and how does this transition work effectively?
7. What is the link or transition between the conclusion and the rest of the essay?
8. How does the conclusion relate to the thesis and to the steps in the essay?
9. How does the title relate to the content of the essay?
10. What is the effect of repeating in the concluding line the idea from the opening line of the essay?

Analysis

If you were misled by the tone of this essay and read it at face value, you would be puzzled by its purpose. After all, who would really want to write badly, insult readers, and be illogical? As you quickly realized, the essay is **ironic;** that is, it says one thing while meaning another.

This essay is complex because of its irony, but most process analyses of "how to" are straightforward. What makes "How to Use Less Communication" challenging isn't the process it describes but the ironic tone in which it is written.

1. Based on your reading of this essay, what would you say are the correct steps to communicating effectively?
2. A **pun** is a play on words: words that say two things at once. Explain the pun in the title.
3. Why must writers be aware of readers? The essay talks about frustration, confusion, an and "air of superiority." Why are these negative things? Why should they be avoided by good writers?
4. An essay can be written in a humorous, serious, sarcastic, or ironic tone. How does the ironic tone of this essay create humour?
5. What does the term *cri de coeur* mean? Is the author using this term with an air of superiority?

Writing Strategy

Here is a list of steps on how to compose a "how to" process. These numbered steps can be applied to writing analyses ranging from a lab experiment to directions for finding something to a detailed manual of instructions. Once you've read this list, apply it to the essay "How to Use Less Communication" to determine how closely the writer followed the ten steps.

1. Start with a list. Outline, in steps, what materials you may need and/or what you are going to do.
2. Define your purpose. Why are you doing this? Define your result. What do you want in the end?
3. Are your lists complete? Do some steps or materials need to be dropped? Have you made clear all the things you must do to achieve your result? Do your lists relate clearly to the process you are to describe?
4. Order your steps chronologically, first things first. Do some steps happen at the same time as others?
5. Ask yourself: What must my readers know to repeat these steps? Are any background details or definitions of terms needed?
6. Write up the process. Are three main stages best? Are paragraphs more suitable to readers than a numbered list? How should readers be addressed? By simple commands? Through anecdotes and examples? Through long descriptive passages?
7. Write a thesis statement. Name the process you will analyze. State your purpose and desired result.
8. Write an introduction, mentioning your process and any information that would clarify why or how the process is written.
9. Revise your process analysis. Check for unity and coherence. Be aware of dates, times, measurements, transitions (e.g., *while, at the same time, before, after, first, then, at the end*).
10. Write a conclusion. Restate your purpose, summarize your stages, review the desired result.

Here is the second type of process analysis. It explains how something happens.

Reading Strategy

Because it first appeared in a newspaper and was intended to tell the general reader how something happened, this article by Leslie C. Smith uses informal language. In spite of its slang expressions and light-hearted tone, the article, a brief history of blue jeans, is very formal in its structure.

The first paragraph presents a clear thesis statement preceded by an attention-getting question: "What do an 1850s California gold miner, Marlon Brando and you have in common?" Once readers have moved on to the second paragraph, Smith's purpose and pattern of organizing her information become apparent: she is presenting a **process analysis** that traces the development of blue jeans, step by step. Since Smith is interested in a historical subject, readers are aware that this process is descriptive in nature and that its purpose is to help readers understand a series of significant events which began in the past and still have influence today. In reading a process analysis, it is essential to note how a writer arranges ideas in separate units or steps and that these units are usually arranged in a time sequence, a chronology. Notice how Smith uses dates to define the stages of blue jeans' development from the canvas tent to the designer pant.

Readers of process analysis should also be aware of how transitions are used—such words as then, only recently, until—to clarify the chronology. Examples and reasons are also essential to process analysis as they show readers *how* and *why* steps occurred. To recognize the pattern of organization in a process analysis, readers should find the thesis, note transitions, and identify separate steps.

Blue Jeans Born to Last

By Leslie C. Smith

Question: What do an 1850s California gold miner, Marlon Brando and you have in common? The answer is jeans—those ubiquitous blue pants that have become, within the short span of a baby boomer's lifetime, the very keystone of our casual wear wardrobes.

Jeans weren't intended to reshape the way we wear clothes. In fact, they didn't start out as pants at all. In 1853, they were a mere wagon load of brown canvas cloth, carted over the Sierras by a young, enterprising Bavarian immigrant by the name of Levi Strauss.

Strauss had it in mind to turn the canvas into miners' tents, and so make his fortune. But when he reached the California gold fields, an old prospector shook his head and said, "You should have brought pants." It seems regular trousers couldn't quite cut the mustard in the rough-and-tumble world of gold mining.

Being a clever businessman, Strauss immediately revised his plans and had a tailor cut the canvas up into tough workpants. From then on, it was a race to keep his supply in line with the enormous demand. The button-flied, brown canvas trousers were alternately dubbed "Levi's" because of their designer's name, or simply "501s," which was the material's lot number for reordering.

At the close of the 1850s, a sturdy French cotton, *serge de Nîmes* (hence "denim"), replaced the canvas cloth. By this time, however, many people had started calling Levi Strauss's pants "jeans," a corruption of *Genes,* the French name for Genoa—a rather oblique reference to the cotton-twill trousers worn by Italian sailors.

Jeans did not become blue until the year 1873. After much experimentation, Strauss decided that indigo was the best dye for his workpants, as that colour remained entirely consistent throughout the dyeing process. Around this time, too, he added brass rivets to the pants' pockets for better reinforcement.

Less precisely documented is the moment when Strauss first chose to add the decorative wing-shaped stitching to the back pockets of his 501s. This was a tribute to his new land of opportunity—America, whose intrepid spirit is symbolized by the bald eagle.

Jeans, in their own right, began to symbolize the rugged endurance of the American West. The favoured garb of cowboys, by the 1930s they were an established icon—one that Easterners, fresh from their vacations on popular dude ranches, were happy to appropriate.

Yet it took until the 1950s before jeans really took off. In that decade, their rough individuality made them the uniform of nonconformists, as typified by film stars James Dean in *Rebel Without a Cause* and Marlon Brando in *The Wild One.*

Anti-establishment chic carried jeans through the turbulent 1960s; and by the 1970s, they had become so much a part of our lives that they moved, along with flower children, into the mainstream. Like their wearers, they, too, were caught up in the excesses of the Me Decade: wherein designers, catering to Yuppie desires, raised jeans (and their own bank accounts) to ever more outrageous heights.

Only recently have we seen the wisdom in returning to the original, no-frills, five-pocket jeans. They speak to us of true value—not just of price, but of the tradition they represent.

Jeans are functional and down-to-earth, apolitical and unisexual. They are also fundamental: They provide a plain blue backdrop for a wealth of wardrobe options. Such versatility makes them acceptable whether worn well-pressed and dressed-up with a blazer and tie, or faded and torn with a T-shirt and sneakers. And because they tend to conform to our bodies over time, we know that they are ultimately as individual as ourselves.

Perhaps the main reason for jeans' enduring popularity is the difficulty of pigeon-holing them. There are no set dress regulations governing the wearing of jeans, no denim dos and don'ts to bone up on. Jeans can go wherever and howsoever one wishes. Jeans are, through every fibre of their being, true wardrobe rebels.

•

Comprehension

1. Locate the thesis statement in the essay and paraphrase it. Could the essay begin without a thesis statement? If not, how could it begin effectively to lead readers through the process?
2. How many separate steps are mentioned in the development of blue jeans? Number them.
3. Using skimming and scanning, answer the following True or False questions.
   a. Everybody owns a pair of blue jeans. _____
   b. Levi Strauss was the inventor of blue jeans. _____
   c. The first jeans were made from tent canvas. _____
   d. The name "jeans" was introduced in 1850. _____
   e. The word "denim" came from Genoa. _____

f. Indigo was used to reinforce jeans in 1873. _____
g. Blue jeans became more popular in the 1950s because they represented rebellion. _____
h. Today, blue jeans are regarded as a basic item of clothing. _____

Analysis

1. How does the title of this article relate to its content? to its structure?
2. How would you explain the popularity of blue jeans? What do you think of the reasons Leslie C. Smith presents for their popularity? Are they valid reasons?
3. Do you think blue jeans really are ubiquitous?
4. Why do you think a national newspaper would print an article like this one?
5. Could the story of blue jeans have been as effective if Smith had reversed the order of her steps, starting with the popularity of blue jeans today and going back into history, to the California gold rush? Why or why not?
6. How effective is Smith in holding the reader's attention throughout the article? What devices does she use to keep interest in the subject? Does she use anecdote? Does she ask questions? Does she use supporting examples effectively?

Writing Strategy

As with the "how to do something" process, in preparing to write the process of how something happened, the first thing you must do is make a list of the steps involved. You must determine where the process starts and where it ends.

In Leslie C. Smith's essay, the start of the process was 1853, when blue jeans were born from canvas tents.

You must also ask yourself if anything needs to be explained—background information—before you start writing down the steps of the process. What do readers need to know *before* the process is explained? For instance, if you were to explain how a car engine works, would you have to define the main components of the engine before you began? Would readers need to know a brief history of combustion as a preface to the process? What did Leslie C. Smith do? She provided a brief description of the use of canvas in the California gold rush. This background led the reader to the first step, which described how Levi Strauss "had a tailor cut the canvas up into tough workpants."

The *thesis statement* must state clearly the focused subject and identify where the process begins. Smith stated her thesis in the opening paragraph by answering the question she wrote in her brief introduction. She then stated in her second paragraph the idea that jeans weren't intended to reshape the way people dress. This led to her first step in the historical process.

The *body paragraphs* of the process are made up of the chronological steps that you determined in your list. Examples, anecdotes, and definitions may be included to sustain reader interest and to clarify how and why a step occurred.

Steps must develop logically. When writing the body, do not write each step separately. Group steps into *stages,* each stage making up a separate paragraph. Smith arranged her steps into three major stages. She began with details illustrating the birth of jeans in the Gold Rush. Her second stage traced the evolution of jeans as popular clothing due to the influence of Hollywood movie stars. Her final stage discussed jeans in their maturity, as essential clothing for people from all walks of life.

To create unity and coherence, each stage should be defined. Smith used dates in her essay to define her stages, but transition words and phrases also clarify stages for readers. To clarify her chronology, Smith combined with her dates words like *yet, after,* and *recently.*

Writing Suggestions

1. Write a humorous and ironic article that tells somebody how *not* to do something, making sure you give explicit instructions but using the appropriate tone.
2. Have you ever asked yourself where an object comes from? How was it manufactured, and where and by whom? (Think about your VCR, for instance. Who designed it? Where and how was it made?) Write a process analysis explaining how something you own was made.
3. Read ahead to Unit Six, on the research paper. You might want to write a historical process similar to Smith's article on blue jeans and will need to do research in a library. Ever wondered why or how a war occurred? What was the birth and development of the car?

III. Essay of Comparison and Contrast

Any act of comparison means making a value judgment. How do you decide which shirt to wear? If you have a lot of clothes, you make a series of judgments about colours, pattern, sleeve length, and coordination. For some, the choice may lie between clean and dirty; nevertheless, a decision has been made based on comparison.

Making the reader draw a conclusion or arrive at a value judgment is the purpose of writing an essay of **comparison and contrast.** The conclusion simply may be to see things in a new way because they have been set side by side.

The introduction to comparison and contrast presents the two subjects side by side and states or implies that a comparison or contrast will follow. Because readers easily recognize comparison and contrast, we begin our study of this rhetorical mode with writing strategy, through careful reading of student Sandra Stewart's essay, *"Aladdin* and *Beauty and the Beast."*

Writing Strategy

The essay of comparison or contrast presents two subjects side by side. A **comparison** shows how the two subjects are alike or similar; a **contrast** demonstrates the differences between the two subjects. Some essays of comparison and contrast (Sandra Stewart's, for example) deal with both similarities and differences.

When composing this sort of essay you must consider why you are comparing or contrasting two subjects. What is your purpose in showing the reader how the two subjects are alike or different? Do you want to demonstrate, for example, that a Big Mac is better than a cheeseburger from Burger King? Do you want to persuade your reader to adopt Marketing Strategy A rather than Marketing Strategy B? Do you want to shed new light on Tom Cruise by comparing him to, or contrasting him with, Paul Newman?

In the introduction to any essay of comparison/contrast you must clearly identify your two subjects and your purpose for considering them together. Then you must establish your approach. There are two methods of organizing your materials for an essay of comparison/contrast: block method and point method.

Block Method

With this method you concentrate on your first subject; you present all of your key ideas and supporting details as they relate to this subject. When you finish subject one, you turn to subject two and follow the same procedure.

> *subject 1 – apples*   *subject 2 – oranges*
> *Introduction to apples & oranges + thesis statement*
> *Block 1 – Apples*   *– taste*
>   *– cost*
>   *– storage*
> *Block 2 – Oranges*   *– taste*
>   *– cost*
>   *– storage*
> *Conclusion to apples & oranges*

Point Method

With this method you discuss the two subjects together in relation to point one, the first of your key ideas. Then you discuss the same two subjects in relation to point two, your second key idea. In this way you go back and forth between your two subjects until you have finished discussing your key ideas.

> *subject 1 – apples*   *subject 2 – oranges*
> *Introduction to apples & oranges + thesis statement*
> *Point 1 – taste*   *– apples & oranges*
> *Point 2 – cost*   *– apples & oranges*
> *Point 3 – storage*   *– apples & oranges*
> *Conclusion to apples & oranges*

The following essay by student Sandra Stewart uses the point-by-point method. As you answer the following questions, you are teaching yourself how to organize an essay of comparison and contrast.

Aladdin and *Beauty and the Beast*

By Sandra Stewart

There seems to be a trend in movies recently: more interest in the human element, less in hi-tech spectacle. Ironically, two of the best movies I've seen in the last couple of years that explore the area of human relationships are cartoons. Both are Disney productions exemplifying the highest standards of artwork, complex musical scores, and a strong storyline. *Beauty and the Beast* and *Aladdin* are alike in these ways, but *Beauty and the Beast,* unlike *Aladdin,* is a movie with a message.

Both movies open with a narrative voice-over, setting the scene. In each the artwork is wonderful. The story *Aladdin* begins with the terrifying Tiger-God set against a deep, dark sky sparkling with stars. Even though it's all drawings, you feel the emptiness of the open spaces, and you know that the villain, Jafar, is really evil. *Beauty and the Beast* opens by moving the viewer through a forest. You really feel as if you are part of the scenery. Even though it's all a cartoon, the camera leads the eyes of the audience deeper through the tangled growth of forest bushes. What amazes me is how the cartoonists managed to give depth and perspective to that forest. In *Aladdin* the artwork is at its most brilliant in the wild carpet-rides, first through the cave of treasures and then in the romantic flight over the countryside that Aladdin and Jasmine take. In the case of *Aladdin,* the star is undoubtedly the Genie. The changes in his shape and size are so fast. This is amazing, especially when fluid movement is not sacrificed to that rapid pace. *Beauty and the Beast* excels in the flowing movements of all its characters, but especially Belle. She moves like a real ballerina with none of the jerkiness you'd expect from watching Saturday morning cartoons. In addition, Belle's face is so expressive. Her acting is better than some Hollywood movie stars. Moods are shown and she has this unruly lock of hair that is always falling across her face and which she brushes aside gracefully. It is this attention to "real" detail that makes this movie so brilliant technically.

The quality of the music in each movie is another example of attention to detail. Part of the energy in *Aladdin* comes from its musical score. The songs, with the exception of the beautiful and romantic "New World," are really lively and entertaining. My particular favourites are the ones my little brother likes best, "Prince Ali" and "A Friend Like Me." The talents of Robin Williams, who plays the Genie, are really outstanding. Just as *Aladdin* allows real actors a chance to shine, so does *Beauty and the Beast.* The spectacular "Be Our Guest" would be a showstopper on stage. Jerry Orbach sings his heart out as Lumière in this particular song. The romantic ballad "Beauty and the Beast" is so melodic that my little brother, who was only three and a half at the time, came out of the movie theatre singing it.

Both of the movies are based on really well-loved fairy stories. They have strong plots which everyone knows and the Disney writers have adapted to suit today's society. In *Aladdin,* Princess Jasmine isn't only a "girl" expecting to be married off. She has her own strong personality and demands the right to choose whom she'll marry. She also helps Aladdin overcome the evil Jafar, so that they can "live happily ever after." However, it is in *Beauty and the Beast* that the most powerful changes to the fairy tale have been made. Belle is definitely the star of this movie, and again she's not a weak little girl. In the movie, Belle is a more fully developed character than in the fairy story. She's an active, intelligent modern woman who respects education more than good looks. She really despises the "macho" Gaston. Gaston is an addition to the original fairy story and this character really modernizes the plot. Through Gaston, the movie is able to make us think about "jock" behaviour, mob violence, and propaganda. It's critical of all of these things. *Beauty and the Beast* has a moral that *Aladdin* doesn't. It's more than a story. This is the real difference between the two movies. *Beauty and the Beast* shows how powerful and fragile love is. Even my little brother knew that this movie showed us that real love is for what a person is and not what a person looks like. He could see that the Beast became a handsome Prince only because he and Belle loved each other.

Well, I hope I've convinced you to see these movies. They're both on video now. Believe me you'll enjoy both of them not only because they are spectacular and entertaining but also because they teach you something about human relationships in a very realistic way. If you're embarrassed renting them, borrow a kid to accompany you to the video store. You'll be glad you did.

•

Introduction

1. In her introductory paragraph, Stewart identifies her two subjects. What are they?
2. What is her thesis?
3. What are the key ideas she will use to compare/contrast her two subjects?
4. What does Stewart say is her purpose in making this comparison/contrast?

Body Paragraphs

In this section of her essay, Stewart takes each key idea and develops it point by point in a paragraph of its own. She discusses both movies in each paragraph, comparing them on the basis of a key idea.

5. Based on your identification of the key ideas in the essay's introduction, find the topic sentence in each paragraph.
6. If she had chosen the block-by-block method of development, Stewart would have concentrated first on *Aladdin* and then on *Beauty and the Beast*. Using Stewart's key ideas and her supporting details write an outline for this essay using the block-by-block method.

Columbus and the Moon

By Tom Wolfe

1   The National Aeronautics and Space Administration's moon landing 10 years ago today was a Government project, but then so was Columbus's voyage to America in 1492. The Government, in Columbus's case, was the Spanish Court of Ferdinand and Isabella. Spain was engaged in a sea race with Portugal in much the same way that the United States would be caught up in a space race with the Soviet Union four and a half centuries later.

2   The race in 1492 was to create the first shipping lane to Asia. The Portuguese expeditions had always sailed east, around the southern tip of Africa. Columbus decided to head due west, across open ocean, a scheme that was feasible only thanks to a recent invention—the magnetic ship's compass. Until then ships had stayed close to the great land masses even for the longest voyages. Likewise, it was only thanks to an invention of the 1940's and early 1950's, the high-speed electronic computer, that NASA would even consider propelling astronauts out of the Earth's orbit and toward the moon.

3   Both NASA and Columbus made not one but a series of voyages. NASA landed men on six different parts of the moon. Columbus made four voyages to different parts of what he remained convinced was the east coast of Asia. As a result both NASA and Columbus had to keep coming back to the Government with their hands out, pleading for refinancing. In each case the reply of the Government became, after a few years: "This is all very impressive, but what earthly good is it to anyone back home?"

4   Columbus was reduced to making the most desperate claims. When he first reached land in 1492 at San Salvador, off Cuba, he expected to find gold, or at least spices. The Arawak Indians were awed by the strangers and their ships, which they believed had descended from the sky, and they presented them with their most prized possessions, live parrots and balls of cotton. Columbus soon set them digging for gold, which didn't exist. So he brought back reports of fabulous riches in the form of manpower; which is to say, slaves. He was not speaking of the Arawaks, however. With the exception of criminals and prisoners of war, he was supposed to civilize all natives and convert them to Christianity. He was talking about the Carib Indians, who were cannibals and therefore qualified as criminals. The Caribs would fight down to the last unbroken bone rather than endure captivity, and few even survived the voyages back to Spain. By the end of Columbus's second voyage, in 1496, the Government was becoming testy. A great deal of wealth was going into voyages to Asia, and very little was coming back. Columbus made his men swear to return to Spain saying that they had not only reached the Asian mainland, they had heard Japanese spoken.

5   Likewise by the early 1970's, it was clear that the moon was in economic terms pretty much what it looked like from Earth, a gray rock. NASA, in the quest for appropriations, was reduced to publicizing the "spinoffs" of the space program. These included Teflon-coated frying pans, a ballpoint pen that would write in a weightless environment, and a computerized biosensor system that would enable doctors to treat heart patients without making house calls. On the whole, not a giant step for mankind.

6   In 1493, after his first voyage, Columbus had ridden through Barcelona at the side of King Ferdinand in the position once occupied by Ferdinand's late son, Juan. By 1500, the bad-mouthing of Columbus had reached the point where he was put in chains at the conclusion of his third voyage and returned to Spain in disgrace. NASA suffered no such ignominy, of course, but by July 20, 1974, the fifth anniversary of the landing of Apollo 11, things were grim enough. The public had become gloriously bored by space exploration. The fifth anniversary celebration consisted mainly of about 200 souls, mostly NASA people, sitting on folding chairs underneath a camp-meeting canopy on the marble prairie outside the old Smithsonian Air Museum in Washington listening to speeches by Neil Armstrong, Michael Collins, and Buzz Aldrin and watching the caloric waves ripple.

7   Extraordinary rumors had begun to circulate about the astronauts. The most lurid said that trips to the moon, and even into earth orbit, had so traumatized the men, they had fallen victim to religious and spiritualist manias or plain madness. (Of the total 73 astronauts chosen, one, Aldrin, is known to have suffered from depression, rooted, as his own memoir makes clear, in matters that had nothing to do with space flight. Two teamed up in an evangelical organization, and one set up a foundation for the scientific study of psychic phenomena—interests the three of them had developed long before they flew in space.) The NASA budget, meanwhile, had been reduced to the light-bill level.

8   Columbus died in 1509, nearly broke and stripped of most of his honours as Spain's Admiral of the Ocean, a title he preferred. It was only later that history began to look upon him not as an adventurer who had tried and failed to bring home gold—but as a man with a supernatural sense of destiny, whose true glory was his willingness to plunge into the unknown, including the remotest parts of the universe he could hope to reach.

9   NASA still lives, albeit in reduced circumstances, and whether or not history will treat NASA like the admiral is hard to say.

10   The idea that the exploration of the rest of the universe is its own reward is not very popular, and NASA is forced to keep talking about things such as bigger communications satellites that will enable live television transmission of European soccer games at a fraction of the current cost. Such notions as "building a bridge to the stars for mankind" do not light up the sky today—but may yet.

•

Comprehension

1. Which two things are being compared in this essay?
2. Identify the thesis of this essay.
3. Is this essay developed by using the point-by-point or the block-by-block method?
4. What points of comparison does Wolfe make between Columbus's voyages and NASA's forays into space?
5. Why and how were the governments involved in each of these explorations?

6. What is the purpose of the various anecdotes Wolfe uses?
7. How did rumour affect the reputations of Columbus and the astronauts?
8. How optimistic is Wolfe about NASA's future? What clues led to your answer?

Analysis

1. What revelation does the reader experience from the comparison of Columbus's voyages with NASA's space travels?
2. What is the purpose in comparing these two subjects?
3. Explain the allusion in paragraph five, "On the whole, not a giant step for mankind."
4. Were the voyages of Columbus glorious achievements or merely self-serving exploits? What is Tom Wolfe's position on this? How do you know?
5. What is the implication of placing the "exploration of the rest of the universe" alongside the idea of transmitting "European soccer games at a fraction of the current cost"?

Rachel Carson draws comparisons and contrasts in her essay, "A Fable for Tomorrow," using the block method.

A Fable for Tomorrow

By Rachel Carson

1   There was once a town in the heart of America where all life seemed to live in harmony with its surroundings. The town lay in the midst of a checkerboard of prosperous farms, with fields of grain and hillsides of orchards where, in spring, white clouds of bloom drifted above the green fields. In autumn, oak and maple and birch set up a blaze of color that flamed and flickered across a backdrop of pines. The foxes barked in the hills and deer silently crossed the fields, half hidden in the mists of the fall mornings.

2   Along the roads, laurel, viburnum and alder, great ferns and wildflowers delighted the traveler's eye through much of the year. Even in winter the roadsides were places of beauty, where countless birds came to feed on the berries and on the seed heads of the dried weeds rising above the snow. The countryside was, in fact, famous for the abundance and variety of its bird life, and when the flood of migrants was pouring through in spring and fall people traveled from great distances to observe them. Others came to fish the streams, which flowed clear and cold out of the hills and contained shady pools where trout lay. So it had been from the days many years ago when the first settlers raised their houses, sank their wells, and built their barns.

3   Then a strange blight crept over the area and everything began to change. Some evil spell had settled on the community: mysterious maladies swept the

flocks of chickens; the cattle and sheep sickened and died. Everywhere was a shadow of death. The farmers spoke of much illness among their families. In the town the doctors had become more and more puzzled by new kinds of sickness appearing among their patients. There had been several sudden and unexplained deaths not only among adults but even among children, who would be stricken suddenly while at play and die within a few hours.

4   There was a strange stillness. The birds, for example—where had they gone? Many people spoke of them, puzzled and disturbed. The feeding stations in the backyards were deserted. The few birds seen anywhere were moribund; they trembled violently and could not fly. It was a spring without voices. On the mornings that had once throbbed with the dawn chorus of robins, catbirds, doves, jays, wrens, and scores of other bird voices there was no sound; only silence lay over the fields and woods and marsh.

5   On the farms the hens brooded, but no chicks hatched. The farmers complained that they were unable to raise any pigs—the litters were small and the young survived only a few days. The apple trees were coming into bloom but no bees droned among the blossoms, so there was no pollination and there would be no fruit.

6   The roadsides, once so attractive, were now lined with browned and withered vegetation as though swept by fire. These, too, were silent, deserted by all living things. Even the streams were now lifeless. Anglers no longer visited them, for all the fish had died.

7   In the gutters under the eaves and between the shingles of the roofs, a white granular powder still showed a few patches; some weeks before it had fallen like snow upon the roofs and the lawns, the fields and streams. No witchcraft, no enemy action had silenced the rebirth of new life in this stricken world. The people had done it themselves.

8   This town does not actually exist, but it might easily have a thousand counterparts in America or elsewhere in the world. I know of no community that has experienced all the misfortunes I describe. Yet every one of these disasters has actually happened somewhere, and many real communities have already suffered a substantial number of them. A grim specter has crept upon us almost unnoticed, and this imagined tragedy may easily become a stark reality we all shall know.

•

Analysis

1. Carson begins her essay without a formal introduction. What are her two subjects? Because she develops the essay in block method, she concentrates on subject one before turning to subject two. Which paragraphs discuss subject two?
2. Is there a thesis statement? If so, where does Carson place it?
3. Identify Carson's key ideas in each block.
4. Why does Carson devote so much of her supporting detail to bird life?
5. What is her purpose in discussing the "town in the heart of America"?

6. Identify the order of her key ideas in her first subject. What is the order of the key ideas in the block of paragraphs discussing her second subject?
7. The discussion of her second subject is substantially longer than her discussion of the first. What details does she add?
8. Her final two paragraphs provide an explanation, a cause for the changes discussed in the essay. What effect does Carson produce by placing this information at the end of her essay?
9. Do you think this essay could have the same impact if it had been written point-by-point?

Writing Suggestions

1. Compare and contrast two movies, TV shows, or books that you have enjoyed—or not enjoyed.
2. "There are things I will tell my children that my parents never told me." Compare and contrast the attitudes and behaviours of your generation with those of your parents' generation.

IV. Essay of Analogy

"Life is like a bowl of cherries; sometimes it's the pits."

Analogy is a device related to comparison and contrast. When you use an analogy you compare two apparently unlike terms (life and the bowl of cherries). The purpose of the comparison is to explain only the "real" subject (life), not the other item (a bowl of cherries). The comparison, because it is a surprising one, forces the reader to think about the "real" subject in a new way.

In the following brief article by Anthony Lukas, life and pinball are compared. After his first sentence, Lukas doesn't mention life (the "real" subject) directly again until the final sentence. He lets his discussion of pinball represent what he wants to say about life.

As you read through the article, list the similarities between the game of pinball and "the game of life" as Lukas sees them.

In what order does Lukas present these comparisons? Do you think Lukas could have strengthened his analogy by pointing out the contrasts between pinball and life?

Pinball

By J. Anthony Lukas

Pinball is a metaphor for life, pitting man's skill, nerve, persistence, and luck against the perverse machinery of human existence. The playfield is rich with rewards: targets that bring huge scores, bright lights, chiming bells, free balls, and extra games. But it is replete with perils, too: culs-de-sac, traps, gutters, and gobble holes down which the ball may disappear forever.

Each pull of the plunger launches the ball into a miniature universe of incalculable possibilities. As the steel sphere hurtles into the eclipse at the top of the playfield, it hangs for a moment in exquisite tension between triumph and disaster. Down one lane lies a hole worth thousands, down another a sickening lurch to oblivion. The ball trembles on the lip, seeming to lean first one way, then the other.

A player is not powerless to control the ball's wild flight, any more than man is powerless to control his own life. He may nudge the machine with hands, arms, or hips, jogging it just enough to change the angle of the ball's descent. And he is armed with "flippers" which can propel the ball back up the playfield, aiming at the targets with the richest payoffs. But, just as man's boldest strokes and bravest ventures often boomerang, so an ill-timed flip can ricochet the ball straight down "death alley," and a too vigorous nudge will send the machine into "tilt." Winning pinball, like a rewarding life, requires delicate touch, fine calibrations, careful discrimination between boldness and folly.

●

Sometimes the comparison in the analogy is implied, that is, it is not stated directly.

The Bonfire and the Ants

By Alexander Solzhenitsyn

I threw a rotten log onto the fire without noticing that it was alive with ants.

The log began to crackle, the ants came tumbling out and scurried around in desperation. They ran along the top and writhed as they were scorched by the flames. I gripped the log and rolled it to one side. Many of the ants then managed to escape onto the sand or the pine needles.

But, strangely enough, they did not run away from the fire.

They had no sooner overcome their terror than they turned, circled and some kind of force drew them back to their forsaken homeland. There were many who climbed back onto the burning log, ran about on it, and perished there.

●

Solzhenitsyn has returned to his native Russia after years of living in exile in the United States. He is a writer noted for his criticisms of the former Communist regime, and in particular for his book *The Gulag Archipelago*, on the imprisonment and death of millions of Russians in Siberia. He himself was sent there as a prisoner and experienced the regime's repression while working in a slave-labour camp. When he first lived in Russia before fleeing to America, he was forced to write his political criticisms in coded form, in some cases using analogy as he did in the selection above.

1. Whom do you think the ants represent in this story? The log? The fire? Why do people want to leave their native country?
2. Is it always a case of politics? Is this story about love or hatred of one's homeland?

In much science fiction writing and movies, an implicit criticism of our society is given by comparing it to an imagined alien culture. James C. Rettie sets his essay within that framework. "But a Watch in the Night" is an example of an extended analogy.

"But a Watch in the Night": A Scientific Fable

By James C. Rettie

1   Out beyond our solar system there is a planet called Copernicus. It came into existence some four or five billion years before the birth of our Earth. In due course of time it became inhabited by a race of intelligent men.

2   About 750 million years ago the Copernicans had developed the motion picture machine to a point well in advance of the stage that we have reached. Most of the cameras that we now use in motion picture work are geared to take twenty-four pictures per second on a continuous strip of film. When such film is run through a projector, it throws a series of images on the screen and these change with a rapidity that gives the visual impression of normal movement. If a motion is too swift for the human eye to see it in detail, it can be captured and artificially slowed down by means of the slow-motion camera. This one is geared to take many more shots per second—ninety-six or even more than that. When the slow-motion film is projected at the normal speed of twenty-four pictures per second, we can see just how the jumping horse goes over a hurdle.

3   What about motion that is too slow to be seen by the human eye? That problem has been solved by the use of the time-lapse camera. In this one, the shutter is geared to take only one shot per second, or one per minute, or even one per hour—depending upon the kind of movement that is being photographed. When the time-lapse film is projected at the normal speed of twenty-four pictures per second, it is possible to see a bean sprout growing up out of the ground. Time-lapse films are useful in the study of many types of motion too slow to be observed by the unaided, human eye.

4   The Copernicans, it seems, had time-lapse cameras some 757 million years ago and they also had superpowered telescopes that gave them a clear view of what was happening upon this Earth. They decided to make a film record of the life history of Earth and to make it on the scale of one picture per year. The photography has been in progress during the last 757 million years.

5   In the near future, a Copernican interstellar expedition will arrive upon our Earth and bring with it a copy of the time-lapse film. Arrangements will be made

for showing the entire film in one continuous run. This will begin at midnight of New Year's Eve and continue day and night without a single stop until midnight of December 31. The rate of projection will be twenty-four pictures per second. Time on the screen will thus seem to move at the rate of twenty-four years per second; 1440 years per minute, 86,400 years per hour; approximately two million years per day; and sixty-two million years per month. The normal life-span of individual man will occupy about three seconds. The full period of earth history that will be unfolded on the screen (some 757 million years) will extend from what the geologists call Pre-Cambrian times up to the present. This will, by no means, cover the full time-span of the earth's geological history but it will embrace the period since the advent of living organisms.

6   During the months of January, February, and March the picture will be desolate and dreary. The shape of the land masses and the oceans will bear little or no resemblance to those that we know. The violence of geological erosion will be much in evidence. Rains will pour down on the land and promptly go booming down to the seas. There will be no clear streams anywhere except where the rains fall upon hard rock. Everywhere on the steeper ground the stream channels will be filled with boulders hurled down by rushing waters. Raging torrents and dry stream beds will keep alternating in quick succession. High mountains will seem to melt like so much butter in the sun. The shifting of land into the seas, later to be thrust up as new mountains, will be going on at a grand scale.

7   Early in April there will be some indication of the presence of single-celled living organisms in some of the warmer and sheltered coastal waters. By the end of the month it will be noticed that some of these organisms have become multicellular. A few of them, including the Trilobites, will be encased in hard shells.

8   Toward the end of May, the first vertebrates will appear, but they will still be aquatic creatures. In June about 60 per cent of the land area that we know as North America will be under water. One broad channel will occupy the space where the Rocky Mountains now stand. Great deposits of limestone will be forming under some of the shallower seas. Oil and gas deposits will be in the process of formation—also under shallow seas. On land there will still be no sign of vegetation. Erosion will be rampant, tearing loose particles and chunks of rock and grinding them into sand and silt to be spewed out by the streams into bays and estuaries.

9   About the middle of July the first land plants will appear and take up the tremendous job of soil building. Slowly, very slowly, the mat of vegetation will spread, always battling for its life against the power of erosion. Almost foot by foot, the plant life will advance, lacing down with its root structures whatever pulverized rock material it can find. Leaves and stems will be giving added protection against the loss of the soil foothold. The increasing vegetation will pave the way for the land animals that will live upon it.

10   Early in August the seas will be teeming with fish. This will be what geologists call the Devonian period. Some of the races of these fish will be breathing by means of lung tissue instead of through gill tissues. Before the month is over, some of the lung fish will go ashore and take on a crude lizard-like appearance. Here are the first amphibians.

11   In early September the insects will put in their appearance. Some will look like huge dragonflies and will have a wing spread of 24 inches. Large portions of the land masses will now be covered with heavy vegetation that will include

the primitive spore-propagating trees. Layer upon layer of this plant growth will build up, later to appear as the coal deposits. About the middle of this month, there will be evidence of the first seed-bearing plants and the first reptiles. Heretofore, the land animals will have been amphibians that could reproduce their kind only by depositing a soft egg mass in quiet waters. The reptiles will be shown to be freed from the aquatic bond because they can reproduce by means of a shelled egg in which the embryo and its nurturing liquids are sealed and thus protected from destructive evaporation. Before September is over, the first dinosaurs will be seen—creatures destined to dominate the animal realm for about 140 million years and then to disappear.

12   In October there will be series of mountain uplifts along what is now the eastern coast of the United States. A creature with feathered limbs—half bird and half reptile in appearance—will take itself into the air. Some small and rather unpretentious animals will be seen to bring forth their young in a form that is a miniature replica of the parents and to feed these young on milk secreted by mammary glands in the female parent. The emergence of this mammalian form of animal life will be recognized as one of the great events in geologic time. October will also witness the high water mark of the dinosaurs—creatures ranging in size from that of the modern goat to monsters like Brontosaurus that weighed some 40 tons. Most of them will be placid vegetarians, but a few will be hideous-looking carnivores, like Allosaurus and Tyrannosaurus. Some of the herbivorous dinosaurs will be clad in bony armor for protection against their flesh-eating comrades.

13   November will bring pictures of a sea extending from the Gulf of Mexico to the Arctic in space now occupied by the Rocky Mountains. A few of the reptiles will take to the air on bat-like wings. One of these, called Pteranodon, will have a wingspread of 15 feet. There will be a rapid development of the modern flowering plants, modern trees, and modern insects. The dinosaurs will disappear. Toward the end of the month there will be a tremendous land disturbance in which the Rocky Mountains will rise out of the sea to assume a dominating place in the North American landscape.

14   As the picture runs on into December it will show the mammals in command of the animal life. Seed-bearing trees and grasses will have covered most of the land with a heavy mantle of vegetation. Only the areas newly thrust up from the sea will be barren. Most of the streams will be crystal clear. The turmoil of geologic erosion will be confined to localized areas. About December 25 will begin the cutting of the Grand Canyon of the Colorado River. Grinding down through layer after layer of sedimentary strata, this stream will finally expose deposits laid down in Pre-Cambrian times. Thus in the walls of that canyon will appear geological formations dating from recent times to the period when the Earth had no living organisms upon it.

15   The picture will run on through the latter days of December and even up to its final day with still no sign of mankind. The spectators will become alarmed in the fear that man has somehow been left out. But not so; sometime about noon on December 31 (one million years ago) will appear a stooped, massive creature of man-like proportions. This will be Pithecanthropus, the Java ape man. For tools and weapons he will have nothing but crude stone and wooden clubs. His children will live a precarious existence threatened on the one side by hostile animals and on the other by tremendous climatic changes. Ice sheets—

in places 4000 feet deep—will form in the northern parts of North America and Eurasia. Four times this glacial ice will push southward to cover half the continents. With each advance the plant and animal life will be swept under or pushed southward. With each recession of the ice, life will struggle to re-establish itself in the wake of the retreating glaciers. The woolly mammoth, the musk ox, and the caribou all will fight to maintain themselves near the ice line. Sometimes they will be caught and put into cold storage—skin, flesh, blood, bones and all.

16   The picture will run on through supper time with still very little evidence of man's presence on the earth. It will be about 11 o'clock when Neanderthal man appears. Another half hour will go by before the appearance of Cro-Magnon man living in caves and painting crude animal pictures on the walls of his dwelling. Fifteen minutes more will bring Neolithic man, knowing how to chip stone and thus produce sharp cutting edges for spears and tools. In a few minutes more it will appear that man has domesticated the dog, the sheep and, possibly, other animals. He will then begin the use of milk. He will also learn the arts of basket weaving and the making of pottery and dugout canoes.

17   The dawn of civilization will not come until about five or six minutes before the end of the picture. The story of the Egyptians, the Babylonians, the Greeks, and the Romans will unroll during the fourth, the third, and the second minute before the end. At 58 minutes and 43 seconds past 11:00 PM (just 1 minute and 17 seconds before the end) will come the beginning of the Christian era. Columbus will discover the new world 20 seconds before the end. The Declaration of Independence will be signed just 7 seconds before the final curtain comes down.

18   In those few moments of geologic time will be the story of all that has happened since we became a nation. And what a story it will be! A human swarm will sweep across the face of the continent and take it away from the ... red men. They will change it far more radically than it has ever been changed before in a comparable time. The great virgin forests will be seen going down before ax and fire. The soil, covered for eons by its protective mantle of trees and grasses, will be laid bare to the ravages of water and wind erosion. Streams that had been flowing clear will, once again, take up a load of silt and push it toward the seas. Humus and mineral salts, both vital elements of productive soil, will be seen to vanish at a terrifying rate. The railroads and highways and cities that will spring up may divert attention, but they cannot cover up the blight of man's recent activities. In great sections of Asia, it will be seen that man must utilize cow dung and every scrap of available straw or grass for fuel to cook his food. The forests that once provided wood for this purpose will be gone without a trace. The use of these agricultural wastes for fuel, in place of returning them to the land, will be leading to increasing soil impoverishment. Here and there will be seen a dust storm darkening the landscape over an area a thousand miles across. Man-creatures will be shown counting their wealth in terms of bits of printed paper representing other bits of a scarce but comparatively useless yellow metal that is kept buried in strong vaults. Meanwhile, the soil, the only real wealth that can keep mankind alive on the face of this earth, is savagely being cut loose from its ancient moorings and washed into the seven seas.

19   We have just arrived upon this earth. How long will we stay?

Comprehension

1. How many paragraphs does Rettie use for his introduction? Why does he need so many?
2. The thesis statement is implied. Write one of your own for Rettie's essay.
3. The body of this essay is a process analysis. What process is analyzed?
4. In paragraph seventeen, Rettie introduces into his process a profound irony. What is it?
5. What does Rettie say is the only real wealth of the earth? Why does he make this claim?
6. Rettie's conclusion is written in two short sentences. How do they relate to the implied thesis?

Analysis

1. What analogy does Rettie exploit in this essay?
2. Rettie is an American and is writing for an American audience. How can you tell this from this essay?
3. Why does Rettie spend so much time describing the earth's evolution before turning to his "real" subject (civilization)?
4. What relationship does Rettie establish between geologic time and the final seven seconds?
5. Is his last question rhetorical?
6. A **fable** is a short story that teaches a lesson or a moral. What lesson can readers learn from Rettie's essay?
7. What is the source of the first part of Rettie's title? How then does the title relate to his content? What allusions are conjured up by this title?

Writing Suggestions

1. Use an analogy to discuss your attitude to life.
2. Interpret a current event using an analogy.

Simile and Metaphor

A **simile** makes a comparison using *like* or *as*. "My love is like a red rose."

A **metaphor** states a comparison directly. "Life's but a walking shadow, a poor player that struts and frets his hour upon the stage, and then is heard no more ..."

Shall I Compare Thee to a Summer's Day?

By William Shakespeare

Shall I compare thee to a summer's day?
Thou art more lovely and more temperate.
Rough winds do shake the darling buds of May,
And summer's lease hath all too short a date:
Sometime too hot the eye of heaven shines,
And often is his gold complexion dimm'd;
And every fair from fair some time declines,
By chance, or nature's changing course, untrimm'd;
But thy eternal summer shall not fade
Nor lose possession of that fair thou ow'st;
Nor shall Death brag thou wand'rest in his shade,
When in eternal lines to time thou grow'st.
So long as men can breathe or eyes can see,
So long lives this, and this gives life to thee.

Comprehension

1. Shakespeare opens with a question to his love. List the ways in which his love is like a summer's day.
2. Does he use similes and metaphors? Where?
3. Line nine opens with the word "But." How is his love *not* like a summer's day?
4. The last two lines of the poem are the conclusion. Paraphrase them.
5. What is the "eye of heaven" in line five?
6. How could the gold complexion of the sun be dimmed?
7. In line eleven, Shakespeare capitalizes the word "Death," making it a proper noun. This is the use of **personification,** giving inanimate objects or abstract qualities human characteristics. What does Shakespeare say Death will not be able to do? Why not?

Analysis

A sonnet has only fourteen lines, yet it is a complex form. Shakespeare compares his love to a summer's day, but she is more beautiful and will survive because he has written about her. This sonnet in fact praises poetry itself, for it can preserve ideas and feelings about love for all time. Thus, poetry becomes the "real" subject of this work through Shakespeare's expression. Ultimately, Shakespeare praises his own creative artistry by proving that his lines and their expression of love will endure. This is a paraphrase of the poem's ideas. Find the lines in the poem that relate to each idea.

V. Essay of Classification

Classification is a process of arranging information about people, places, things, and ideas into categories sharing common traits. A strong organizing principle determines the kind and number of traits used.

The Plot against People

By Russell Baker

1   Inanimate objects are classified scientifically into three major categories—those that break down, those that get lost, and those that don't work. The goal of all inanimate objects is to resist us and ultimately to defeat us, and the three major classifications are based on the method each object uses to achieve its purpose. As a general rule, any object capable of breaking down at the moment when it is most needed will do so. The automobile is typical of the category.

2   With the cunning peculiar to its breed, the automobile never breaks down while entering a filling station which has a large staff of idle mechanics. It waits until it reaches a downtown intersection in the middle of the rush hour, or until it is fully loaded with family and luggage on the Ohio Turnpike. Thus it creates maximum inconvenience, frustration, and irritability, thereby reducing its owner's lifespan.

3   Washing machines, garbage disposals, lawn mowers, furnaces, TV sets, tape recorders, slide projectors—all are in league with the automobile to take their turn at breaking down whenever life threatens to flow smoothly for their enemies.

4   Many inanimate objects, of course, find it extremely difficult to break down. Pliers, for example, and gloves and keys are almost totally incapable of breaking down. Therefore, they have had to evolve a different technique for resisting us.

5   They get lost. Science has still not solved the mystery of how they do it, and no one has ever caught one of them in the act. The most plausible theory is that they have developed a secret method of locomotion which they are able to conceal from human eyes.

6   It is not uncommon for a pair of pliers to climb all the way from the cellar to the attic in its single-minded determination to raise its owner's blood pressure. Keys have been known to burrow three feet under mattresses. Women's purses, despite their great weight, frequently travel through six or seven rooms to find hiding space under a couch.

7   Scientists have been struck by the fact that things that break down virtually never get lost, while things that get lost hardly ever break down. A furnace, for example, will invariably break down at the depth of the first winter cold wave, but it will never get lost. A woman's purse hardly ever breaks down; it almost invariably chooses to get lost.

8   Some persons believe this constitutes evidence that inanimate objects are not entirely hostile to us. After all, they point out, a furnace could infuriate you even more thoroughly by getting lost than by breaking down, just as a glove could upset you far more by breaking down than by getting lost.

9   Not everyone agrees, however, that this indicates a conciliatory attitude. Many say it merely proves that furnaces, gloves, and pliers are incredibly stupid.

10   The third class of objects—those that don't work—is the most curious of all. These include such objects as barometers, car clocks, cigarette lighters, flashlights and toy train locomotives. It is inaccurate, of course, to say that they *never* work. They work once, usually for the first few hours after being brought home, and then quit. Thereafter, they never work again.

11   In fact, it is widely assumed that they are built for the purpose of not working. Some people have reached advanced ages without ever seeing some of these objects—barometers, for example—in working order. Science is utterly baffled by the entire category. There are many theories about it. The most interesting holds that the things that don't work have attained the highest state possible for an inanimate object, the state to which things that break down and things that get lost can still only aspire.

12   They have truly defeated us by conditioning us never to expect anything of them. When a cigarette lighter won't light or a flashlight fails to illuminate, it does not raise blood pressure. Objects that don't work have given us the only peace we receive from inanimate society.

Reading Strategy

Russell Baker classifies objects into categories or types and begins his essay with a thesis statement that states his focused subject (inanimate objects) and his three specific categories—objects that break down, get lost, and don't work. You can see that he also defines his organizing principle—the idea on which he has based his categories and their shared traits: the method each object uses to defeat mankind.

In a classification essay, the thesis statement alerts the reader to the *number* of types to be discussed and the *principle* upon which the types have been chosen.

Russell Baker wrote this essay to be humorous. Much of his humour depends on personification, a technique that writers use to give inanimate objects human aspects. In describing objects as having malicious intentions, Baker emphasizes his own frustration with the material world around him. His use of this technique also aids him in outlining the traits or characteristics of the objects that annoy him. Notice how in the first three supporting paragraphs—the ones discussing objects that break down—Baker uses examples to illustrate *how* and *why* the objects behave as they do. Note in the first supporting paragraph how Baker concentrates solely on the car, telling the reader specific instances when it "breaks down" and the aftermath: "Thus it creates maximum inconvenience, frustration, and irritability ..."

Baker uses contrast as a transitional device. He directs readers from objects that break down to ones that get lost, ending his supporting paragraph three with a statement of fact that contrasts the style of one type of object with another. Some objects "find it extremely difficult to break down," while others "have had to evolve a different technique."

To add irony to his essay, Baker supplements his humour with allusions to science. He writes parts of his essay as if it were a scientific study and uses the language of a more formal, serious essay that might be found in a scientific journal or a magazine on psychology. Baker imitates such scientific language with phrases such as "struck by the fact" and "constitutes evidence."

The conclusion of Baker's essay is actually a discussion of his third category. Baker considers his last category special because he calls it the "most curious of all," showing that this last type of object is the ultimate one for defeating mankind. Irony once again is used to finish. In spite of the fact that objects of this kind cause frustration, it is ironic to discover an unexpected reversal of effect: "Objects that don't work have given us the only peace we receive from inanimate society." This use of irony strengthens Baker's point of view and reminds readers that he retains a distrust of the objects that surround him.

Comprehension

1. According to Baker's thesis statement, inanimate objects frustrate people because of a shared attitude. What is that attitude?
2. All the objects discussed in this essay are found in a certain environment. Which one?
3. Find three instances in the essay where Baker uses irony to create a comic effect.
4. Personification is a literary device wherein an inanimate object is given human qualities. Find three instances where Baker uses this device. To what effect?
5. Keys, pliers, and purses share a secret method for irritating humans. What is this method?
6. What key trait does the automobile possess that makes it a true enemy of humanity?

Analysis

1. What is the ultimate defeat suffered by humanity in "the plot against people"? Do you share Baker's belief in objects' ability to defeat us?
2. Would Baker's essay be as effective without the use of personification? How does personification create humour?
3. How effective is Baker's use of humour in negating frustration? Do you find humour a useful device for combatting stress and tension?
4. **Satire**, the humorous criticism of events and people to expose their folly, is used by writers like Baker to provoke readers to think and change. What is exposed here? What problems does Baker attack with his satire? Is there a remedy in his humour?

Writing Strategy

You classify all the time. Look around at your fellow students. How would you type them? Put them into categories? By gender, height, clothing style, major program? Consider the world of business and government. Employees are classified according to the work they do and are paid for. What do you think the "pay equity" initiative is based on? That's right—job classification!

In order to classify information, you need to begin your process by asking questions specific to categorization:

1. Can my subject be focused and written about adequately enough in a short essay?
2. Can my subject be broken down into distinct categories, each category having a separate series of related traits?
3. Can my categories relate to one another based on an organizing principle?

To demonstrate how you could classify a subject and create valid categories, traits, and a working organizing principle, let's pick the subject of students. The following questions and answers provide an outline of the information you will later compose as sentences and paragraphs.

Subject: STUDENTS

1. *Can this subject be focused?*
   Which students: preschool, public, private, high school, college?
2. *Can one of these focused subjects be organized into groups?*
   College students can be full-time or part-time. Some college students hold down jobs, live at home, and go to school. Others have temporarily left a job to continue schooling, live on their own, and take classes. What about adult learners? They are a distinct group with their own needs, backgrounds, and goals.
3. *Can you label or sort students based on a principle of organization?*
   For instance, could you organize students according to their behaviour and attitudes? The browner, the workaholic, the party animal, the rebel, the whiner?

All groupings must have an organizing principle upon which to define traits and to limit the scope of the type. When you write out your focused subject and your types or groups, be sure to find an organizing principle that will lend unity and coherence to your essay.

Organizing principle

An **organizing principle** defines a purpose that is common to a group. To determine your organizing principle, ask yourself these questions:

a. What is the purpose behind a group's activities or behaviour?
b. What motivates action or thought?
c. What background is shared by the persons and ideas involved?

Once information has been generated, you can begin by writing the thesis statement. A thesis statement for a classification essay must:

a. state the focused subject
b. outline the groups to be discussed
c. state the organizing principle

If you were to write an essay on types of students in the classroom based on behaviour, you might say:

College students behave in different ways both in and out of the classroom. Three common types are the browner, the workaholic, and the party animal.

In composing the paragraphs for a classification essay, it is essential to discuss each group separately. Your paragraphs would open with topic sentences that state the groups to be discussed. The supporting details would be the *traits* shared by members of the groups. The traits are common characteristics and they must relate to the organizing principle in the thesis. For instance, if you were to discuss the workaholics, talking about how such people stay up late, study for ten hours a day, tend to be quiet and studious, and never hand in work late, you would be certain these traits related to the *behaviour* of each group member. If, however, you talked about what workaholics *feel* about work, or what their religious beliefs were, you would be off topic. These traits do not relate to your organizing principle and would be, for this particular essay, unnecessary information for your reader.

Your conclusion could paraphrase your thesis statement or it could make a comment on the reasons why student behaviour exists in your groups. In the classification essay, the conclusion is written to emphasize one feature of your process. In the essay on student behaviour, you might conclude by pointing out that all behaviour is motivated by needs—for some it is a need for recognition, for others a need to release tension and anxiety.

In the following essay by Lionel Ruby, "What Kind of Language Are You Using?" note that Ruby uses a three-point thesis statement and a series of short paragraphs that outline the traits of each function he assigns to language. Note, as well, that his organizing principle rests on his analysis of levels of spoken language.

What Kind of Language Are You Using?

By Lionel Ruby

1   Language has more than one purpose. We might say that language operates on different levels, except that the word "levels" suggests higher and lower planes in a scale of value, and this is not intended here. We shall deal with three functions: the informative, the expressive, and the directive. To say that language has these three functions is to say that there are three different reasons for speaking. One reason, or purpose, is to communicate factual information. This is the informative function. We speak also in order to express our feelings, to "blow off steam," or to stir the feelings and attitudes of the person we are talking to. We shall call this the expressive or "emotive" function. And, finally, we speak in order to get people to act. This is the directive function.

2   Some illustrations are in order. A book on astronomy describes the solar system and the stars. We learn that the diameter of the earth is about 8,000 miles; that of the sun, about 800,000 miles; a ratio of 100 to 1. We learn that the star Betelgeuse has a diameter three hundred times that of the sun. This means that if the earth is represented by a baseball, about three inches in diameter, then Betelgeuse would have a diameter of almost a mile and a half. We may learn that there are as many stars in the heavens as there are grains of sand on all the seashores of the world. I have just been using language to communicate information.

3   Expressive language is a second type. When I talk about the United States Senator I like least, I may let off some steam, and relieve my pent-up feelings. I may even infect you with my feelings, making you feel as I feel. The poet, of course, is a specialist in expressive language, as in the lines:

> Comes the blind Fury with th' abhorred shears
> And slits the thin-spun life.

These lines give expression to John Milton's feelings and perhaps make us feel as he felt. When we tell our friends a funny story, to get a laugh, we express our feelings, too, and affect theirs.

4   The third type, directive or action-provoking speech, is illustrated by examples like: "Do unto others as you would have others do unto you," or "Praise the Lord, and pass the ammunition!" We say these things to get action. Ceremonial language, such as "I am happy to meet you," "What a beautiful baby!" and conversation about the weather, also have a directive purpose: to establish social rapport, and to get a friendly response.

5   There are, then, at least three different purposes of discourse. We may also make a somewhat similar classification for words, that is, for words taken by themselves. A basic distinction here is between what we shall call neutral words and emotive words. Neutral words merely convey ideas to us, as when I say, "The sun rose at six this morning." The words in this sentence do not arouse our emotions. But words like "God," "love," "freedom," and "communism" are so closely connected with our total attitudes to life that they are likely to arouse emotional reactions. This division of words into neutral and emotive, however, is relative to our personal experiences, for there is nothing in the word itself which makes it neutral or emotive. If a word conveys nothing but an idea to you, then it is neutral to you; if it arouses your emotions, then it is emotive to you. The word "bread" is a neutral word to me, but to a "fat boy" or a starving man, it may be fraught with emotion. Nevertheless there are some words which can be counted on to make almost everyone "see red," so to speak, like the word "traitor."

6   This classification of words is independent of our classification of the functions of language, for those who wish to inform may use either type, as may those who want to express their feelings, or to get action. In general, however, neutral words will be used when we wish merely to inform, emotive words when we wish to be expressive.

•

Comprehension

1. According to his thesis statement, what types of language does Ruby intend to discuss?
2. Ruby differentiates between kinds of language and kinds of languages! Paraphrase his discussion.
3. What example does Ruby use to illustrate the informative function of language?
4. How many examples illustrate expressive language?
5. Into how many types is directed language subdivided?
6. In paragraph five, Ruby approaches his subject differently by doing what?
7. How does Ruby relate the functions of language to the classification of words?
8. Consider Ruby's conclusion. Does it summarize, restate, or add new information?

Analysis

1. Before reading this essay, you were probably aware of levels of language: the casual talk of friends, the semi-formal level of the classroom, etc. What types of vocabulary and sentence structure do you associate with the casual, semiformal, and formal uses of language?
2. Consider the following speakers. What level(s) of language do you associate with each? (a) news anchor, (b) disc jockey, (c) politician, (d) religious leader
3. Some words are loaded (Ruby calls these emotive words), some are neutral. Look up articles in a newspaper and locate the two kinds of words. Look also at Chodirker's essay in Unit Two to see what it says about loaded words.

In our third essay of classification, by Judith Viorst, you will notice how the author introduces a number of elements to clarify her groups. First, she uses numbers and titles to define each group. She also bases her data on personal experience. In reading through Viorst's essay, note that she divides and categorizes the people she knows into types.

Viorst is very clear as to how much her friends mean to her and how certain ones belong very much to certain groups. Viorst's focused subject is complicated, yet she is able to simplify her groupings and make them accessible to her readers. In particular, she divides her groups very clearly, making sure there is no overlap from one to another. She defines for each group a unifying principle or *central trait* and then adds other traits and examples to fill out her analysis. Notice she does not use generalizations. That is, Viorst avoids making vague statements about her types of friends. Each type is portrayed with specific and individual details.

Friends, Good Friends—and Such Good Friends

By Judith Viorst

Women are friends, I once would have said, when they totally love and support and trust each other, and bare to each other the secrets of their souls, and run— no questions asked—to help each other, and tell harsh truths to each other (no, you can't wear that dress unless you lose ten pounds first) when harsh truths must be told.

Women are friends, I once would have said, when they share the same affection for Ingmar Bergman, plus train rides, cats, warm rain, charades, Camus, and hate with equal ardor Newark and Brussels sprouts and Lawrence Welk and camping.

In other words, I once would have said that a friend is a friend all the way, but now I believe that's a narrow point of view. For the friendships I have and the friendships I see are conducted at many levels of intensity, serve many different functions, meet different needs and range from those as all-the-way as the friendship of the soul sisters mentioned above to that of the most nonchalant and casual playmates.

Consider these varieties of friendship:

1. Convenience friends. These are the women with whom, if our paths weren't crossing all the time, we'd have no particular reason to be friends: a next-door neighbor, a woman in our car pool, the mother of one of our children's closest friends or maybe some mommy with whom we serve juice and cookies each week at the Glenwood Co-op Nursery.

Convenience friends are convenient indeed. They'll lend us their cups and silverware for a party. They'll drive our kids to soccer when we're sick. They'll take us to pick up our car when we need a lift to the garage. They'll even take our cats when we go on vacation. As we will for them. But we don't, with convenience friends, ever come too close or tell too much; we maintain our public face and emotional distance. "Which means," says Elaine, "that I'll talk about being overweight but not about being depressed. Which means I'll admit being mad but not blind with rage. Which means I might say that we're pinched this month but never that I'm worried sick over money."

But which doesn't mean that there isn't sufficient value to be found in these friendships of mutual aid, in convenience friends.

2. Special-interest friends. These friendships aren't intimate, and they needn't involve kids or silverware or cats. Their value lies in some interest jointly shared. And so we may have an office friend or a yoga friend or a tennis friend or a friend from the Women's Democratic Club.

"I've got one woman friend," says Joyce, "who likes, as I do, to take psychology courses. Which makes it nice for me—and nice for her. It's fun to go with someone you know and it's fun to discuss what you've learned, driving back from the classes." And for the most part, she says, that's all they discuss.

"I'd say that what we're doing is *doing* together, not being together," Suzanne says of her Tuesday-doubles friends. "It's mainly a tennis relationship, but we play together well. And I guess we all need to have a couple of playmates."

I agree.

My playmate is a shopping friend, a woman of marvelous taste, a woman who knows exactly *where* to buy *what,* and furthermore is a woman who always knows beyond a doubt what one ought to be buying. I don't have the time to keep up with what's new in eyeshadow, hemlines and shoes and whether the smock look is in or finished already. But since (oh, shame!) I care a lot about eyeshadow, hemlines and shoes, and since I don't *want* to wear smocks if the smock look is finished, I'm very glad to have a shopping friend.

3. Historical friends. We all have a friend who knew us when ... maybe way back in Miss Meltzer's second grade, when our family lived in that three-room flat in Brooklyn, when our dad was out of work for seven months, when our brother Allie got in that fight where they had to call the police, when our sister married the endodontist from Yonkers and when, the morning after we lost our virginity, she was the first, the only, friend we told.

The years have gone by and we've gone separate ways and we've little in common now, but we're still an intimate part of each other's past. And so whenever we go to Detroit we always go to visit this friend of our girlhood. Who knows how we looked before our teeth were straightened. Who knows how we talked before our voice got unBrooklyned. Who knows what we ate before we learned about artichokes. And who, by her presence, puts us in touch with an earlier part of ourself, a part of ourself it's important never to lose.

"What this friend means to me and what I mean to her," says Grace, "is having a sister without sibling rivalry. We know the texture of each other's lives. She remembers my grandmother's cabbage soup. I remember the way her uncle played the piano. There's simply no other friend who remembers those things."

4. Crossroads friends. Like historical friends, our crossroads friends are important for *what was*—for the friendship we shared at a crucial, now past, time of life. A time, perhaps, when we roomed in college together; or worked as eager young singles in the Big City together; or went together, as my friend Elizabeth and I did through pregnancy, birth and that scary first year of new motherhood.

Crossroad friends forge powerful links, links strong enough to endure with not much more contact than once-a-year letters at Christmas. And out of respect for those crossroads years, for those dramas and dreams we once shared, we will always be friends.

5. Cross-generational friends. Historical friends and crossroads friends seem to maintain a special kind of intimacy—dormant but always ready to be revived—and though we may rarely meet, whenever we do connect, it's personal and intense. Another kind of intimacy exists in the friendships that form across generations in what one woman calls her daughter–mother and her mother–daughter relationships.

Evelyn's friend is her mother's age—"but I share so much more than I ever could with my mother"—a woman she talks to of music, of books and of life. "What I get from her is the benefit of her experience. What she gets—and enjoys—from me is a youthful perspective. It's a pleasure for both of us."

I have in my own life a precious friend, a woman of 65 who has lived very hard, who is wise, who listens well; who has been where I am and can help me understand it; and who represents not only an ultimate ideal mother to me but also the person I'd like to be when I grow up.

In our daughter role we tend to do more than our share of self-revelation; in our mother role we tend to receive what's revealed. It's another kind of pleasure—playing wise mother to a questing younger person. It's another very lovely kind of relationship.

6. Part-of-a-couple friends. Some of the women we call our friends we never see alone—we see them as part of a couple at couples' parties. And though we share interests in many things and respect each other's views, we aren't moved to deepen the relationship. Whatever the reason, a lack of time or—and this is more likely—a lack of chemistry, our friendship remains in the context of a group. But the fact that our feeling on seeing each other is always, "I'm *so* glad she's here" and the fact that we spend half the evening talking together says that this too, in its own way, counts as a friendship.

(Other part-of-a-couple friends are the friends that came with the marriage, and some of these are friends we could live without. But sometimes, alas, she married our husband's best friend; and sometimes, alas, she *is* our husband's best friend. And so we find ourself dealing with her, somewhat against our will, in a spirit of what I'll call *reluctant* friendship.)

7. Men who are friends. I wanted to write just of women friends, but the women I've talked to won't let me—they say I must mention man–woman friendships too. For these friendships can be just as close and as dear as those that we form with women. Listen to Lucy's description of one such friendship:

"We've found we have things to talk about that are different from what he talks about with my husband and different from what I talk about with his wife. So sometimes we call on the phone or meet for lunch. There are similar intellectual interests—we always pass on to each other the books that we love—but there's also something tender and caring too." In a couple of crises, Lucy says, "He offered himself, for talking and for helping. And when someone died in his family he wanted me there. The sexual, flirty part of our friendship is very small, but *some*—just enough to make it fun and different." She thinks—and I agree—that the sexual part, though small, is always there when a man and a woman are friends. It's only in the past few years that I've made friends with men, in the sense of a friendship that's *mine,* not just part of two couples. And achieving with them the ease and the trust I've found with women friends has value indeed. Under the dryer at home last week, putting on mascara and rouge, I comfortably sat and talked with a fellow named Peter. Peter, I finally decided, could handle the shock of me minus mascara under the dryer. Because we care for each other. Because we're friends.

8. There are medium friends, and pretty good friends, and very good friends indeed, and these friendships are defined by their level of intimacy. And what we'll reveal at each of these levels of intimacy is calibrated with care. We might tell a medium friend, for example, that yesterday we had a fight with our husband. And we might tell a pretty good friend that this fight with our husband made us so mad that we slept on the couch. And we might tell a very good friend that the reason we got so mad in that fight that we slept on the couch had something to do with that girl who works in his office. But it's only to our very best friends that we're willing to tell all, to tell what's going on with that girl in his office.

The best of friends, I still believe, totally love and support and trust each other, and bare to each other the secrets of their souls, and run—no questions asked—to help each other, and tell harsh truths to each other when they must be told.

But we needn't agree about everything (only 12-year-old girl friends agree about *everything*) to tolerate each other's point of view. To accept without judgment. To give and to take without ever keeping score. And to *be* there, as I am for them and as they are for me, to comfort our sorrows, to celebrate our joys.

●

Comprehension

1. Paraphrase Viorst's definition of friendship as stated in her introduction.
2. Is Viorst's thesis statement stated directly or is it implied? If implied, write out a thesis for her article.
3. Could one compare "convenience" friends with "special-interest friends"? On what grounds? Take your details from Viorst's examples.
4. What points of similarity exist between "historical" friends and "crossroads" friends?
5. What problem in friendships between men and women is identified by the author?
6. The author uses a conversational style. Based on your reading of the Ruby essay, why do you think Viorst chose to write in this fashion? Does she ever use loaded (emotive) words?

Analysis

1. Which of Viorst's categories are most meaningful to you? Why?
2. Classification can lead to stereotyping. Do you think the author avoids this danger? What do you think of her treatment of men?
3. On what principles would you classify your friends? Is this an appropriate way of thinking about your friends? Define friendship and tell what it means to you.

Writing Suggestions

1. How would you classify your own personal goals? Short-term, long-term, immediate? Discuss.
2. Read Viorst's essay and then make up your own categories of friends. Find an organizing principle that is based on personal experience. Or, if you wish, take Viorst's principle and apply it to your friends. Do not, however, use her titles. Make up your own.
3. Classify emotions. Here, you could use research methods discussed in the final unit of this text and discuss types of emotions. Make references to

your own life and to characters you've read about in fiction to add detail to your classification.

Stereotype

A **stereotype** is a particular kind of classification. When we classify people (e.g., students as browners, whiners, and workaholics), we have to keep in mind that each category is composed of individuals who will vary from the norm we have established. In the case of a stereotype, the category has become fixed as an accepted image and it represents all the people, ideas, or things that belong to that category. In its oversimplification and falsification, a stereotype is an invalid form of classification.

Stereotypes are most often based on gender, race, or religion. Examples of such are "the dumb blonde" or "the uptight WASP." When a person is denied individuality because of stereotyping, then bigotry and prejudice result. Jokes based on stereotypes, while they seem harmless, are nonetheless pernicious because they dehumanize the persons involved.

The following essay by Neil Bissoondath, "I'm Not Racist But ...," discusses the dehumanizing effect of stereotypes.

"I'm Not Racist But ..."

By Neil Bissoondath

1   Someone recently said that racism is as Canadian as maple syrup. I have no argument with that. History provides us with ample proof. But, for proper perspective, let us remember that it is also as American as apple pie, as French as croissants, as Jamaican as ackee, as Indian as aloo, as Chinese as chow mein, as ... Well, there's an entire menu to be written. This is not by way of excusing it. Murder and rape, too, are international, multicultural, as innate to the darker side of the human experience. But we must be careful that the inevitable rage evoked does not blind us to the larger context.

2   The word "racism" is a discomforting one: It is so vulnerable to manipulation. We can, if we so wish, apply it to any incident involving people of different colour. And therein lies the danger. During the heat of altercation, we seize, as terms of abuse, on whatever is most obvious about the other person. It is, often, a question of unfortunate convenience. A woman, because of her sex, easily becomes a female dog or an intimate part of her anatomy. A large person might be dubbed "a stupid ox," a small person "a little" whatever. And so a black might become "a nigger," a white "a honky," an Asian "a paki," a Chinese "a chink," an Italian "a wop," a French-Canadian "a frog."

3   There is nothing pleasant about these terms; they assault every decent sensibility. Even so, I once met someone who, in a stunning surge of naiveté, used them as simple descriptives and not as terms of racial abuse. She was horrified

to learn the truth. While this may have been an extreme case, the point is that the use of such patently abusive words may not always indicate racial or cultural distaste. They may indicate ignorance or stupidity or insensitivity, but pure racial hatred—such as the Nazis held for Jews, or the Ku Klux Klan for blacks—is a thankfully rare commodity.

4   Ignorance, not the willful kind but that which comes from lack of experience, is often indicated by that wonderful phrase, "I'm not racist but ..." I think of the mover, a friendly man, who said, "I'm not racist, but the Chinese are the worst drivers on the road." He was convinced this was so because the shape of their eyes, as far as he could surmise, denied them peripheral vision.

5   Or the oil company executive, an equally warm and friendly man, who, looking for an apartment in Toronto, rejected buildings with East Indian tenants not because of their race—he was telling me this, after all—but because he was given to understand that cockroaches were symbols of good luck in their culture and that, when they moved into a new home, friends came by with gift-wrapped roaches.

6   Neither of these men thought of himself as racist, and I believe they were not, deep down. (The oil company executive made it clear he would not hesitate to have me as a neighbour; my East Indian descent was of no consequence to him, my horror of cockroaches was.) Yet their comments, so innocently delivered, would open them to the accusation, justifiably so if this were all one knew about them. But it is a charge which would undoubtedly be wounding to them. It is difficult to recognize one's own misconceptions.

7   True racism is based, more often than not, on willful ignorance, and an acceptance of—and comfort with—stereotype. We like to think, in this country, that our multicultural mosaic will help nudge us into a greater openness. But multiculturalism as we know it indulges in stereotype, depends on it for a dash of colour and the flash of dance. It fails to address the most basic questions people have about each other: Do those men doing the Dragon Dance really all belong to secret criminal societies? Do those women dressed in saris really coddle cockroaches for luck? Do those people in dreadlocks all smoke marijuana and live on welfare? Such questions do not seem to be the concern of the government's multicultural programs, superficial and exhibitionistic as they have become.

8   So the struggle against stereotype, the basis of all racism, becomes a purely personal one. We must beware of the impressions we create. A friend of mine once commented that, from talking to West Indians, she has the impression that their one great cultural contribution to the world is in the oft-repeated boast that "We (unlike everyone else) know how to party."

9   There are dangers, too, in community response. We must be wary of the self-appointed activists who seem to pop up in the media at every given opportunity spouting the rhetoric of retribution, mining distress for personal, political and professional gain. We must be skeptical about those who depend on conflict for their sense of self, the non-whites who need to feel themselves victims of racism, the whites who need to feel themselves purveyors of it. And we must be sure that, in addressing the problem, we do not end up creating it. Does the *Miss Black Canada Beauty Contest* still exist? I hope not. Not only do I find beauty contests offensive, but a racially segregated one even more so. What would the public reaction be, I wonder, if every year CTV broadcast the *Miss White Canada*

Beauty Pageant? We give community-service awards only to blacks: Would we be comfortable with such awards only for whites? In Quebec, there are The Association of Black Nurses, The Association of Black Artists, The Congress of Black Jurists. Play tit for tat: The Association for White Nurses, White Artists, White Jurists: visions of apartheid. Let us be frank, racism for one is racism for others.

10   Finally, and perhaps most important, let us beware of abusing the word itself.

•

Comprehension

1. In his introduction the author begins with a series of stereotypes. On what basis are they alike?
2. Where does the author actually define racism?
3. What TV events does the author refer to in order to discuss the theme of his essay? How would you define "inverse racism"?
4. How many specific examples does the author use of loaded (emotive) language?
5. The author talks about the use of emotive and neutral words, terms you read about in Ruby's essay. Where does Bissoondath show an example of these two levels of word use?

Analysis

1. Why does the author use so many rhetorical questions in paragraph seven?
2. What is the purpose of the anecdote about the cockroach?
3. Read the opening sentence in paragraph eight. Do you think Bissoondath is right?
4. Is it really possible to abuse the word racism? How has the author convinced you of this fact?
5. When you read the title, what was your initial expectation as a reader? Did the essay fulfil your expectation? Who is the author's intended audience?
6. Why do so many people make use of stereotypes?
7. The author implies that multiculturalism is a form of stereotyping, if not racism. Is he right?

VI. Essay of Cause and Effect

Cause and effect writing explains why things happen and what results follow. Cause and effect essays link conditions and consequences by showing how and why they are connected.

On Reading Trash

By Bob Swift

1   If you want kids to become omnivorous readers, let them read trash. That's my philosophy, and I speak from experience.

2   I don't disagree with The National Endowment for the Humanities, which says every high school graduate should have read 30 great works of literature, including the Bible, Plato, Shakespeare, Hawthorne, the Declaration of Independence, *Catcher in the Rye, Crime and Punishment* and *Moby Dick.*

3   It's a fine list. Kids should read them all, and more. But they'll be better readers if they start off on trash. Trash? What I mean is what some might call "popular" fiction. My theory is, if you get kids interested in reading books—no matter what sort—they will eventually go on to the grander literature all by themselves.

4   In the third grade I read my first novel, a mystic adventure set in India. I still recall the sheer excitement at discovering how much fun reading could be.

5   When we moved within walking distance of the public library a whole new world opened. In the library I found that wonder of wonders, the series. What a thrill, to find a favorite author had written a dozen or more other titles.

6   I read a series about frontiersmen, learning about Indian tribes, beef jerky and tepees. A Civil War series alternated young heroes from the Blue and the Gray, and I learned about Grant and Lee and the Rock of Chickamauga.

7   One summer, in Grandpa Barrow's attic, I discovered the Mother Lode, scores of dusty books detailing the adventures of Tom Swift, The Rover Boys, The Submarine Boys, The Motorcycle Boys and Bomba the Jungle Boy. It didn't matter that some were written in 1919; any book you haven't read is brand new.

8   Another summer I discovered Edgar Rice Burroughs. I swung through the jungles with Tarzan, fought green Martians with John Carter, explored Pellucidar at the Earth's core, flew through the steamy air of Venus with Carson Napier. Then I came across Sax Rohmer and, for book after book, prowled opium dens with Nayland Smith, in pursuit of the insidious Fu Manchu.

9   In the seventh grade, I ran across Booth Tarkington's hilarious Penrod books and read them over and over.

10   My cousin went off to war in 1942 and gave me his pulp magazines. I became hooked on Doc Savage, The Shadow, G8 and His Battle Aces, The Spider, Amazing Stories. My folks wisely did not object to them as trash. I began to look in second-hand book shops for past issues, and found a Blue Book Magazine, with an adventure story by Talbot Mundy. It led me back to the library, for more of Mundy's Far East thrillers. From Mundy, my path led to A. Conan Doyle's *The Lost World,* Rudyard Kipling's *Kim,* Jules Verne, H.G. Wells and Jack London.

11   Before long I was whaling with Herman Melville, affixing scarlet letters with Hawthorne and descending into the maelstrom with Poe. In due course came Hemingway, Dos Passos, *Hamlet, The Odyssey, The Iliad, Crime and Punishment.* I had discovered "real" literature by following the trail of popular fiction.

12   When our kids were small, we read aloud to them from *Doctor Dolittle* and *Winnie-the-Pooh.* Soon they learned to read, and favored the "Frog and Toad" and "Freddie the Pig" series.

13   When the old Doc Savage and Conan the Barbarian pulps were reissued as paperbacks, I brought them home. The kids devoured them, sometimes hiding them behind textbooks at school, just as I had. They read my old Tarzan and Penrod books along with Nancy Drew and *The Black Stallion.*

14   Now they're big kids. Each kid's room is lined with bookshelves, on which are stacked, in an eclectic mix, Doc Savage, Plato, Louis L'Amour westerns, Thomas Mann, Gothic romances, Agatha Christie, Sartre, Edgar Allen Poe, science-fiction, Saul Bellow, Shakespeare, Pogo, Greek tragedies, Hemingway, Kipling, Tarzan, *Zen and the Art of Motorcycle Maintenance,* F. Scott Fitzgerald, *Bomba the Jungle Boy,* Nietzsche, *The Iliad, Dr. Dolittle,* Joseph Conrad, Fu Manchu, Hawthorne, Penrod, Dostoevsky, Ray Bradbury, Herman Melville, Fitzgerald, Conan the Barbarian ... more. Some great literature, some trash, but all good reading.

●

Reading Strategy

Bob Swift's essay claims that children who are encouraged to read popular fiction will become, as a result, avid lifetime readers. His thesis statement is the opening line of his essay. Using personal anecdotes from his own childhood, Swift illustrates how and why he became a reader. Note how he uses specific examples of the books he discovered and what effect they had on his way of seeing the world: "Another summer I discovered Edgar Rice Burroughs. I swung through the jungles with Tarzan, fought green Martians with John Carter ..."

Swift relates a chronology of discoveries, charting the times and the books he read as his curiosity for reading grew. His method is simple: he states a single cause and then shows the multiple effects that followed. In support of paragraph nine, Swift points out that his cousin introduced him to pulp magazines. As a result, Swift became "hooked on Doc Savage," and he began searching for more books of the same kind in second-hand bookstores. His interest led him back to the public library, where he became acquainted with more sophisticated writing: the stories of Jules Verne, H.G. Wells, and Jack London.

Swift selects examples that prove the connection between his reading trash (e.g., pulp magazines) and his subsequent desire to explore new books. The final consequence of his devouring of popular fiction was the discovery of "real" literature—the works of Hemingway and Shakespeare.

Comprehension

1. In paragraphs one to four, what does Swift claim is the immediate effect of reading trash?
2. If kids fall in love with reading trash, what happens next?
3. How many of the works listed have you read? How many have you never heard of? Why are so many of them unfamiliar to readers today?

4. What do all the titles of the trash have in common?
5. How many personal anecdotes does Swift use?
6. Give Swift's reasons why kids should read trash.
7. How does Swift's conclusion relate to his thesis?
8. What other ways of teaching kids to read does Swift implicitly reject?

Analysis

1. Do you agree with Swift that all reading—trash and great literature—is good reading?
2. Trash is an emotive word. Why does Swift use it more often than the neutral "popular fiction"?
3. This article was written for a newspaper to be read by the "general public of readers." What assumptions has Swift made about his reading audience?
4. Did you read trash as a kid? Did you go on to read greater things as Swift did? Tell how and why. If you didn't read trash, or were forbidden to do so, how did you learn to read and like reading? Do you like reading, in fact? If not, why?

Writing Strategy

In writing a cause and effect essay it is essential to state from the beginning what your subject is and how it creates a connection between causes and effects.

Writing cause and effect essays requires a number of careful approaches:

1. Make sure the cause and effect relationship between two or more things is logical and valid, and not just based on coincidence.

EXAMPLE: For years it was rumoured that cigarette smoking caused cancer. Without evidence to back up the claim, the statement was regarded as mere coincidence. Now there are ample scientific data to prove there is a real and logical link between the cigarette and lung cancer.

2. In writing out a cause and effect essay, be sure to gather adequate data and examples.

EXAMPLE: Bob Swift wrote his essay using book titles and memories from his own life to prove his cause and effect thesis. His data were valid evidence that reading popular fiction can result in an increased desire to read better works. Evidence is essential in cause and effect writing, for without it false assumptions and claims can be presented as truth.

3. Do not create a connection between causes and effects if none readily exists.

EXAMPLE: Sometimes writers say "this is the cause because ... here is the effect." No clear connection has been established. There is crime in a neighbourhood;

therefore, there are drugs being sold. Such an assumption may be false. It is tempting to assume proof or to depend on bias, but evidence must be shown before a cause and effect relationship can be considered valid. Consider this situation: If a strict teacher fails you on an essay-answer test, is it because that teacher is unfair and picky? Or is the grade based on errors you missed in proofreading your final copy? The causes might be a combination of both the teacher's methods and your exam fatigue, a combination difficult to measure. Do not assume that because one event follows another, the first *causes* the second. If you inhale and cough, your cigarette may be the cause of your sudden hacking. But there is the possibility that you may have asthma or an allergy and one of those may be the actual reason for your cough.

4. In writing cause and effect essays be aware that there are types of causes:
   a. immediate causes—causes that on first glance are obviously related to effects
   b. ultimate causes—causes that stand out above all others as main motivations

EXAMPLE: If a child is crying, the immediate cause could be a skinned knee. If a child skins a knee frequently and cries, the ultimate cause might be a poor sense of balance or a low pain threshold.

5. Try to balance causes and effects in equal numbers. If that is not possible, realize that a sequence of causes may bring about further causes that then lead on to certain consequences.

EXAMPLE: The firing of two employees caused much anxiety in the company, which in turn caused low morale in the office. The results were decreased productivity and an increase in absenteeism on Fridays and Mondays.

In the following essay by Malcolm X, notice how the author describes multiple causes that led to his becoming an educated man.

Prison Studies

By Malcolm X

Many who today hear me somewhere in person, or on television, or those who read something I've said, will think I went to school far beyond the eighth grade. This impression is due entirely to my prison studies.

It had really begun back in the Charlestown Prison, when Bimbi first made me feel envy of his stock of knowledge. Bimbi had always taken charge of any conversation he was in, and I had tried to emulate him. But every book I picked up had few sentences which didn't contain anywhere from one to nearly all of the words that might as well have been in Chinese. When I just skipped those words, of course, I really ended up with little idea of what the book said. So I had come to the Norfolk Prison Colony still going through only bookreading motions. Pretty soon, I would have quit even these motions, unless I had received the motivation that I did.

I saw that the best thing I could do was get hold of a dictionary—to study, to learn some words. I was lucky enough to reason also that I should try to improve my penmanship. It was sad. I couldn't even write in a straight line. It was both ideas together that moved me to request a dictionary along with some tablets and pencils from the Norfolk Prison Colony school.

I spent two days just riffling uncertainly through the dictionary's pages. I'd never realized so many words existed! I didn't know which words I needed to learn. Finally, to start some kind of action, I began copying.

In my slow, painstaking, ragged handwriting, I copied into my tablet everything printed on that first page, down to the punctuation marks.

I believe it took me a day. Then, aloud, I read back, to myself, everything I'd written on the tablet. Over and over, aloud, to myself, I read my own handwriting.

I woke up the next morning, thinking about those words—immensely proud to realize that not only had I written so much at one time, but I'd written words that I never knew were in the world. Moreover, with a little effort, I also could remember what many of these words meant. I reviewed the words whose meanings I didn't remember. Funny thing, from the dictionary first page right now, that "aardvark" springs to my mind. The dictionary had a picture of it, a long-tailed, long-eared, burrowing African mammal, which lives off termites caught by sticking out its tongue as an anteater does for ants.

I was so fascinated that I went on—I copied the dictionary's next page. And the same experience came when I studied that. With every succeeding page, I also learned of people and places and events from history. Actually the dictionary is like a miniature encyclopedia. Finally the dictionary's A section had filled a whole tablet—and I went on into the B's. That was the way I started copying what eventually became the entire dictionary. It went a lot faster after so much practice helped me to pick up handwriting speed. Between what I wrote in my tablet, and writing letters, during the rest of my time in prison I would guess I wrote a million words.

I suppose it was inevitable that as my word-base broadened, I could for the first time pick up a book and read and now begin to understand what the book was saying. Anyone who has read a great deal can imagine the new world that opened. Let me tell you something; from then until I left that prison, in every free moment I had, if I was not reading in the library, I was reading on my bunk. You couldn't have gotten me out of books with a wedge. Between Mr. Muhammad's teachings, my correspondence, my visitors—usually Ella and Reginald—and my reading of books, months passed without my even thinking about being imprisoned. In fact, up to then, I never had been so truly free in my life. ...

As you can imagine, especially in a prison where there was heavy emphasis on rehabilitation, an inmate was smiled upon if he demonstrated an unusually intense interest in books. There was a sizable number of well-read inmates, especially the popular debaters. Some were said by many to be practically walking encyclopedias. They were almost celebrities. No university would ask any student to devour literature as I did when this new world opened to me, of being able to read and *understand.*

I read more in my room than in the library itself. An inmate who was known to read a lot could check out more than the permitted maximum number of books. I preferred reading in the total isolation of my own room.

When I had progressed to really serious reading, every night at about ten p.m. I would be outraged with the "lights out." It always seemed to catch me right in the middle of something engrossing.

Fortunately, right outside my door was a corridor light that cast a glow into my room. The glow was enough to read by, once my eyes adjusted to it. So when "lights out" came, I would sit on the floor where I could continue reading in that glow.

At one-hour intervals the night guards paced past every room. Each time I heard the approaching footsteps, I jumped into bed and feigned sleep. And as soon as the guard passed, I got back out of bed onto the floor area of that light-glow, where I would read for another fifty-eight minutes—until the guard approached again. That went on until three or four every morning. Three or four hours of sleep a night was enough for me. Often in the years in the streets I had slept less than that.

I have often reflected upon the new vistas that reading opened to me. I knew right there in prison that reading had changed forever the course of my life. As I see it today, the ability to read awoke inside me some long dormant craving to be mentally alive. I certainly wasn't seeking any degree, the way a college confers a status symbol upon its students. My homemade education gave me, with every additional book that I read, a little bit more sensitivity to the deafness, dumbness, and blindness that was afflicting the black race in America. Not long ago, an English writer telephoned me from London, asking questions. One was, "What's your alma mater?" I told him, "Books." You will never catch me with a free fifteen minutes in which I'm not studying something I feel might be able to help the black man. ...

Every time I catch a plane, I have with me a book that I want to read—and that's a lot of books these days. If I weren't out here every day battling the white man, I could spend the rest of my life reading, just satisfying my curiosity—because you can hardly mention anything I'm not curious about. I don't think anybody ever got more out of going to prison than I did. In fact, prison enabled me to study far more intensively than I would have if my life had gone differently and I had attended some college. I imagine that one of the biggest troubles with colleges is there are too many distractions, too much panty-raiding, fraternities, and boola-boola and all of that. Where else but in prison could I have attacked my ignorance by being able to study intensely sometimes as much as fifteen hours a day?

Comprehension

1. How did Bimbi inspire Malcolm X to become better educated?
2. Malcolm X outlines the process by which he taught himself to read. Summarize it in your own words.
3. What was the effect of Malcolm's copying the dictionary?
4. What caused Malcolm X to feel so "truly free" in prison?

5. To what effect did Malcolm X put his new-gained ability to read?
6. On what grounds does Malcolm X compare his prison studies with a college education?
7. What made those who met Malcolm X believe he was university educated?
8. Throughout this essay, Malcolm X uses a lot of slang. Find five examples and paraphrase them.

Analysis

1. What is the conclusion of this essay? How does Malcolm X finally end his story of his life in prison? How effective is this ending?
2. For whom did Malcolm X write this essay? What assumptions did he make about his audience? How well do you think he addressed this audience?
3. In what ways do you identify with Malcolm X's self-improvement process? Have you ever taught yourself to do something difficult? Outline the process, if you have, and compare it with the attitude Malcolm X expressed in his essay.
4. Malcolm X claims that prison allowed him to be free. In what ways was that true? Have you ever felt that being held down by something actually helped you to grow and change?
5. In what ways did Malcolm X show his belief in the dignity of humankind—white or black? Do you think he was a revolutionary man? How does his essay relate to current race relations among Canada's various groups?

Writing Suggestions

1. What conditions or causes resulted in your coming to college?
2. Define an issue, see if it can be discussed using cause and effect analysis, and then write an essay.

Unit Five

"Observe always that everything is the result of a change." (Marcus Aurelius)

Writing That Affects the Reader:

Description, Narration, Argumentation/Persuasion

The following rhetorical techniques—description, narration, and argumentation/persuasion—are used not only to explain but also to create an effect upon readers' feelings, ideas, and actions.

Description

Description is a means of conveying information vividly. It appeals to a reader's senses—sight, touch, taste, hearing—as it attempts to reproduce through words the physical qualities of a previous experience. Affecting a reader's senses heightens emotion.

Descriptive writing depends upon conveying feeling using adjectives, adverbs, similes, metaphors, and other rhetorical devices.

Curtain Up

By Catherine George

1   Sit back, relax and enjoy. It's showtime in Ontario. And you're in for an eye-popping treat. In the next few weeks, right here on our country stage, the curtain will rise on a color spectacle to rival the flashiest of show-biz extravaganzas.

2   Watch Mother Nature, the star of the show, in her role as leading lady. Like a classy Vegas showgirl, she'll do a quick change right before your eyes. She'll coyly shed her subdued summer wardrobe and, with a flourish, transform into a brightly-painted vixen, boldly strutting her stuff centre stage.

3   She'll blaze across the hills and down the valleys in a flamboyant cloak of many colors, oranges, crimsons, purples, and a crown of gold, in a season finale that's sure to get rave reviews from even the most jaded of critics. Best of all, everyone gets a free front-row seat.

4   Though the travelling show isn't officially due to open in southern Ontario for a couple of weeks, you can catch a sneak preview in the hardwood forests farther north where the elevations are higher and the climate change occurs a little earlier.

5   And, contrary to what some of us have been told, Jack Frost doesn't have a thing to do with changing the color of the leaves. In fact, he is often the spoiler if he arrives too soon, causing them to shrivel and drop before they get a chance to flaunt their fiery hues. What it takes is sufficient rainfall, cool (not frosty) nights and bright sunny days that cause the sugars in the leaves to produce those red, orange and yellow pigments.

6   With the exception of a few remote areas in Asia, no place on earth puts on an autumn display to rival the one you'll see in Ontario, Quebec, the Maritimes, and over the border in New England and northern New York state. Though no one can predict for certain, late September through Thanksgiving weekend should be the best time for leaf peepers to plan a jaunt into the countryside.

7   If you watch the ads you'll find a number of bus tour operators offering foliage tours in Ontario, Quebec and across the border. Cruise boats operate regularly on the Muskoka, Kawartha and Haliburton lakes, a pleasant day's outing for the family. It's probably too late this year but for next autumn you might think about renting a houseboat and taking the family for a color cruise on the Trent-Severn waterways system.

8   Algoma Central runs a train trip from Sault Ste. Marie into the spectacular Agawa canyon until mid-October. Some of the conservation areas such as the Kortright Centre near Kleinburg sponsor autumn color walks. So there are plenty of ways you can put a touch of color in your life.

9   But the best bet for catching the scenery is in the family car. All you need is a tank of gas, a picnic basket and your camera. When the mood strikes or a particular setting appeals you can stop for lunch under a cathedral of color, buy a pumpkin at a roadside stand or pick up a fresh apple pie at a country bakery.

10   You might try to plan your jaunt to coincide with one of the agricultural fairs or harvest festivals taking place in the small communities all across Ontario from now until Thanksgiving.

•

Comprehension

1. George's thesis is "In the next few weeks ... showbiz extravaganzas." With what sorts of examples does she develop her supporting details?

2. What is the analogy established in the thesis and operating throughout this essay?
3. In paragraphs two and five there are examples of personification. What are they?
4. What is the comparison made between Mother Nature and Jack Frost?
5. Find five examples of George's use of vivid language. George describes a colour spectacle. What specific words does she use? How many colours does she present in the first five paragraphs?
6. Does she make use of simile and metaphor? Find examples of each.
7. In the last five paragraphs, George makes a number of suggestions to her readers about how to get a "free front-row seat." What are they?

Analysis

1. What level of language does George use and why did she choose the level of vocabulary in the article? Is it appropriate to her subject? Give examples that show the level of language and vocabulary.
2. This article was written for *The Toronto Star*, and its intended audience was the general reading public. What effects did the writer want to produce in her audience?
3. George places side by side two apparent opposites, comparing the still natural world of the woods to the flamboyant artificial Las Vegas floor show. How and why does this comparison work?

Essays that are solely descriptive are rare. Rather, description is a technique employed to enhance the style of a piece of writing—whether it be a process analysis or a comparison and contrast.

The Shack

By Margaret Laurence

1   The most loved place, for me, in this country has in fact been many places. It has changed throughout the years, as I and my circumstances have changed. I haven't really lost any of the best places from the past, though. I may no longer inhabit them, but they inhabit me, portions of memory, presences in the mind. One such place was my family's summer cottage at Clear Lake in Riding Mountain National Park, Manitoba. It was known to us simply as The Lake. Before the government piers and the sturdy log staircases down to the shore were put in, we used to slither with an exhilarating sense of peril down the steep homemade branch and dirt shelf-steps, through the stands of thin tall spruce

and birch trees slender and graceful as girls, passing moss-hairy fallen logs and the white promise of wild strawberry blossoms, until we reached the sand and the hard bright pebbles of the beach at the edge of the cold spring-fed lake where at nights the loons still cried eerily, before too much humanshriek made them move away north.

2 My best place at the moment is very different, although I guess it has some of the attributes of that long-ago place. It is a small cedar cabin on the Otonabee River in southern Ontario. I've lived three summers there, writing, birdwatching, river-watching. I sometimes feel sorry for the people in speedboats who spend their weekends zinging up and down the river at about a million miles an hour. For all they're able to see, the riverbanks might just as well be green concrete and the river itself flowing with molten plastic.

3 Before sunup, I'm wakened by birdvoices and, I may say, birdfeet clattering and thumping on the cabin roof. Cursing only slightly, I get up *temporarily,* for the pre-dawn ritual of lighting a small fire in the old black woodstove (mornings are chilly here, even in summer) and looking out at the early river. The waters have a lovely spook quality at this hour, entirely mist-covered, a secret meeting of river and sky.

4 By the time I get up to stay, the mist has vanished and the river is a clear ale-brown, shining with sun. I drink my coffee and sit looking out to the opposite shore, where the giant maples are splendidly green now and will be trees of flame in the fall of the year. Oak and ash stand among the maples, and the grey skeletons of the dead elms, gauntly beautiful even in death. At the very edge of the river, the willows are everywhere, water-related trees, magic trees, pale green in early summer, silvergreen in late summer, greengold in autumn.

5 I begin work, and every time I lift my eyes from the page and glance outside, it is to see some marvel or other. The joyous dance-like flight of the swallows. The orange-black flash of the orioles who nest across the river. The amazing takeoff of a red-winged blackbird, revealing like a swiftly unfolded fan the hidden scarlet in those dark wings. The flittering of the goldfinches, who always travel in domestic pairs, he gorgeous in black-patterned yellow feathers, she (alas) drabber in greenish grey-yellow.

6 A pair of great blue herons have their huge unwieldy nest about half a mile upriver, and although they are very shy, occasionally through the open door I hear a sudden approaching rush of air (yes, you can *hear* it) and look up quickly to see the magnificent unhurried sweep of those powerful wings. The only other birds which can move me so much are the Canada geese in their autumn migration flight, their far-off wilderness voices the harbinger of winter.

7 Many boats ply these waterways, and all of them are given mental gradings of merit or lack of it, by me. Standing low in the estimation of all of us along this stretch of the river are some of the big yachts, whose ego-tripping skippers don't have the courtesy to slow down in cottage areas and whose violent wakes scour out our shorelines. Ranking highest in my good books are the silent unpol-

luting canoes and rowboats, and next to them, the small outboard motorboats put-putting along and carrying patient fishermen, and the homemade houseboats, unspeedy and somehow cosy-looking, decorated lovingly with painted birds or flowers or gaudy abstract splodges.

8   In the quiet of afternoon, if no boats are around, I look out and see the half-moon leap of a fish, carp or muskie, so instantaneous that one has the impression of having seen not a fish but an arc of light.

9   The day moves on, and about four o'clock Linda and Susan from the nearby farm arrive. I call them the Girls of the Pony Express. Accompanied by dogs and laughter, they ride their horses into my yard, kindly bringing my mail from the rural route postbox up the road. For several summers it was Old Jack who used to drive his battered Volkswagen up to fetch the mail. He was one of the best neighbours and most remarkable men I've ever known. As a boy of eighteen, he had homesteaded a hundred miles north of Regina. Later, he'd been a skilled toolmaker with Ford. He'd travelled to South America and done many amazing things. He was a man whose life had taught him a lot of wisdom. After his much-loved wife died, he moved out here to the river, spending as short a winter as possible in Peterborough, and getting back into his cottage the first of anyone in the spring, when the river was still in flood and he could only get in and out, hazardously, by boat. I used to go out in his boat with him, late afternoons, and we would dawdle along the river, looking at the forest stretches and the open rolling farmlands and vast old barns, and at the smaller things close by, the heavy luxuriance of ferns at the water's rim, the dozens of snapping turtles with unblinking eyes, all sizes and generations of the turtle tribe, sunning themselves on the fallen logs in the river. One summer, Old Jack's eighty-fourth, he spent some time planting maple saplings on his property. A year later, when I saw him dying, it seemed to me he'd meant those trees as a kind of legacy, a declaration of faith. Those of us along the river, here, won't forget him, nor what he stood for.

10   After work, I go out walking and weed-inspecting. Weeds and wildflowers impress me as much as any cultivated plant. I've heard that in a year when the milkweed is plentiful, the Monarch butterflies will also be plentiful. This year the light pinkish milkweed flowers stand thick and tall, and sure enough, here are the dozens of Monarch butterflies, fluttering like dusky orange-gold angels all over the place. I can't identify as many plants as I'd like, but I'm learning. Chickweed, the ragged-leafed lambs' quarters, the purple-and-white wild phlox with its expensive-smelling perfume, the pink and mauve wild asters, the two-toned yellow of the tiny butter-and-eggs flowers, the burnt orange of devil's paint-brush, the staunch nobility of the huge purple thistles, and, almost best of all, that long stalk covered with clusters of miniature creamy blossoms which I finally tracked down in my wildflower book—this incomparable plant bears the armorial name of the Great Mullein of the Figwort Family. It may not be the absolute prettiest of our wildflowers, but it certainly has the most stunning pedigree.

11   It is night now, and there are no lights except those of our few cottages. At sunset, an hour or so ago, I watched the sun's last flickers touching the rippling river, making it look as though some underwater world had lighted all its candles down there. Now it is dark. Dinner over, I turn out the electric lights in the cabin so I can see the stars. The black skydome (or perhaps skydom, like kingdom) is alive and alight.

12   Tomorrow the weekend will begin, and friends will arrive. We'll talk all day and probably half the night, and that will be good. But for now, I'm content to be alone, because loneliness is something that doesn't exist here.

•

Comprehension

1. The first two paragraphs act as Laurence's introduction based on her opening line, "The most loved place ..." What is this place and how do you know?
2. What was the first place she loved most?
3. What is the controlling pattern of organization Laurence uses from paragraph three to the end? How does she organize her supporting details within this pattern?
4. Paraphrase her "pre-dawn ritual."
5. Paragraph four focuses on the trees around Laurence's cabin. Find examples of simile and metaphor at work here.
6. The bird is often used as a symbol of our imagination. In paragraph five what is the implied analogy that Laurence uses?
7. In paragraph seven how many classifications of boats does Laurence present to her readers?
8. In paragraph nine Laurence pauses in her description of her day to tell an anecdote about Old Jack. What kind of anecdote is it?
9. In paragraph ten Laurence employs cause and effect. Find examples of this pattern of organization.
10. Do you think Laurence's final sentence could stand as her thesis statement? Why or why not?

Analysis

1. Do you think there is a distinction between being lonely and being alone? How does Laurence's essay support your point of view?

2. Laurence has succeeded in condensing the details of Old Jack's life into a single paragraph. How is it that we feel we know him and "what he stood for"?

3. Compare Laurence's attitude to nature to that of Catherine George. You might wish to consider their word choice and techniques.

4. "The black skydome (or perhaps skydom, like kingdom) is alive and alight." The play on words—skydome/skydom—is a *pun*. What does Laurence achieve by the use of this pun?

5. Laurence presents a typical day at her cabin. These simple everyday events through their repetition—both in action and words—take on a greater significance for Laurence; that is, they become a *ritual*. Remember, a **ritual** is a form of celebration or praise, often with spiritual overtones. To what extent is this true in Laurence's account of her day? What rituals are important to you? What do they celebrate?

Writing Strategy

Margaret Laurence had a keen eye. She saw shadows, colours, and shapes, and she drew comparisons. She knew the names of objects and animals, and she knew how to talk about what they did and why they existed. Her descriptions are full of details that express her strong love of the Canadian outdoors.

To use description effectively, you must first of all observe closely. Descriptive writing rests on details—colours, smells, sounds, and shapes. It is important to select details for effect. What *main effect* do you wish to create for the reader? Do you wish to re-create a scene in its physical dimension or do you want to describe a moment in time and the feelings you experienced? Description must rely on a selection of details that will be most useful for creating the main effect. A writer must also decide on a point of view in using descriptive details. Should you re-create in words the entire scene in front of you or only a part? If you were to describe an object, would you begin your description at the top or the bottom?

Above all, descriptive writing must be concrete. You must use specific words and a variety of details in order to create a vivid impression. For example, compare the two passages below. The first is by Laurence. The second is a paraphrase of her passage written in a vague and general style.

> *LAURENCE:* By the time I get up to stay, the mist has vanished and the river is a clear ale-brown, shining with sun. ... Oak and ash stand among the maples, and the grey skeletons of the dead elms, gauntly beautiful even in death.

> *PARAPHRASE:* By the time I'm up, the river is clear and the sun is shining. I look at trees, some of which are dead.

Writing Suggestions

1. Describe in detail a favourite place where you have recently spent time. Use as many words as you can to relate to readers the colours, smells, shapes, and sizes found in this place.
2. Describe your feelings for a person by telling the reader the concrete effects that person has on you. For instance, how do you physically react when you first see someone you really like or despise? Do you blush? Do you feel hot and cold at the same time? What happens to the palms of your hands, the pit of your stomach?
3. Describe a vivid memory of an incident in your childhood and then describe your feelings about it. How would you describe joy or anger, for instance?

Narration

Narration is a story-telling technique. It can be as brief as an anecdote, as casual as a joke, as exciting as gossip about the weekend.

Reading Strategy

What you will notice with all narrative is that there is a beginning, a middle, and an end. Readers are impelled by the forward movement and development of a story. They become increasingly interested in "what happens next" when a clear chronological ordering of events is presented. A narrative may be interrupted from time to time by a flashback, a foreshadowing, a description of a scene, yet readers have an expectation that the events in the story will eventually reach some kind of end or resolution. Narrative writing arranges events in time to make a point. A joke, for instance, leads a listener through a series of events and moments up to a punchline. The events must be selected and related carefully and accurately for the punchline to make sense. Narrative depends on logical order, clear detail, effective transitions, and a believable outcome.

The following story by the brothers Grimm is very simple, at first. The plot structure—the order of key events—is linear; one event follows another in a simple line of cause and effect.

The appearance of simplicity is deceptive, for this is a story of profound implications. As you read it, see if you can detect the turning point, that is, the moment when the story takes a change of direction and meaning. Ask yourself whether the end met your initial expectations.

The Old Man and His Grandson

By Jacob and Wilhelm Grimm

There was once a very old man, whose eyes had become dim, his ears dull of hearing, his knees trembled, and when he sat at table he could hardly hold the spoon, and spilled the broth on the tablecloth or let it run out of his mouth. His son and his son's wife were disgusted at this, so at last they made the old grandfather sit in the corner behind the stove, and they gave him his food in an earthenware bowl, and not even enough of it. And he used to look toward the table with his eyes full of tears. Once, too, his trembling hands could not hold the bowl, and it fell to the ground and broke. The young wife scolded him, but he said nothing and only sighed. Then they bought him a wooden bowl for a few pennies out of which he had to eat.

They were once sitting thus when the little grandson of four years old began to gather together some bits of wood on the ground. "What are you doing there?" asked the father. "I am making a little trough," answered the child, "for father and mother to eat out of when I am big."

The man and his wife looked at each other for a while and presently began to cry. Then they took the old grandfather to the table and henceforth always let him eat with them and likewise said nothing if he did spill a little of anything.

•

Comprehension

1. In paragraph one, what background details are you given? Summarize the facts.
2. The facts in paragraph one provide the **setting** for the story. Setting tells readers when and where the story happens. It can also inform the reader of the social, economic, and political status of the characters. Setting can also convey an emotional atmosphere. How firmly can you establish where and when the story took place?
3. In paragraph two, what has the child learned from observing his parents' treatment of the grandfather?
4. Although this is a simple story, readers can discover complex motivations for the characters' actions. Why do the man and wife start crying?
5. List in point form the plot of the story.

Analysis

1. A story is not only its plot; it has a central **theme**, an idea that it develops. What is the theme of this story? Look at the title for a clue. Why does the title exclude mention of the parents?
2. An **archetype** is an assumed ideal pattern used as a model. Could this story be read as an archetype of family life?
3. What lesson does this folk tale teach us about human behaviour?
4. Folk tales often transcend time and culture. Does this story succeed in doing so?
5. This narrative is told in the **third-person** point of view (using *he, she, they, it*). The narrator may or may not be directly involved in the events of the story. The **first-person** point of view uses *I, my, we* and tells the story either as a participant or an observer. Retell this story from the first-person point of view of one of the characters. Compare your version with those of your classmates.

Writing Strategy

Most stories in everyday life have already happened before they are told on paper. Thus, the use of the *past tense* is common in writing a narrative. Events in a story are arranged by writers in chronological order—the order in which they occurred in time. Some narrative structures reverse the order of events—going from last to first to make a certain point—but this structure is rare. Often narrative requires some background information. Readers need to know details about the people in a story before the actual events are described.

If you use narrative in essay form, you must have a central point. Telling a joke without a punchline would be similar to writing a narrative without a reason. If you wish to tell a story, say, about a friend who won a lottery, the point of your story could be to show what the friend did with the money. You would have to restrict your narrative to the events that are crucial to the friend's winning of the jackpot, pointing out in concrete detail the series of events that took place once the money was in your friend's hands. The point of your story would be to show readers what happened to your friend; perhaps it'd tell how sudden wealth brought both happiness and despair.

John Allemang's essay tells a first-person story consisting of a series of anecdotes.

Bedtime Stories

By John Allemang

1   In my nine years as official family storyteller, I figure I've taken on about 727 parts. Before a fidgety audience of two, I've played genies, princesses, bickering hippopotami, a Teutonic witch (the movie role went to Anjelica Huston), God, the Hardy Boys, an Alsatian chef, neurotic mice, two nuns and, my personal favourite, Nancy "Boss" Chicken, failed telephone operator.

2   Of all the nice surprises lying in wait for parents—outweighing the nasty ones, you'll be happy to hear, if only because sleepless nights come as no surprise—one of the nicest has been bedtime. Late at night, I've discovered, my children will listen to me. This is the next thing to a miracle, as you'll know if you've ever tried to tell a child not to inspect his baseball cards in the middle of the road.

3   For someone whose stage career never got much beyond the role of Lettuce in the Grade 1 production of Peter Rabbit, there is a wonderful pleasure in giving a nightly performance. And my audience gives me the actor's supreme compliment: they stay awake. Now I realize that what my children enjoy hearing are the squawks and howls and bad French accents, not the moral at the end of the story. But I like to think of it as a softening up. Listen to my rendition of The Church Mice 50 times and you'll pay closer attention next time I tell you to take your feet off the table.

4   What both children and adults enjoy about bedtime stories is that they are make-believe. They are a quick escape from a way of life that no longer tolerates many fantasies or escapes. And that's why I was surprised when my six-year-old daughter said to me the other night, after I'd sent my son off to his room, "Daddy, tell me a story about when you were little."

5   Playing a pompous chicken in front of your child is easy. Playing yourself is much harder. I have this odd feeling that my children admire me more the less I'm like myself. Part of the pleasure in reading stories comes from convincing these hereditary skeptics that their meek father really is part-genie, part-witch, that he is able to turn into whatever he pleases.

6   The past imposes its own limits, and I don't always like to remind myself of them. We didn't have an enchanted wardrobe or a magic looking glass when I was young. We had shopping centres and open ditches and three transit connections to downtown Toronto. It is not a past I want to escape—it seemed like paradise at the time—but as a realm of fantasy, it always seemed to be lacking.

7   But my daughter was asking, and she must have had her reasons. I turned out the lights, thought hard, and came up with a memory of my grandparents' garden in the Niagara peninsula. I told her about climbing cherry trees and playing hide-and-go-seek among the sunflowers, and before long the discarded bits

and pieces of this ordinary life started coming back together again. I remembered for my daughter the stale, musty smell of the basement where my grandfather, who was a dentist, had his office. I talked about the crisp, new comic books that my grandmother kept ready for our surprise visits, and the ancient organ we pretended to play, and the earaches we got after a summer's swimming in Lake Erie.

8   These stories have no end, as my wily daughter must have known. She was trying to match the 1,001 Arabian Nights for staying power. Every night since my debut I have felt a little dread when the storybook comes to an end and I have to improvise my life. How can I hope to match the last book we read, which was about a giant who collected dreams and blew them into children's ears and saved the world?

9   But the plain, simple stories that leave my mouth enter my daughter's ears almost as a dream. I remember the trivia from my childhood, but she hears myths. "Once upon a time …" I should say, as I begin my tales of breakfast hamburgers at Woolworth's and babysitters who died on the job and the boy who crossed the busy street against the rule so he could buy his Mom a present.

10   Not a princess anywhere. But for my daughter, who hears stories about princesses and giants every night, family stories have their unreal charm. And at the very worst (such were the joys) they put her to sleep.

•

Comprehension

1. What is the central point of Allemang's essay?
2. Allemang tells the story of himself telling stories. How many separate stories are told within this framework?
3. What setting is presented in the first paragraph?
4. Explain the allusion to the actress Anjelica Huston. Can you explain any of Allemang's other references to children's stories?
5. Give examples of how Allemang makes this a funny narrative.
6. Find an example of Allemang's use of cause and effect.
7. How does he compare storybook stories to stories about when he was little?
8. "The past imposes its own limits." What does this mean?
9. In paragraph nine, Allemang refers to the "giant who collected dreams." How does Allemang implicitly compare himself to that giant?
10. How many different audiences is Allemang addressing in this essay?

Analysis

1. In spite of its humour, how do you know this is a serious essay?
2. Allemang says people enjoy stories because "they are a quick escape from a way of life that no longer tolerates many fantasies or escapes." Do you think this is true? Do you find it ironic that Allemang offers so many escapes?
3. Even though this was written for a North American reading audience (just look at all those allusions), do you think this essay can appeal to people worldwide? Why?
4. Almost every family has its official storyteller. Who told you your stories and what were they about?
5. "I remember the trivia from my childhood, but she hears myths." What does Allemang mean by this?
6. Many writers, including Shakespeare, claim that literature gives humankind a sense of the eternal. In "Bedtime Stories," simple, mundane events of one's life are transformed into stories that engage the imagination. How important is imagination in your life? Does telling stories make your life more meaningful to you? Do you think telling stories can give people both a history and a future?

In this final narrative essay, by Maya Angelou, the author appears to be telling a simple story about a group of people listening to a boxing match on the radio. In fact, Angelou tells a number of stories at the same time—each one relating directly to the boxing match and its effect on the people in the room.

The Fight

By Maya Angelou

The last inch of space was filled, yet people continued to wedge themselves along the walls of the Store. Uncle Willie had turned the radio up to its last notch so that youngsters on the porch wouldn't miss a word. Women sat on kitchen chairs, dining-room chairs, stools and upturned wooden boxes. Small children and babies perched on every lap available and men leaned on the shelves or on each other.

The apprehensive mood was shot through with shafts of gaiety, as a black sky is streaked with lightning.

"I ain't worried 'bout this fight. Joe's gonna whip that cracker like it's open season."

"He gone whip him till that white boy call him Momma."

At last the talking was finished and the string-along songs about razor blades were over and the fight began.

"A quick jab to the head." In the Store the crowd grunted. "A left to the head and a right and another left." One of the listeners cackled like a hen and was quieted.

"They're in a clench, Louis is trying to fight his way out."

Some bitter comedian on the porch said, "That white man don't mind hugging that niggah now, I betcha."

"The referee is moving in to break them up, but Louis finally pushed the contender away and it's an uppercut to the chin. The contender is hanging on, now he's backing away. Louis catches him with a short left to the jaw."

A tide of murmuring assent poured out the doors and into the yard.

"Another left and another left. Louis is saving that mighty right ..." The mutter in the Store had grown into a baby roar and it was pierced by the clang of a bell and the announcer's "That's the bell for round three, ladies and gentlemen."

As I pushed my way into the Store I wondered if the announcer gave any thought to the fact that he was addressing as "ladies and gentlemen" all the Negroes around the world who sat sweating and praying, glued to their "master's voice."

There were only a few calls for R.C. Colas, Dr. Peppers, and Hire's root beer. The real festivities would begin after the fight. Then even the old Christian ladies who taught their children and tried themselves to practice turning the other cheek would buy soft drinks, and if the Brown Bomber's victory was a particularly bloody one they would order peanut patties and Baby Ruths also.

Bailey and I lay the coins on top of the cash register. Uncle Willie didn't allow us to ring up sales during a fight. It was too noisy and might shake up the atmosphere. When the gong rang for the next round we pushed through the near-sacred quiet to the herd of children outside.

"He's got Louis against the ropes and now it's a left to the body and a right to the ribs. Another right to the body, it looks like it was low ... Yes, ladies and gentlemen, the referee is signalling but the contender keeps raining the blows on Louis. It's another to the body, and it looks like Louis is going down."

My race groaned. It was our people falling. It was another lynching, yet another Black man hanging on a tree. One more woman ambushed and raped. A Black boy whipped and maimed. It was hounds on the trail of a man running through slimy swamps. It was a white woman slapping her maid for being forgetful.

The men in the Store stood away from the walls and at attention. Women greedily clutched the babes on their laps while on the porch the shufflings and smiles, flirtings and pinching of a few minutes before were gone. This might be the end of the world. If Joe lost we were back in slavery and beyond help. It would all be true, the accusations that we were lower types of human beings. Only a little higher than the apes. True that we were stupid and ugly and lazy and dirty and, unlucky and worst of all, that God Himself hated us and ordained us to be hewers of wood and drawers of water, forever and ever, world without end.

We didn't breathe. We didn't hope. We waited.

"He's off the ropes, ladies and gentlemen. He's moving towards the center of the ring." There was no time to be relieved. The worst might still happen.

"And now it looks like Joe is mad. He's caught Carnera with a left hook to the head and a right to the head. It's a left jab to the body and another left to the head. There's a left cross and a right to the head. The contender's right eye is bleeding and he can't seem to keep his block up. Louis is penetrating every block. The referee is moving in, but Louis sends a left to the body and it's the uppercut to the chin and the contender is dropping. He's on the canvas, ladies and gentlemen."

Babies slid to the floor as women stood up and men leaned toward the radio.

"Here's the referee. He's counting. One, two, three, four, five, six, seven … Is the contender trying to get up again?"

All the men in the Store shouted, "NO."

"—eight, nine, ten." There were a few sounds from the audience, but they seemed to be holding themselves in against tremendous pressure.

"The fight is all over, ladies and gentlemen. Let's get the microphone over to the referee … Here he is. He's got the Brown Bomber's hand, he's holding it up … Here he is …"

Then the voice, husky and familiar, came to wash over us—"The winnah, and still heavyweight champeen of the world … Joe Louis."

Champion of the world. A Black boy. Some Black mother's son. He was the strongest man in the world. People drank Coca-Colas like ambrosia and ate candy bars like Christmas. Some of the men went behind the Store and poured white lightning in their soft-drink bottles, and a few of the bigger boys followed them. Those who were not chased away came back blowing their breath in front of themselves like proud smokers.

It would take an hour or more before the people would leave the Store and head for home. Those who lived too far had made arrangements to stay in town. It wouldn't do for a Black man and his family to be caught on a lonely country road on a night when Joe Louis had proved that we were the strongest people in the world.

•

Comprehension

1. How does Angelou set the scene to let readers know this is an important event?

2. The events of the story are interspersed with dialogue. What is the effect of the dialogue on the telling of the story?
3. Explain the reference to "their 'master's voice.'"
4. What is the dramatic effect Angelou creates by describing the people's reactions to the radio commentary on the Joe Louis fight?
5. How many stories are actually told here? Identify each one.
6. "The real festivities ... Baby Ruths also." Explain the irony in this passage.
7. In the paragraph beginning "My race groaned," Angelou uses syntactical repetition ("It was ..."). What is the effect of this?
8. What are the implications of the phrase "hewers of wood and drawers of water, forever and ever, world without end"? What does the phrase allude to?
9. A lot of brand names of products are included in the story. What do these tell you about the young narrator?
10. What is the reaction of the crowd in the store to the Brown Bomber's victory?

Analysis

1. Joe Louis has become a symbol for his people. What passages or single details demonstrate this in the story?
2. What are the people in the store really like? What is their social standing? What are their fears and dreams? What is their daily life like? Base your answer on the details Angelou provides.
3. What does the store represent to the people in the story?
4. Angelou presents this narrative based on her own childhood memories. Just like Allemang she shapes those memories for a purpose. Define it.
5. Discuss the irony in the final paragraph.

Writing Suggestions

1. Write a narrative about a very happy moment in your life. Tell it first in third person and then in first person.
2. Write a simple narrative about a series of events that had several meanings. For example, write about your high-school graduation but point out how the actions in that story had broader implications in your life.
3. Write a narrative about a time in your life when you were misunderstood by someone.

Argumentation and Persuasion

Argumentation or **persuasion** is written with the express purpose of influencing the reader by effecting a change in the reader's opinions, attitude, or actions. The essay of argumentation or persuasion issues a challenge. To be successful, this type of essay may exploit all of the other patterns of organization and prose techniques. Written effectively, such an essay will sway the reader to think, feel, and act differently.

Read the following essay by Barbara Lawrence, "Four-Letter Words Can Hurt You." How does it make you feel? Does it issue a challenge to your way of thinking?

Four-Letter Words Can Hurt You

By Barbara Lawrence

Why should any words be called obscene? Don't they all describe natural human functions? Am I trying to tell them, my students demand, that the "strong, earthy, gut-honest"—or, if they are fans of Norman Mailer, the "rich, liberating, existential"—language they use to describe sexual activity isn't preferable to "phony-sounding, middle-class words like 'intercourse' and 'copulate'?" "Cop You Late!" they say with fancy inflections and gagging grimaces. "Now, what is *that* supposed to mean?"

Well, what is it supposed to mean? And why indeed should one group of words describing human functions and human organs be acceptable in ordinary conversation and another, describing presumably the same organs and functions, be tabooed—so much so, in fact, that some of these words still cannot appear in print in many parts of the English-speaking world?

The argument that these taboos exist only because of "sexual hangups" (middle-class, middle-age, feminist), or even that they are a result of class oppression (the contempt of the Norman conquerors for the language of their Anglo-Saxon serfs), ignores a much more likely explanation, it seems to me, and that is the sources and functions of the words themselves.

The best known of the tabooed sexual verbs, for example, comes from the German *ficken*, meaning "to strike"; combined, according to Partridge's etymological dictionary *Origins*, with the Latin sexual verb *futuere*; associated in turn with the Latin *fustis*, "a staff or cudgel"; the Celtic *buc*, "a point, hence to pierce"; the Irish *bot*, "the male member"; the Latin *battuere*, "to beat"; the Gaelic *batair*, "a cudgeller"; the Early Irish *bualaim*, "I strike"; and so forth. It is one of what etymologists sometimes call "the sadistic group of words for the man's part in copulation."

The brutality of this word, then, and its equivalents ("screw," "bang," etc.), is not an illusion of the middle class or a crotchet of Women's Liberation. In their origins and imagery these words carry undeniably painful, if not sadistic, implications, the object of which is almost always female. Consider, for example, what a "screw" actually does to the wood it penetrates; what a painful, even mutilating, activity this kind of analogy suggests. "Screw" is particularly interesting in this context, since the noun, according to Partridge, comes from words meaning "groove," "nut," "ditch," "breeding sow," "scrofula" and "swelling," while the verb, besides its explicit imagery, has antecedent associations to "write on," "scratch," "scarify," and so forth—a revealing fusion of a mechanical or painful action with an obviously denigrated object.

Not all obscene words, of course, are as implicitly sadistic or denigrating to women as these, but all that I know seem to serve a similar purpose: to reduce the human organism (especially the female organism) and human functions (especially sexual and procreative) to their least organic, most mechanical dimensions; to substitute a trivializing or deforming resemblance for the complex human reality of what is being described.

Tabooed male descriptives, when they are not openly denigrating to women, often serve to divorce a male organ or function from any significant interaction with the female. Take the words "testes," for example, suggesting "witnesses" (from the Latin *testis*) to the sexual and procreative strengths of the male organ; and the obscene counterpart of this word, which suggests more than a mechanical shape. Or compare almost any of the "rich," "liberating" sexual verbs, so fashionable today among male writers, with that much-derided Latin word "copulate" ("to find or join together") or even that Anglo-Saxon phrase (which seems to have had no trouble surviving the Norman Conquest) "make love."

How arrogantly self-involved the tabooed words seem in comparison to either of the other terms, and how contemptuous of the female partner. Understandably so, of course, if she is only a "skirt," a "broad," a "chick," a "pussy," or a "piece." If she is, in other words, no more than her skirt, or what her skirt conceals; no more than a breeder, or the broadest part of her; no more than a piece of human being or a "piece of tail."

The most severely tabooed of all the female descriptives, incidentally, are those like a "piece of tail," which suggest (either explicitly or through antecedents) that there is no significant difference between the female channel through which we are all conceived and born and the anal outlet common to both sexes—a distinction that pornographers have always enjoyed obscuring.

This effort to deny women their biological identity, their individuality, their humanness, is such an important aspect of obscene language that one can only marvel at how seldom, in an era preoccupied with definitions of obscenity, this fact is brought to our attention. One problem, of course, is that many of the people in the best position to do this (critics, teachers, writers) are so reluctant today to admit that they are angered or shocked by obscenity. Bored, maybe, unimpressed, aesthetically displeased but—no matter how brutal or denigrating the material—never angered, never shocked.

And yet how eloquently angered, how piously shocked many of these same people become if denigrating language is used about any minority group other than women; if the obscenities are racial or ethnic, that is, rather than sexual. Words like "coon," "kike," "spic," "wop," after all, deform identity, deny individuality and humanness in almost exactly the same way that sexual vulgarisms and obscenities do.

No one that I know, least of all my students, would fail to question the values of a society whose literature and entertainment rested heavily on racial or ethnic pejoratives. Are the values of a society whose literature and entertainment rest as heavily as ours on sexual pejoratives any less questionable?

Comprehension

1. What is the effect of Barbara Lawrence's starting her essay with a series of questions?
2. Before she gets to her thesis statement, Lawrence disposes of two counter-arguments. What are they?
3. How many etymological examples of taboo words does she include in her introduction?
4. What is the relationship between the title and the thesis statement?
5. Paraphrase what Lawrence says is the purpose of obscene words.
6. What does Lawrence say is the effect on a person who is represented by a part of the body?
7. What relationship does Lawrence suggest between pornography and four-letter words?
8. How does the author express her criticism of society in general?
9. Is Lawrence logical or emotional in her argument? What vocabulary does she use to support her position?
10. Why does Lawrence near the end of her argument include racial epithets?
11. How does Lawrence write her conclusion? How does it relate to her opening paragraphs?

Analysis

1. In what ways does Bissoondath's argument (Unit Four) on stereotyping support Lawrence's position on "four-letter words"?
2. How does Lawrence achieve such a rational argument given her highly emotive subject?

3. Explain the pun on the word hurt in the title by looking at Lawrence's evidence to support her argument.
4. Compile a list of "four-letter" words relating to women and one relating to men. What do these two lists tell you about society? How do your observations relate to Lawrence's position on such words?
5. In her conclusion Lawrence equates sexism with racism. Do you think this is a valid position to take?

Writing Strategy

The essay of argumentation or persuasion can be written in the five-paragraph format. The thesis statement of such an essay is often called a proposition, main position, or main premise. Each of those terms in effect states the focus and direction of the essay and gives readers an indication of the essay's content.

Paragraphs begin with topic sentences and develop ideas using examples and other support devices. There are, however, a number of aspects to writing argumentation or persuasion that differ from those most often associated with expository writing. Argumentation or persuasion essays use patterns of organization such as cause and effect and comparison/contrast. Think of a lawyer arguing to protect a client wrongly accused of a crime. The lawyer may choose to build his case exclusively on relating the causes that led up to the events of the crime and the victim's innocence. The lawyer, however, would also use techniques commonly associated with persuasion. These include **appeals, evidence,** and **induction/deduction.**

Before we define these terms, consider the following analogy. Suppose you are a lawyer preparing a case and must present your argument to a jury. Your role is to persuade the jury of the innocence or guilt of a client. As you have seen on television and in the movies, a lawyer may make an appeal to the jury's sense of justice. Or the lawyer may try to arouse the feelings of jurors to vote for or against the client, appealing to the jurors' personal feelings. Once emotions or a sense of justice has been aroused, the lawyer presents proof—the evidence of the case. He may tell a story, or point out contrasts in the behaviour of his client in certain situations. The lawyer takes a stand—states his point of view or his premise: "The defendant is guilty," or "My client is innocent."

To make sure his evidence was sound, the lawyer would tell the facts of the case, use witnesses and hard evidence (e.g., the murder weapon), and attempt to counter charges against his client. In other words, the lawyer would try to refute claims made against his client that he felt were unfair and untrue. Finally, the lawyer would sum up his points, in a concluding statement, and once again make an appeal to the jurors. He might end by asking them to make an honest, moral judgment.

The analogy of trial by jury can teach you much about writing an argumentation or persuasion essay. Similar methods and presentation of data are useful in setting up your essay of persuasion.

Consider Barbara Lawrence's essay, "Four-Letter Words Can Hurt You." Could you imagine this as being a lawyer's speech presented in a courtroom? Look ahead in this section and read Michele Landsberg's essay on capital punishment. Notice how she presents her subject and her evidence. What does she appeal to in her audience?

Appeals

An important feature in argumentation or persuasion is respect for your audience. How you wish to influence your readers is based on three means of **appeal**: logical, ethical, and emotional.

What appeal did Barbara Lawrence use in her essay, "Four-Letter Words Can Hurt You?" Did she use only one of the three above or did she combine them? Argumentation and persuasion can combine all three depending on the content of the essay and its dominant patterns of organization.

1. Logical
The **logical appeal** is based upon reason: objective facts, figures, and statistics are of key importance. A clear relationship between your stated position (your thesis statement) and reasons for adhering to it must be established. Evidence and proof are of prime importance in this appeal. As in the writing of an expository essay, you must have verifiable data. See the section that follows, on evidence.

2. Ethical
The **ethical appeal** rests on a system of defined values or a code of morality shared by both writer and audience. In the analogy of the lawyer, the jury's beliefs in justice and fair play should complement those of the lawyer. As part of your position you must clearly define your set of values. Readers will find your argument *credible* if your principles are clear. Credibility, in fact, is important in ethical appeals, as your audience must believe that you are not only knowledgeable but honest and fair-minded. Ethical appeals require proof and evidence as much as any other appeal. Simply stating an opinion without back-up facts can destroy your credibility as a writer of argument.

3. Emotional
The **emotional appeal** is one made first of all on the basis of your feelings for or against some idea or issue. Second, you must appeal to your readers' feelings. You may want to arouse their feelings of shame or anger concerning an

issue, and thus attempt to use facts and examples that would make them react with their hearts. For instance, read Michele Landsberg's essay and see how her language and her examples appeal to our emotions. She also uses logic in her argument, but she combines it with examples that arouse shame and doubt. This is a popular appeal: you will see it in newspaper editorials, and in television lawyer dramas, as most audiences act on how they feel—their gut reactions!

Evidence

Often writers separate argumentation into the logical category and persuasion into the emotional, but this division is based on personal choice and is not an established rule. Persuasion, for instance, can combine both logical and emotional appeals. Likewise, the ethical category can be included in both, or used exclusively on its own.

In constructing an essay of argumentation or persuasion, the evidence you present is crucial. Logical appeals, for example, must have verifiable facts. Opinions must be examined for their validity and cross-referenced to make sure they are not lies. Facts in an argument must be logically arranged. In arguing for or against an idea or a belief, you may need to find **primary sources**: first-hand evidence from interviews or personal observations. **Secondary sources** are also valuable—records and reports. Evidence must be *reliable* as well; verifying your facts often depends on doing research and cross-referencing (that is, looking up the same facts as reported by another person or book). Some of the techniques for locating data for the research paper would be helpful in argumentation (see Unit Six).

Evidence in the form of supporting details is grounded in three general areas:

1. **Authority** is citing, quoting, or summarizing the views of a well-known and respected person or institution.
   EXAMPLE: In arguing for a sandbox in a local day-care, one could cite the ideas of Jean Piaget, a noted child psychologist. In persuading citizens of your small town against hunting, you could biblically proclaim: "Thou Shalt Not Kill."
   EXAMPLE: Barbara Lawrence quotes from Partridge the etymology of the German word *ficken* to prove her point.
2. **Experience** can be presented by personal anecdote or as a historical example. The process of the experience—how something happened—or the cause and effect relationship between historical events could be related.
   EXAMPLE: In arguing for an improvement in the college's registration process you could recount the horrors of your first day, starting with the

line-ups you had to endure. To persuade readers that scientific discoveries are often simple, retell the story of Sir Isaac Newton and the apple.

EXAMPLE: Barbara Lawrence starts her essay by talking about her own students' reactions to words describing sexual activities.

3. **Facts** are information that can be validated or verified. All argumentation and persuasion rests on the use of clear facts. To argue that the ancient Egyptians were great engineers, one need only cite the proportions of the pyramids. To persuade the public against smoking, the government has made tobacco manufacturers include health warnings on packages.

Once information, wording, and appeal have been determined, the overall structure of the essay must be designed. Such structure will depend on the issue you wish to discuss, how much you decide to appeal to logic or emotion, and the needs of your audience. Classical logic presents writers with two forms of setting up an argument: deduction and induction.

Deduction

Deduction accepts a *general principle* (the **main premise** or thesis statement of the essay) as true, then applies it to a specific case or cases (the **minor premises** explored in the body paragraphs) and arrives at a rational **conclusion**. This three-part form is called a **syllogism**. It is used in argumentation to clarify the placement of evidence and to test the validity of the appeal to the audience. In a simple format, the syllogism can be expressed as follows:

MAJOR PREMISE:	*All humans are mortal.*
MINOR PREMISE:	*Tom Cruise is human.*
CONCLUSION:	*Tom Cruise is mortal.*

In building an argument on a syllogism you must be careful, when examining your evidence and deciding on your appeal, not to make the mistake of using faulty reasoning. Here is an example where the syllogism can work against itself:

MAJOR PREMISE:	*All mothers are women.*
MINOR PREMISE:	*Mary is a woman.*
CONCLUSION:	*Mary is a mother.*

These examples are simplified, of course, to show you how the structure of deduction can be applied to information and thought. You must be careful in using deduction not to lead your audience to a false conclusion. Your evidence must be logical and not contradictory.

Induction

Induction examines particular cases and then formulates a general principle or conclusion based on those cases. Induction is often called the *scientific method* and is commonly used in such things as lab experiments and mathematical problem-solving. Lawyers use induction to prove guilt or innocence. To be sure your inductive reasoning is sound, you have to substantiate your evidence. Induction depends on facts and dependable supporting information and cannot rely on hearsay, opinion, rumour, or false evidence.

Lawyers who prosecute a murder suspect must have dependable and verifiable data to prove guilt. As we know from television, false evidence is misleading and unacceptable. Lawyers often try to appeal to our emotions or our sense of morality when they want to persuade us of their client's innocence, but the inductive approach must rest on solid evidence or no amount of emotion can sway us to believe in the lawyer's case.

Try the following exercises to test deduction, induction, and conclusion.

Missing Premises/Conclusions

In the following sentences, determine what the missing statement is and whether it is a premise or conclusion.

1. All of my students are intelligent, so Kevin can't be one of my students.
2. Only roses grow in the east garden, and those flowers on the table were picked from there this morning.
3. The woman who committed the robbery had long blonde hair, but Heather is a curly-haired brunette.
4. Dictatorial people aren't popular, so Delphine can't be dictatorial.
5. Tony dresses very stylishly, and we know what that implies because all successful businessmen dress stylishly.
6. Someone must be burning leaves because the scent of burning leaves is in the air.
7. Dr. Kent can't be a psychiatrist because his name isn't listed in the Medical Directory.
8. You know the saying "None but the brave deserve the fair," and Bruce's bravery is beyond question.
9. Whenever it snows, Mai Li gets excited about skiing, and it's snowing now.
10. This can't be a rosebush because it doesn't have thorns.

Fallacies

Finally, to make sure your argument is sound, you must be aware of what are known as **fallacies**. In presenting an argument, writers sometimes get caught up in their own feelings or their overwhelming sense of right and wrong. Unknowingly, they may "bend" their facts to suit their premise, or express a bias in their choice of data. A lawyer might do this, for instance, in order to win a case, leaving out certain details or overstating others. The lawyer may make personal remarks that appeal to a jury's prejudices. To avoid being accused of lying or distortion, be wary of the following:

Hasty generalization: Generalizations are assumptions based on weak or incomplete evidence. They lead readers toward false or irrelevant conclusions:
EXAMPLE: Corporations are evil and do not benefit society because all they want to do is make a profit at the expense of the environment.

Begging the question or **Arguing in a circle:** A writer presents an argument proving nothing because it gives no clear reasons but simply restates the original premise.
EXAMPLE: No one who cares about children will oppose the building of a new day-care because a day-care is something that those who love children know is necessary.

Non sequitur or **Unclear reasoning:** Non sequitur is a Latin term meaning "It does not follow." Writers present hidden or unclear assumptions that make the conclusion or the order of the argument unclear, illogical.
EXAMPLE: Playing a lot of sports builds stamina and speed. Thus, sports is the best way to teach young men manners and morality.

Ad hominem or **Attacking the person:** A writer makes personal, even untrue, remarks about a person or an idea rather than presenting facts against the issue.
EXAMPLE: All politicians are criminals and have never done any good for the people of Canada.

Bandwagon emotionalism or **Ad populum:** Writers appeal to popular prejudices or claim that since everyone thinks in a certain way, that way must be true.
EXAMPLE: Everyone knows today that governments are out to tax honest people to death—just look at the increase in consumer and private income taxes over the past few years!

Refutation

Refutation, another structural device in the essay of argumentation or persuasion, means being able to recognize and deal with counter-arguments by proving how they are in error. In taking into account opposing views, even presenting the opposition's full case, you can demonstrate that you are willing to acknowledge two sides to an issue and are able to show how your argument is truthful. This technique helps to establish your fairness and credibility. It can also give you the opportunity to demolish the argument of the opposition.

The following essay by journalist Michele Landsberg is about an emotional issue—capital punishment. Examine how Landsberg appeals to readers' emotions but avoids fallacies that could mar the credibility of her point of view. Note, also, how she uses the inductive method to build her argument and *refutation*.

Let's Just Shamble Back to the Cave for Some Bone Gnawing

By Michele Landsberg

It's not because I have any special compassion for murderers that I oppose the death penalty—I enjoy, as much as anyone, the national fantasy of putting a bullet through Clifford Olson's brain—but because it's so useless.

The death penalty turns a country into a nation of fools. What has the long, wavering struggle of civilization been but an effort to control, shape and raise us above our most primitive impulses? Now we are about to commit our political energies to a protracted debate on capital punishment, and, according to an Angus Reid survey, 75 per cent of Canadians hope to reinstate the killing of murderers. We might as well shamble back to the cave and gnaw on bones if we are going to the distort the whole structure of the law to enshrine our thirst for vengeance.

And vengeance it is, because there is no logical basis for the death penalty. This does not seem to have occurred to many pro-death penalty Canadians.

Some say it's a waste of good tax money to keep murderers alive in jail. Wrong. At a conservative estimate, every death sentence costs the U.S. Government $2-million in court costs, legal fees, endless appeals and delays, more than twice as much as it costs to keep a killer in jail for life. Right now, each Canadian pays $23 a year for all federal correctional services. We would have to kill off the whole population of a penitentiary to cut the cost significantly.

Canadians seem to think that an execution is a painless, modern and scientific way to rid ourselves of an inconvenient human who will never be worth saving. Amnesty International, now campaigning against the death penalty (only two Western nations, the United States and Turkey, have it), says that even the most streamlined methods of gassing, strangling, burning and poisoning entail gruesome agony.

In Alabama in 1983, it took three charges of 1,900 volts over a period of 14 minutes to kill a prisoner—smoke and flames erupted from his flesh before he died. A Mississippi murderer writhed in convulsions for eight minutes after he was gassed, until finally the legal witnesses were asked to leave. Prison officials have blocked their nostrils with Vaseline so they won't smell the burning flesh of electrocuted men. In Florida last year, a prison doctor and six guards engaged in a long and brutal struggle to subdue a frantic prisoner and force him into the electric chair.

It isn't neat and scientific: it's grotesque, filled with stench and horror, and we turn officials and doctors into legal torturers—"Is he dead yet, doctor?" "No, give him more voltage"—to carry out our fantasy of revenge.

Canadians who favor the death penalty think it's only fair to kill those who kill others. But fairness in capital punishment is a sick joke. In the United States, it's the poor, unemployed and black who are executed. There's irrefutable bias in sentencing. Kill a white person and you have more than doubled your chances of being executed. A study of 11,000 U.S. executions shows only two cases of whites put to death for killing a black man. In fact, U.S. law officials have pointed out that the application of the death penalty is freakishly quixotic: accomplices have been electrocuted while the trigger-puller went free; the retarded and mentally ill and even those who committed crimes as juveniles are gassed; and a man's life or death often depends on a legal labyrinth of technicalities and accidents.

Do Canadians think we will never execute people out of racial prejudice? Do we assume that our court officials and legal procedures are free of stupid mistakes, malfeasance and public pressure for conviction? Do we think we would never be capable of hanging an innocent man? Donald Marshall, Donald Marshall, Donald Marshall.

If you've ever been in court, you'll know there's truth in the cliché about one law for the rich and one for the poor. If Canada had the death penalty, we could well see a parade of the colored to the hanging room—native Indians, Sikhs, Haitians—while the Helmuth Buxbaums pay a million dollars for expensive lawyers and live. Is this what we want?

Many people think the death sentence is a deterrent, but all the evidence points the other way. After Florida reinstated the death penalty, the homicide rate went from a record low to a record high; in non-executing states and in Canada, the murder rate, since abolition, has fallen. The causes of murder are far more complex than the simple absence of capital punishment.

And there's an ominous sidelight: only a tiny fraction of those who spend time on death row are eventually executed. Many of the others literally go crazy in their tiny isolation cells—and then they are released. Life sentences may be safer for society.

We seem to be in the grip of a fevered delusion, fed perhaps by U.S. media violence. Canadians believe the murder rate is seven times higher than it really is. We use "compassion for the victim's families" as our excuse for insisting on death for the murderers, but, if we genuinely cared about victims, we would spend our time and resources on prevention of the economic and family stresses that lead to murder.

Why, when it offends reason and reality, do we turn now to such a pointless debate? We are angry people living in a frightening time. Never have so many felt so threatened, with so much reason. What a spectacle: "The gods are rumbling. Let's smear on the woad and have a human sacrifice." The death penalty is our magic dance, the superstition of savages.

•

Comprehension

1. Unlike Barbara Lawrence, Michele Landsberg introduces her thesis statement (main premise) immediately. What precisely is her thesis?
2. State the first point in her argument against the death penalty.
3. How does she refute the argument that it's expensive to keep murderers alive?
4. With what evidence does Landsberg refute the argument that modern execution is painless and scientific?
5. What appeal does Landsberg make in her fourth point? How does she refute this particular argument?
6. What comparative evidence does Landsberg provide to refute the notion of the death sentence as a deterrent to crime?
7. What impact does the United States have on how Canadians see themselves, according to Landsberg?
8. What powerful emotional images of humanity does the author conjure up in her last two sentences?
9. Explain the allusions to the following: Clifford Olson, Donald Marshall, Helmuth Buxbaum.
10. Only two Western nations—the United States and Turkey—retain the death penalty. Why does Landsberg state this fact?
11. Why does Landsberg use only American examples of executions?

Analysis

1. The structure of Landsberg's essay is logical. Her appeal is also to logic. How then does this essay achieve its highly emotional tone and effect?
2. The author in her title and conclusion writes differently from the evidence in the body paragraphs. How and why?
3. "Life sentences may be safer for society." Do you agree?
4. After reading Landsberg's argument, was your mind changed?

In the following essay, by Judy Syfers, the subject is serious. Unlike Lawrence and Landsberg, however, the author chooses to treat her subject with irony and humour.

I Want a Wife

By Judy Syfers

I belong to that classification of people known as wives. I am A Wife. And, not altogether incidentally, I am a mother.

Not too long ago a male friend of mine appeared on the scene fresh from a recent divorce. He had one child, who is, of course, with his ex-wife. He is obviously looking for another wife. As I thought about him while I was ironing one evening, it suddenly occurred to me that I, too, would like to have a wife. Why do I want a wife?

I would like to go back to school so that I can become economically independent, support myself, and, if need be, support those dependent upon me. I want a wife who will work and send me to school. And while I am going to school I want a wife to keep track of the children's doctor and dentist appointments. And to keep track of mine, too. I want a wife to make sure my children eat properly and are kept clean. I want a wife who will wash the children's clothes and keep them mended. I want a wife who is a good nurturant attendant to my children, who arranges for their schooling, makes sure that they have an adequate social life with their peers, takes them to the park, the zoo, etc. I want a wife who takes care of the children when they are sick, a wife who arranges to be around when the children need special care, because, of course, I cannot miss classes at school. My wife must arrange to lose time at work and not lose the job. It may mean a small cut in my wife's income from time to time, but I guess I can tolerate that. Needless to say, my wife will arrange and pay for the care of the children while my wife is working.

I want a wife who will take care of *my* physical needs. I want a wife who will keep my house clean. A wife who will pick up after me. I want a wife who will keep my clothes cleaned, ironed, mended, replaced when need be, and who will see to it that my personal things are kept in their proper place so that I can find what I need the minute I need it. I want a wife who cooks the meals, a wife who is a *good* cook. I want a wife who will plan the menus, do the necessary grocery shopping, prepare the meals, serve them pleasantly, and then do the cleaning up while I do my studying. I want a wife who will care for me when I am sick and sympathize with my pain and loss of time from school. I want a wife to go along when our family takes a vacation so that someone can continue to care for me and my children when I need a rest and a change of scene.

I want a wife who will not bother me with rambling complaints about a wife's duties. But I want a wife who will listen to me when I feel the need to explain a rather difficult point I have come across in my course of studies. And I want a wife who will type my papers for me when I have written them.

I want a wife who will take care of the details of my social life. When my wife and I are invited out by my friends, I want a wife who will take care of the babysitting arrangements. When I meet people at school that I like and want to entertain, I want a wife who will have the house clean, will prepare a special meal, serve it to me and my friends, and not interrupt when I talk about the things that interest me and my friends. I want a wife who will have arranged that the children are fed and ready for bed before my guests arrive so that the children do not bother us. I want a wife who takes care of the needs of my guests so that they feel comfortable, who makes sure that they have an ashtray, that they are passed the hors d'oeuvres, that they are offered a second helping of the food, that their wine glasses are replenished when necessary, that their coffee is served to them as they like it.

And I want a wife who knows that sometimes I need a night out by myself.

I want a wife who is sensitive to my sexual needs, a wife who makes love passionately and eagerly when I feel like it, a wife who makes sure that I am satisfied. And, of course, I want a wife who will not demand sexual attention when I am not in the mood for it. I want a wife who assumes the complete responsibility for birth control, because I do not want more children. I want a wife who will remain sexually faithful to me so that I do not have to clutter up my intellectual life with jealousies. And I want a wife who understands that *my* sexual needs may entail more than strict adherence to monogamy. I must, after all, be able to relate to people as fully as possible.

If, by chance, I find another person more suitable as a wife than the wife I already have, I want the liberty to replace my present wife with another one. Naturally, I will expect a fresh, new life; my wife will take the children and be solely responsible for them so that I am left free.

When I am through with school and have a job, I want my wife to quit working and remain at home so that my wife can more fully and completely take care of a wife's duties.

My God, who *wouldn't* want a wife?

Comprehension

1. What motivated Syfers to want a wife?
2. Is her major premise simply, I want a wife?
3. What minor premises (key ideas) does Syfers give for wanting a wife? What major pattern of organization is used to structure these minor premises?
4. How would you classify Syfers' appeal: logical, emotional, or ethical? What is her attitude toward her argument? How do you know?
5. From what environment does Syfers draw her evidence? Why does she do so?
6. "I want" is repeated throughout this argument. How does it affect the argument?
7. What is the basis of the irony in this argument?

Analysis

1. Is Syfers in her argument fair in her assessment of a wife's duties?
2. This essay was written in 1970. Is it still relevant to the modern marriage?
3. Has Syfers simply stereotyped a wife? Discuss.
4. Refute Syfers, using her style of argument, claiming I Want a Husband.
5. Has Syfers effectively alienated the male part of her audience?

Judy Syfers treats a serious subject with humour. Like her, Gary Pinder uses humour, but how serious is he?

Clone Farms:
Let's Bring a Capital Idea to 'Life'

By Gary W. Pinder

It is a melancholy object to see each day, on the streets and on the television, the many people wearing prostheses or confined to wheelchairs, the blind or deaf struggling to cope ... victims of drunk drivers, freak accidents, or birth defects due to illicit drug use.

Equally joyless is the increasing number of bedridden souls patiently awaiting organ transplants, dying on expensive waiting lists.

And how sobering are the thousands of people hampered by polluted lungs and livers, the undernourished and the undernutrified, the underdressed and the overstressed, unable to work, made impotent by high cholesterol and low self-esteem, outcast by their deficiencies.

Even more disturbing, in the present deplorable state of the economy, is the additional grievance to society in the form of welfare and health-care costs and workers-compensation payments. Not only do many individuals suffer, but so does society as a whole.

Now, we have just learned, we have the technology to clone human embryos. With what sincere and silent determination, with what furitive ingenuity, with what stealthy creativity this knowledge came upon us. And with what binding obviousness has it been suggested that this is a source for organ donations. Every compassionate taxpayer has an interest in the matter.

I therefore humbly offer it to public consideration that we establish immediately, and with equitable distribution throughout the country, clone farms.

Each member of society should be entitled to his or her own clone. When a person is born, the parents or the government will authorize a clone to be made for that person. This clone would live "its life" on a clone farm. If an individual, for whatever reason, needs a heart, say, or a hand, it would be supplied by the clone. There would be no worry about finding a perfect match. And if that individual should happen to die, total replacement is an option to ease the pain of a grieving family. Or if the family prefers not, the clone could be auctioned or sold, whole or in parts.

Of course, some scrupulous people are likely to censure this idea as a little bordering on cruelty; however, once the overwhelming benefits are explained to them, they will surely give full support to the implementation of this scheme.

First of all, thousands of people will be able to lead happy, healthy, normal lives they otherwise would not have been able to lead, no longer restricted by a dialysis machine or the clumsy self-consciousness of a prosthesis. Think of all the Baby Jane and Baby Moe stories with happy endings. In time, they will not even be stories; they will be a matter of course.

Individuals will enjoy a higher quality of life and be able to fully participate in daily activities once again or for the very first time. They would be able to contribute to a healthy economy. This in itself would cut welfare and health costs. Millions of dollars would be saved in long-term disability payments.

As for the clone farms, they would be entirely self-sustaining. They would not just be farms but places of diverse productivity. Clones would be kept busy with agriculture or working in factories. Their work would pay for their own maintenance, which would be minimal. (Clones can do without steaks and CD players.) All surplus would be split between the "farmers" and the "originals" in the form of dividends, and both would be taxable income, the proceeds of which would go to fight the deficit.

Furthermore, as a source of cheap labour, clone farms would ensure that industry would locate here instead of abandoning Canada for other countries like, say, Mexico. This would lead to the production and consumption of inexpensive, high-quality merchandise here at home and an increase of exports to other countries. The economy would grow to be as healthy and as strong as its citizens.

Some of those same scrupulous people may fear that the pace of change is "too swift." But the apparatus of society, complex as it is, will remain intact. Government commissions formed to develop regulatory policies and industry standards would employ a few people for a few years. New employment opportunities would open for genetic technologists and clone farmers. Clones-rights activists would form lobby groups and demonstrate. Psychologists and self-help groups would help people with identity crises. Lawyers would argue issues of ownership and copyright. Scholars would argue issues of originality, authenticity, and creativity.

Young people could become pen pals with their clones. They would have someone who understands them. They could even take school trips to clone farms.

Parents could better control naughty children: "You can be replaced, you know!" "Settle down, or your clone will get your Christmas presents!"

We can all anticipate the sitcoms, the dramas, the bestsellers and the eventual fabrication of nostalgia for life on the farm.

So, in essence, things would be exactly the same. Only better.

These are not just vain, idle, visionary thoughts. This is a practical and compassionate solution to some of society's problems. We could waste time thinking this through. But we see that after a while, we don't even have to think things through—we just have to take the next step.

Yes, we've come a long way from wooden teeth and wooden legs. Let's not stop now.

•

Comprehension

1. What are the images in Pinder's introduction that lead up to his main premise?
2. What features of Pinder's sentences in the introduction are different from the style of sentences used by Syfers?
3. Paraphrase Pinder's main premise.
4. What benefits would society enjoy as a result of clone farms?
5. How would an individual find his or her life improved as a result of clone farms?
6. Describe how a clone farm would work.
7. Why would it be necessary to create regulatory policies if clone farms were in fact put into practice?
8. At what point in the argument does Pinder make it clear to readers that his proposal is not serious?
9. What types of evidence does Pinder give to readers to make his argument seem valid?
10. Comment on the puns in the subtitle of the article.

Analysis

1. Pinder has written a parody of Jonathan Swift's *A Modest Proposal*. A **parody** is an imitation of the style and composition of another work to create humour. What is Pinder's purpose for doing so?
2. "So, in essence, things would be exactly the same. Only better." Do you agree with Pinder?
3. Although Pinder's proposal is a joke, does it have serious merit?
4. What assumptions has Pinder made about his reading audience? How do you know this?
5. What would you like best about having a clone? Would Judy Syfers perhaps like to have one?

Writing Suggestions

1. Persuade your reader to see a movie. For this assignment, use all of the skills developed in this text. Write a concise thesis statement recommending the movie, with clear reasons for your recommendation. You may choose a movie currently in the theatre or one now on video.

   What is your major premise?

   What was it about this movie that sparked your admiration of it?

   What examples of characters, dialogue, special effects best support your thesis?

   Remember to consider using summary and paraphrase when recounting plot details. Use narrative when necessary. You may also wish to classify the movie by its genre: science fiction, action, drama, western, etc.
2. Argue for or against any one of the essays used in this unit. Be sure to state a strong main premise and to decide on an appeal that is appropriate to your chosen audience.
3. Is there an issue you feel strongly about? First, define it, then structure your argument to persuade readers of the rightness of your position.

Unit Six

"A man will turn over half a library to make one book." (Samuel Johnson)

Reading and Writing from Sources:

The Research Paper

The research paper is your presentation of what others have said about a subject. Regard this challenging task of reading and writing as a long essay in which you present your point of view with a thesis statement, topic sentences, and supporting details *gathered from sources*.

Remember, you have in your control a variety of methods for acquiring information and organizing the facts (see Unit Four). Often a research paper may be organized as a process analysis or a combination of patterns such as comparison/contrast with cause and effect. Student Cecile Dean's research paper in this unit uses comparison, classification, and cause and effect.

1. Assign (or choose) a topic.
2. Focus the subject.
3. Do background research to test viability of focused subject.
4. Take information from sources by skimming, scanning, underlining, note-taking, paraphrasing, summarizing, quoting and citing of sources.
5. Write a working thesis statement and select key ideas from collected data.
6. Read collected data closely and make an outline of your research paper.
7. Write a thesis statement and research paper with proper documentation.

Focusing and Testing the Subject

Whether or not your instructor has assigned a specific topic, you will have to define your subject for this long essay. You may need to brainstorm (see Unit Three), then focus the topic, and finally locate supporting details before you can organize your paper and decide how to pattern your selected information. A research paper may be written using one dominant expository pattern of organization; it may also be persuasive. The form of the paper is defined by your topic and how you wish to express it to your readers.

Let's suppose your instructor assigned a topic related to education. This is a broad field of information; you must narrow it down and find a focus. Let's assume you have brainstormed and decided to discuss math, often a subject either intensely loved or deeply hated. Finding that focused subject still too broad and general, you ultimately choose to centre your research paper on the currently "hot" topic of women and math. A major concern in education, industry, and government today is that at some point during their high-school years, the majority of women become "turned off" by math.

SUBJECT: Women and Math—Why are women turned off? What are the causes, the reasons, the solutions to the problem?

Is this topic viable? You'll need to test the subject to see if it lends itself to a longer paper by heading to the library. Talk to the personnel there. They will help you to locate information in subject catalogues, encyclopedias, indexes, periodicals, and books. By following the questions posed above, you can begin to search for answers in books and articles. Be sure as you begin your library search to keep in mind the focused subject—*women and math*. Do not waste time looking up theories of math or the history of math unless you feel they pertain to your essay. As you go through books and articles, you may find that some are useful and some are not. Research means *searching, selecting,* and *rejecting.*

What you have been doing at this point is background research to test the potential of your focused subject.

A word of advice: as you read through books, look at their lists of works consulted, or bibliographies. There you will find references to additional information that may be useful. Other likely sources are:

- interviews with experts in the field, classmates, friends;
- information from local organizations (on the subject of women and math, try phoning a school board or your old high school), institutions, or government.

Once you've gathered a number of pieces of information—ranging from a book to a series of articles—you must read them. This part of doing research can be time-consuming. Here, *skimming* and *scanning* are very useful reading techniques for getting through your preliminary data. Always keep in mind your focused subject and use it as a guide for selecting articles or books you will later use to write your paper.

When you search for sources, even before you choose which ones you will ultimately use, be sure to keep a record of what you have read. Write down all details you will need for your list of sources, the separate page at the end of your paper that tells readers where you found your details. At this stage of your research it is best to do the following:

- For a book, record—exactly as they are printed—the author's name, the full title, place of publication, name of publisher, date of publication, page numbers.
- For an article in a magazine or newspaper, record—exactly as they are printed—the author's name, title of article (including subtitles under the main title), title of publication, date of the publication, page numbers.

At this early point in your research, it is essential to record these details accurately. Put such information on an index card or on a separate record sheet so you can have easy reference. Later in this unit we will explain how to arrange this information in proper documentation format, using one of two standard methods.

Be sure to be accurate in your recording of data; you won't want to go back to the library to find your source a second time.

If you find a passage that is well expressed and you wish to quote it, copy it out word-for-word or photocopy a few pages. Don't forget to write down the source reference details in the manner discussed above. *Always* record the source information, so that you will not be accused of plagiarism.

Plagiarism

Plagiarism, a serious form of cheating, happens when you claim information written by another as your own. Even unintentional plagiarism can have severe penalties ranging from a grade of zero on the research paper, to failing the course or even expulsion from college.

Plagiarism happens when you write down facts or opinions from someone else but *do not* acknowledge your source. Copying without identification of source is plagiarism. Even if you identify your source, but quote someone without using quotation marks, you are still guilty of plagiarism.

Writing your own paper is difficult and you may find you are overwhelmed by other writers from whom you are taking information. Some research papers rely on sources for eighty percent of their data. How do you then avoid plagiarism? First, be aware that you are selecting data and rearranging it in a new manner—your own, in fact—to make a point or to argue from a different point of view. Think of researched data as raw material from which you will build up your paper. Explain and then use data in quotes or paraphrase form. Don't be alarmed if many of your paragraphs begin with your own topic sentence but then are supported by data from a number of other writers. (For example, see student writer Dean's essay in this unit, particularly paragraph five.) See also in this unit the section on quoting. It explains how selected material can be used creatively in your paper.

But be yourself! Being influenced by a writer you admire is fine, but use your source as a springboard for your own thesis and essay. Take a look at the essay "Clone Farms," from Unit Five, and compare how it reflects but does not copy its famous model, Swift's *A Modest Proposal,* found in the Additional Readings at the end of this book.

Taking Material from Sources

Underlining A word of warning at the start: *do not* underline in library books or journals. Photocopy the passages you need and use your underliner on your own photocopy. Too often, you may find that other students have marked up books with coloured underlining. Such markings can be distracting—not to say "off topic" for *your* essay—let alone damaging to public property.

A problem common to many students is figuring out just what to underline. As a result, more than half an article ends up highlighted. If you underline too much, you ultimately create more work for yourself because you haven't actually read and digested the information you really need.

What should you do?

Underlining is helpful for finding key ideas. Thus, underline the thesis statement and the key ideas in the article. Look at each paragraph and select what you think are pertinent supporting details—ones that relate to or discuss your focused subject. It is helpful if you are systematic in your underlining. For instance:

- Use two lines for the thesis statement and a single line for the key ideas and topic sentences. If the thesis is not directly stated, write out one in your own words and record it next to the opening paragraph.

    Underlining does not simply mean drawing lines or colouring with a highlighter. It also means asking questions, making notations in the margin, numbering ideas for future reference.
- Number the supporting details in each paragraph. Highlight the ones that pertain to your focused subject.
- Record the organizational patterns used by the author (cause and effect, classification, etc.).
- Highlight the key words or terms in the article. Highlight words or terms you don't know and define them on the article for future reference.
- Check or highlight what you agree or disagree with in the article, based on your focused subject. Comment when you feel provoked either

favourably or negatively. These quick comments can be developed later into points of interest or key ideas in your paper.

Try this method on the article "Maths a Plus," by Jennifer Lewington, keeping in mind the focused subject: sometime in their school career, women were "turned off" math. What were the reasons? Are there any solutions?

Maths a Plus, Schoolgirls Assured

By Jennifer Lewington

Above the din of pounding hammers, as a roomful of teen-aged girls build wooden tool boxes, apprentice carpenter Deb Harvey delivers a not-so-subtle message about the importance of math and science in their lives.

"How are you going to read a tape measure?" she says to an inquiring 12-year-old named Susi Porter, who is wielding her hammer with the two-fisted determination of a tennis player.

"How will you know how to read a blueprint?" continues Ms. Harvey. "That's why it's really important to know math."

Ms. Harvey, serving for the day as a role model for women in non-traditional jobs, makes herself heard above the staccato rhythms reverberating from the workshop at Northern Secondary School.

The former telephone operator, courier driver and landscape gardener, now in the second year of her four-year apprenticeship, was one of the hits yesterday at an annual event sponsored by the Toronto Board of Education. The board is trying to break down the barriers that deflect girls from math and science in high school and beyond. Yesterday's workshop came in the wake of a new international study that shows Canadian children have only middling abilities in mathematics and science compared to those in 19 other countries.

"Everything can be fixed …," begins Ms. Harvey, 34, pounding away at her women-can-do theme. But 13-year-old Suzette Marsh, a Grade 8 student at Lord Dufferin Public School and one of 450 Grade 7 and 8 girls from elementary schools across Toronto who spent the day at Northern, finishes the sentence with a grin: "… if you take physics."

Judging by student reaction to the event, a mixture of hands-on activities and speeches, the riddle of women, stereotypes and non-traditional ambitions—such as careers in math and science—becomes less mysterious.

Susi, for example, says she used to "hate" math but now loves it, and science too. Her Grade 7 math teacher "spends a whole lot of time explaining it" and, says Susi, he is patient. Her science teacher, also a man, is "sciency" and "neat." She confides proudly that her teacher has taught the class about the periodic table of the elements, a topic other students do not get until Grade 12.

Self-esteem, says Edite Flaum, a co-chair of the Horizons '92 event, "is at the top of the list" of factors that influence girls to pursue math and science in high school and beyond.

But some old habits, and stereotypes, die hard.

On their way to the carpentry workshop, Susi and Suzette swap stories about their schools. Susi, a Grade 7 student at Winona Drive Public School, is frustrated that her girl friends cannot join the hockey team—there is one for the boys, but not for the girls. She says the girls are not allowed to play tackle football or soccer either.

How does she square that message with the can-do mantra of yesterday's conference? "It's confusing," admits Susi, who has already rejected a career as an actress as too superficial. "We don't need any more pretenders; we need more real people."

Myra Novogrodsky, also co-chair of the event, concedes that a one-day workshop that tries to sell girls on math and science cannot compete with the mixed messages they receive from society in their daily lives.

Janet Reid, a senior physics teacher at Lawrence Park Collegiate Institute, recalls one girl who attended several years ago and switched her career plans from business to engineering. She went on to stand first in her engineering class at the University of Toronto for four years in a row and is now in a master's program.

Ms. Reid says that girls and boys have different attitudes towards success in school, one of the factors that hold young women back from non-traditional academic and career tracks. "Even girls who are very capable don't think of pursuing math and science," she says. "They want to feel assured they will do well."

When asked about her career plans, Suzette rattles off a rich assortment: archeologist, journalist, poet, biologist, part-time ballerina, psychiatrist. Yet she chafes because her father doesn't think women can do heavy lifting and other tasks.

"There are still a lot of men who think carpentry is a man's job," says Suzette.

Ms. Harvey has an answer. Just before the girls leave her workshop, new tool boxes in hand, she tells them how she dealt with the male carpenters who always challenged her—even when she was right.

"They seemed to see a sign on my forehead that said 'Don't believe a thing this woman says,'" she told the girls. "When they argued, I would tell them 'Stop, read my forehead' and it worked." Now, she says, she is proud of her working partnership on the job with the men carpenters.

•

Note-taking   When you first read the article "Maths a Plus" and decided it could be useful, you may have noticed a number of things:

1. It presents a series of anecdotes from "authorities" and high-school girls. How many?
2. The article reports "an annual event sponsored by the Toronto Board of Education." What is that event dedicated to? Why is the event important? Who organized it this year? Who participated in it?
3. The author focuses on a particular role model. Who is this person? Why does the author choose her to represent solutions?

These questions are typical of ones you could use when reading through an article and questioning its viability for your paper. Asking such critical questions helps you absorb the author's content and choose what details you will put into your research paper. Writing out your answers in note form may provide you with necessary supporting details.

One of the most important steps in research is the taking of notes.

Taking notes means reading, questioning, writing down brief answers, selecting pertinent answers based on your focused subject or working thesis statement.

Another aspect of taking notes is **paraphrasing** and **summarizing,** two skills taught in Unit Two. As you read an article, you may find a whole paragraph that could be useful and you will want to summarize its content. Certain passages from paragraphs may strike you as important and may contain ideas you will want to paraphrase. Be careful, however, not to include information that doesn't relate to your subject. For example, Susi in "Maths a Plus" expresses frustration at being denied the chance to play contact sports. While this is an interesting social observation, it is not directly related to the problem of women and math, which is the focus of your research. Such an example may seem pertinent because it shows how Susi was frustrated, as women are with math, but it may not ultimately be useful information and therefore can be rejected.

Quoting   Students often ask, "How much should I quote?" or "How much can I quote?" Quoting is useful as a research device only if it is backed up by analysis. Too often, students include short and long quotations and assume their readers will draw connections between the thesis of the paper and the quotations. Quotations are only *recorded references* and do not stand alone. You as a writer must explain the meaning of the quotation or use it to illustrate a point of your own in the paper. Simply quoting an author is not a part of research writing. Readers want you as the writer to interpret the material you have selected, and this is especially true with quotations.

> *Quote to make a reference, to show readers the tone and wording of an original source.*

A word of warning: when you use quotations, remember that they are included to validate the point you are making. Too often, students string together a series of quotes believing that this proves their point and shows readers they have researched thoroughly. However, this is often a result of mere "padding." Readers may believe that the writer has not thought out the thesis of the essay and has thus included quotations to fill out the length of the paper. Readers may also interpret too many quotations as a sign that the writer is intimidated by the sources chosen as references.

Style

It is important to keep a consistent style in your writing of the research paper. Thus, try to use quotations sparingly and judiciously. Where possible, paraphrase or summarize in your own words to create your own voice in your paper. Always be sure, however, to acknowledge sources. If you need to include a long quotation, you may place the quotation in an indented paragraph of its own in the middle of your paper. Or, if you wish, omit irrelevant sections of the quote by using **ellipses**, devices made of up three dots or four, that show readers you have deleted material. An ellipsis using three dots (...) is used in a passage where a part of a sentence has been removed. An ellipsis using four dots (....) is used in a passage where a complete sentence is quoted but intervening material has been removed. In the following example paragraph, note the two forms. The reference quoted is the essay "Maths a Plus," by Jennifer Lewington. (Note that the number of the page on which the quotation originally appeared is given also.)

> *There are many examples to show that math anxiety can be overcome. "Janet Reid ... recalls one girl who attended several years ago and switched her career plans from business to engineering" (Lewington, "Maths" B1). However, there are problems that remain. "Ms. Reid says that girls and boys have different attitudes towards success in school" (Lewington, "Maths" B1).*

Writing a Working Thesis Statement   Once you have read through your material and decided what you need, it is time to form a thesis statement. You do this in the same manner as taught in Unit Three. Read through the five articles we have chosen as the basis for our model research paper and then read the outline below with its working thesis statement. A working thesis statement is a guide to keep you on track as you write out drafts of your research paper. It may, in fact, become your actual thesis statement and thus be included in your opening paragraph.

Outlining   An outline is like a skeleton. It is the "bare bones" of your essay. These "bones" are the basic structure of the ideas of your paper. Outlines can be written in point form or short sentence form.

1. Write a title and your focused subject.
2. Describe introduction. Write out thesis statement.
3. Draw up a diagram for your paragraphs indicating what key ideas will be discussed. Make sure ideas connect with each other and relate to thesis statement.
4. Finally, write out your conclusion.

This outline may seem simple to do. You can modify it depending on the amount of information you have. Here are two outlines based on student Cecile Dean's research paper on the subject of women and math. One is a working outline, the other an annotated outline.

- Working outline of Cecile Dean's paper, "Math Anxiety: The Real Social Disease."

TITLE: Math Anxiety: The Real Social Disease
FOCUSED SUBJECT: 1. Math anxiety—what is it? Define.
        2. Describe solutions
1. a. define math anxiety.
  b. show its impact on i. individuals
         ii. society
  c. problem recognized: research by individuals and institutions to
    discover causes i. peer pressure
         ii. stereotyping
         iii. gender bias
2. Solutions: deal with causes
  a. educate girls before peer pressure
  b. educate families about stereotyping
  c. provide positive role models
  d. educate teachers about math stereotypes
  e. change curriculum
  f. educate society
3. Conclusion

- Annotated and expanded outline of Cecile Dean's research paper, "Math Anxiety: The Real Social Disease."

In this outline, the "skeleton" has been fleshed out with specific references to the five articles Dean decided to use for her raw material. Note how she refers to specific authors and that she writes in point-form sentences.

TITLE: Math Anxiety: The Real Social Disease

FOCUSED SUBJECT: Women and Math: The reasons why women are "turned off" math. Solutions to the problem in Canada.

INTRODUCTION: A personal anecdote. "I am a pioneer because I am a woman who loves math and escaped the disease of math anxiety." Consider putting here story about Rosalyn Yalow from Jacoby article.

THESIS STATEMENT: Math anxiety has severe repercussions for women and society as a whole. It is a type of "social disease," and in Canada steps are being taken to remedy it.

PARA. ONE: Tell story of Nobel Prize winner Yalow taken from Jacoby article. Idea: not a lot has changed from Yalow's time in 1930s.

PARA. TWO: No one tells girls in the 1990s they can't take physics and must instead be secretaries but attitude still exists: girls stay away from science and math. Quote Finlayson study. Key detail: girls still see math as bad, as a "sickness."

PARA. THREE: Causes for math anxiety: it is a male thing; it is not what girls take to be attractive. Quote Jacoby. Key detail: girls drop out of math by Grade 12; want to avoid being seen as "brains" and competing with guys.

PARA. FOUR: Women and their parents are also to blame for math anxiety. Quote Jacoby on the theory of "conspirators." Social cost of limiting women. Women are cut off from career options because of math anxiety. Key detail: women still see lives in traditional way; women "cut themselves off from careers based on science and math"; an old prejudice exists. Use Finlayson here.

PARA. FIVE: Mention more effects of women seeing themselves only as wives and mothers. Bring in idea of pay equity.

PARA. SIX: Why are girls still turned off math in spite of the research being done? Quote Estrich. Discuss her idea of the "invisible student." Boys are favoured over girls in classroom. Role of teacher is important. Key detail: quote Griffith—"boys learn competence, girls lose it."

PARA. SEVEN: Gender bias adds to the problem. Sexism is institutionalized. But there are initiatives to deal with the problem. Quote Lewington on workshops in Ontario. See Finlayson on reactions to the workshops.

PARA. EIGHT: Discuss role of parents in breaking down the sexism prejudice against girls and math. See Finlayson on the Grade 7 program. Key detail: program attempts to get rid of stereotypes.

PARA. NINE: More examples on workshops. But here, ask question: What is being done to educate teachers about the problem? Quote Estrich and Finlayson. Draw contrast between the ways boys and girls think and learn.

PARA. TEN: Discuss Ministry of Education and Training forum on making math "more fun." Show how it recommends that teachers make math relevant and appealing. See data in "Math Myths."

PARA. ELEVEN: Pose question: are separate schools better for girls to learn math? Quote Estrich. Emphasize that new programs and forums are taking place to help girls, parents, and teachers overcome age-old prejudices.

PARA. TWELVE (CONCLUSION): State the idea that girls can do math well has to be made a reality! Summarize ideas about effects of math anxiety—no career jobs, etc.

The completed essay by Cecile Dean follows:

Math Anxiety: The Real Social Disease

By Cecile Dean

I know I'm stubborn, although I never thought of myself as a pioneer. But that's just what I am. I am a woman: I love math and I'm enrolled in the Environmental program, one of two women. Somehow I escaped the ravages of "math anxiety." "Math anxiety" is the term Susan Jacoby uses to describe the attitude most high school girls have toward this subject. This attitude has severe repercussions not only for the women but for society as a whole. The seriousness of this social "disease" has been recognized and here in Canada steps are being taken to attempt to remedy it.

Jacoby refers to Rosalyn Yalow, who won a Nobel Prize for Physics in the 1930s (2). Rosalyn Yalow was advised to train as a secretary because no university would accept her as a graduate student in physics. What would be the reason for the refusal? Rosalyn Yalow was a woman. Before we become smug and think "we've come a long way baby," let me tell you, things have not changed a great deal since 1930.

No one openly tells girls they can't be physicists and that secretarial courses are more appropriate for them, but somehow this is the message that most girls in high school subliminally pick up. Judith Finlayson quotes research by the Toronto Board of Education.

> ... *even at the introductory level, the ratio of students in computer science courses is two-thirds male to one-third female. By Grade 13, approximately two-thirds of girls in Toronto schools have dropped out of maths and sciences. (Finlayson 8)*

Here we are nearly half way through the 1990s and most girls still see math as a sickness they should avoid. Why?

Jacoby states that the first symptoms of "math anxiety" occur with adolescence. She quotes a 1981 American study on "Female Achievement in Mathematics," which found that girls in Grade 9 typically did well in math. However, by Grade 12, those same girls had lost their ability and desire to succeed in this area. Jacoby identifies two main causes for this: math is considered a "male" subject; also, girls who are "brains" are unattractive to boys, and in order to avoid this classification and direct intellectual competition with males teenage girls drop out of math.

Social stereotyping and peer pressure create "math anxiety." Jacoby goes on to say "the current generation of adolescent girls—and their parents, bred in old expectations about women's interests—are active conspirators in limiting their own intellectual development" (2). These young women are not just limiting their own intellectual development. There is a social cost too. Judith Finlayson points out that high school math is required for admission to many university and community college programs, so many women cut themselves off from career options. Finlayson quotes the conclusion of a 1985 Canadian Advisory Council on the Status of Women report: "adolescent girls still see their lives in very traditional and romanticized terms" (Finlayson 7).

What this means is that most high school girls see their lives in terms of a husband, family and job in the clerical or "helping" professions like nursing, E.C.E. or social work. None of these jobs pays well, as they are traditional "women's work." Failure in math then has severe repercussions that pay equity is only beginning to address.

If all this research has been done, why then are girls still being turned off by math? Susan Estrich goes further than Susan Jacoby in answering this question. Basing her findings on a study done by the American Association of University Women, Estrich claims, "Girls are the invisible students; boys get the bulk of the teachers' time" (39). This study, which focused on the progress of girls in school, showed that regardless of the sex of the teacher, boys are favoured in the classroom. Estrich quotes historian and headmistress Elisabeth Griffith, who says, "boys learn competence, girls lose it" (Estrich 39).

While girls may "conspire" in infecting themselves with math anxiety, as Jacoby points out, the additional problem of gender-bias in education certainly adds to the disease. Sexism is as institutionalized as racism is and only by recognizing that can we begin to deal with it. Fortunately there are a number of initiatives focusing on math in Canada that attempt to deal with the bigger problem of sexism.

For example, each year, the Toronto Board of Education sponsors a workshop for Grade 7 and 8 girls. The annual workshop is an attempt "to break down the barriers that deflect girls from math and science in high school and beyond" (Lewington, "Maths a Plus" A6). The workshop provides those girls with positive role models of women who have succeeded in non-traditional, technical careers. Recognizing that "math anxiety" usually erupts in Grade 9, this workshop is an attempt to inoculate the younger girls against it. The emphasis during the workshop is on the practical applications of math, and a recognition of the girls' need for self-esteem and assurance of success. In the words of Deb Harvey, one of the role models, it shows "why it's really important to know math" (Lewington, "Maths a Plus" A6).

The co-chair of this workshop, Myra Novogrodsky, also runs a program for the parents of girls in Grade 7 and 8. In educating the parents about the deleterious effects of "math anxiety," there is a hope that the parents can be positive role models and provide support for their daughters. The program attempts to remedy the stereotypes that "can seriously undermine the confidence of girls who may have an interest in technical subjects or non-traditional work" (Finlayson, 4).

Workshops and programs like these in Toronto are given across Canada. A real effort is being made to change the ways the girls in high school and their parents view math and sciences. However, what is being done about the teachers of math? As the data quoted by Susan Estrich suggests, part of the problem girls in high school encounter is a direct result of the teaching style. Finlayson also refers to this when she quotes John Clark, coordinator of mathematics at the Toronto Board of Education:

> *Math is usually presented as a search for the right answer rather than as a process of enquiry. Some sociologists believe that females have a more collaborative style. They want to work by consensus and talk with other people. (Finlayson 8)*

An Ontario Math Forum, organized by the Ministry of Education and Training on May 6, 1994, "to make math more relevant, rigorous and fun" (Lewington, "Math Myths" A1), included the recommendation that teachers "develop different teaching strategies to improve the appeal and significance of math." (Lewington, "Math Myths" A1); in addition, clarification and standardization of the provincial curriculum and improvement of the math background for elementary school teachers were recommended. This forum was a response to a recognition that math standards in Canada as a whole are not high enough. However, the discussion and recommendations have definite implications for women. Any changes in curriculum and its presentation will have to consider the "turn-off" factor of "math anxiety."

The answer to "math anxiety" may not be in single-sex schools that Susan Estrich discusses. For now, until the new curriculum is in place, there may be merit in "girls only" math courses as Estrich recommends, since, as she puts it, "the problems of gender bias stubbornly persist" (39). Certainly the contagious idea that math is a "male" subject has got to be wiped out, and there are many initiatives involving the students, parents, and teachers to attempt that eradication. More "hands on" and interactive methods of learning math are recommended by the education experts consulted by Judith Finlayson. Finlayson concludes that

> *hands-on learning validates the children's own observations about the world. It also reinforces their sense of themselves as autonomous problem solvers, a skill linked with success in math. (10)*

Relating math concepts to everyday life makes knowledge of math an obvious necessity. Apart from stressing the practical applications of math, individual problem solving builds the self-esteem and need for success all students, and especially girls, have. The idea that girls "can do" has to be made a reality. Without a background in math, women are cut off from the better-paying professions; they are even precluding themselves from many entry-level jobs. When women are not educated to their full potential, the social implications are great. Good math skills add up to a better future for all.

Works Consulted

Estrich, Susan. "Separate Is Better." *New York Times Magazine* 22 May 1994: 39.

Finlayson, Judith. "Math's Multiple Choices." *Homemaker's Magazine* Jan./Feb. 1988: 4–10.

Jacoby, Susan. "When Bright Girls Decide That Math Is 'a Waste of Time.'" *New York Times* 2 June 1983: 2.

Lewington, Jennifer. "Math Myths Have Got to Go." *Globe and Mail* 7 May 1994: A1.

Lewington, Jennifer "Maths a Plus, Schoolgirls Assured." *Globe and Mail* 8 February 1992: A6.

•

Documentation

The last page of Dean's essay includes a list of the five articles she used to write her research paper. Dean has written her list following the rules of the *MLA Handbook for Writers of Research Papers*, one of two standard handbooks available on formats for recording works consulted. **Documentation** is the final step in preparing a research paper for your readers. Documentation consists of two activities: in-text references and a source list placed at the end of the paper.

Exactly why and how must you document? Well, you must provide proof of your sources to avoid plagiarism. You must follow standard methods of recording information based upon reputable handbooks. You need to show readers that your data are valid. In the text of student writer Dean's paper, you will have noted the use of parentheses, which enclosed references to page numbers and authors of certain works. This form of documentation is the first readers encounter. It is *in-text* documentation. At one time, it was written in the form of footnotes, numbered references at the bottom of a printed page of text. The footnote has been replaced by the *parenthetical reference.* Two formats are commonly used in education and government.

The first of these formats from the Modern Language Association is known as the MLA style. There are numerous editions of this stylesheet and it is best to check with your resource centre or library for the latest. The examples we are using in this unit are based on the third edition, 1988.

The second format is from the American Psychological Association, the APA style. The examples shown in this unit are based on the third edition, 1983.

Parenthetical Reference: Documentation within the Text of the Paper

A parenthetical reference is information about a source placed between parentheses and located within the body of the research paper.

Format I: MLA Style

The MLA style uses parenthetical references in the text after each quotation, paraphrase, and summary of data. Each reference, which begins and ends with a parenthesis, shows readers the author's *last name* or *key words* from the *title* and the *page,* and relates to an entry in the Works Consulted/Cited on a separate page at the end of the research paper.

Once you have determined the content of your parenthetical reference, place the reference at the end of a sentence and place any punctuation marks—period, semicolon—*after* the second parenthesis. When your reference refers to a direct quotation, place it *after* the last quotation mark and *before* the punctuation. Try to fit your reference smoothly into the text to avoid disruption.

Here are three common examples of parenthetical references written in the MLA style:

Author and page   Put the author's name and page number of source inside the parentheses. No comma is needed to separate the two.

With math and women, "*Things have changed since then, but not as much as one would hope*" (Estrich 39).

Author directly named in text   In this case, when the author of the article appears in your sentence, simply put the page number of the author's article in the parentheses.

Susan Estrich has asked, "If schools shortchange girls, why is it surprising when the tests show that they're doing less well?" (39)

Author of more than one reference   If you include two or more articles by the same author in your paper, tell readers which one you refer to in your parentheses by including the author's last name and adding a comma, a short form of the specific article you are referring to, and the page number.

Is anything being done to relieve math anxiety? "The forum, organized by the Ministry of Education and Training ... called for changes in math content, teaching methods and testing" (Lewington, "Math Myths" 1).

Format II: APA Style

The APA style uses parenthetical references after each quotation, summary, and paraphrase but there are differences in what the reference contains compared to the MLA style. Generally, APA style includes in the parentheses the author's *last name,* the *date of publication of the work cited,* and *page* if the reference is specific. References are placed at the end of a sentence, and after the closing quotation mark of a direct quotation with the punctuation—period, semicolon—coming *after* the second parenthesis. The APA style is often used to refer to whole experiments or studies rather than specific page numbers in an article. Often, therefore, the APA style may refer to the entire work and mention no page number.

Here are three common examples of references students use, written in the APA style. (Contrast them with the MLA versions above.)

Author and date   Include the author's name and publication date, separated by a comma.

With math and women, "Things have changed since then, but not as much as one would hope" (Estrich, 1994).

Author directly named in text   In this case, if you name the author in your article, put the date in parentheses right after the author's last name.

Susan Estrich (1994) has asked, "If schools shortchange girls, why is it surprising when the tests show that they're doing less well?"

Author of more than one reference   If you refer to more than one work by an author, put the date of the specific reference of your quotation right after the author's name, as above. If you refer to more than one work by an author in the *same, single* reference, record the author's last name and include the dates of the works you have used, separated by commas.

> *There have been several essays in the past few years that claim math myths must be re-examined and that young girls must be assured math is a suitable subject to study (Lewington, 1992, 1994).*

You can choose in the above case to refer to the author and the dates of the articles directly in your text, and eliminate the parenthetical reference:

> *As Lewington has pointed out in 1992 and 1994, math myths must be re-examined and young girls must be assured math is a suitable subject to study.*

The above examples of in-text documentation remind readers as they read your paper where you found your data. The source list at the end of the paper gives readers the exact location of the complete source by referring to the books and articles you selected.

Works Consulted/References: Documentation at the End of the Paper

The MLA style and the APA style are similar in many ways when it comes to listing the works used in the preparation of your research paper. Students are usually requested to include only works that were directly quoted or summarized in the data of the paper. Often students add long lists of titles to impress readers, but none of those titles refers to any data in the text. This will be seen as a form of "padding," since readers may wonder why so much material was read but not cited.

In any case, it is necessary to tell readers precisely what sources you used to write your paragraphs. Compare and contrast the following MLA and APA styles of presenting source lists.

MLA Style

The MLA style calls this separate sheet of paper at the end of the research paper the *Works Cited* or *Works Consulted*. If your sources list contains only the works referred to in your essay, it is called *Works Cited;* if it contains all the items you found useful in researching your essay, it is called *Works Consulted*. If the sources are all in print, the source list is called a bibliography.

On your list you would present your sources *alphabetically* by authors' last names. If your list has sources with no authors' names, list the title. Put the title *Works Consulted* at the top and centre of your separate sheet, without underline or quotation marks. Begin each entry of your list at the *left* margin but indent each of the next lines (five spaces) so that the authors' names are prominent. Double-space each line, but do not number the entries.

Each entry contains *author's name,* the *title* (and *subtitle*), and *publication information*. Underline titles of books and periodicals. Put titles of articles and short fiction (a short story or poem) in quotation marks. Capitalize all major words in titles and subtitles. Place subtitles after a colon and one space. For an article, do not state the place of publication, only the magazine in which the article appears, volume number, year of publication, and the inclusive page numbers.

APA Style

The APA style calls your source page *References;* this page appears at the end of the paper but before any appendices (notes on experiments, for example). List sources by authors' names, *alphabetically*. If a work has no author named, list title but exclude *the, an, a.* If you cite more than one work by the same author, list the works *chronologically* under the author's last name.

As with the MLA style, this list of sources is placed on a separate page with the word *References* centred at the top, without underline or quotation marks. Begin each entry at the *left* margin; indent the following lines three spaces. Double-space each line.

Each entry contains the *author's name* (unlike the MLA, write out just the *initials of the author's first names*), the *publication date*, the *title and subtitle*, and *publication information*. Underline titles of books and periodicals, but unlike the MLA style do *not* underline or put into quotation marks the titles of articles. For books and article titles, capitalize only the *first* word of the title and subtitle and any proper noun. For a magazine or periodical, name the title only (not the place of publication), the volume or issue underlined, and the inclusive page numbers.

Keeping in mind the differences between the two formats, examine the following. Here are several examples, commonly used by students, of source entries. Contrast the ways each style—the MLA and the APA—records the vital information. For further details on source entries not mentioned here, consult the outline of your own school's handbook, or the style sheets of the MLA and APA in the resource centre or library.

A book written by one author

MLA: Faulkner, William. *The Sound and the Fury*. New York: Vintage Books, 1987.

APA: Faulkner, W. (1987). The sound and the fury. New York: Vintage Books.

A book written by two authors

MLA: Breuer, Michael, and Rosemary Neering. *Historic Alberta*. Toronto: Oxford University Press, 1986.

APA: Breuer, M., & Neering, R. (1986). *Historic Alberta*. Toronto: Oxford University Press.

An article in an encyclopedia

MLA: "Gas, Natural." *Oxford Junior Encyclopaedia*. 1st ed. 1949.

APA: Gas, natural. (1949). *Oxford Junior Encyclopaedia*. 1st ed.

A government publication

MLA: Alberta. Dept. of Agriculture. *Services and Programs 1980–81*. Edmonton, 1981.

APA: Alberta Department of Agriculture. (1981). Services and Programs 1980–81. Edmonton.

An article in a monthly magazine

MLA: Price, Reynolds. "Full Day." *Harper's* Jan. 1991: 56–61.

APA: Price, R. (1991, Jan.). Full day. *Harper's*, pp. 56–61.

An article in a newspaper

MLA: Lewington, Jennifer. "Maths a Plus, Schoolgirls Assured." *Globe and Mail* 8 Feb. 1992, sec. B:1.

APA: Lewington, J. (1992, Feb. 8). Maths a plus, schoolgirls assured. *Globe and Mail*, p. B1.

Whichever style you choose, be sure to be consistent and accurate, and check your work.

Articles

For her research paper, one of Dean's sources was the article "Maths a Plus," by Jennifer Lewington, which is reprinted earlier in this unit. Dean also referred to the following four articles: "Separate Is Better," by Susan Estrich, "Math's Multiple Choices," by Judith Finlayson, "When Bright Girls Decide

That Math Is 'a Waste of Time,'" by Susan Jacoby, and "Math Myths Have Got to Go," by Jennifer Lewington.

Read these articles carefully and see how Dean has used the information in them to write the research paper you have read. Compare her two outlines to her final version, and then compare how her research paper relates to her sources. Once you have done cross-reference reading between Dean's final version and her sources, read and answer the questions that follow the articles.

Separate Is Better

By Susan Estrich

Twenty years ago, when I attended Wellesley College, an all-women's college, coeducation fever was gripping America. Yale and Princeton had just "gone"; Dartmouth "went" next. My freshman year, we were polled on whether we thought Wellesley should join the stampede. What did I know? I said yes. But now I know I was wrong, and I'm glad my vote didn't change anything.

This year, 60 percent of the National Merit Scholarship finalists are boys, because boys outscored on the Preliminary Scholastic Assessment Test (P.S.A.T.), which determines eligibility for the scholarships. The test doesn't ask about sports; it does ask about math and science, though, and that's where the differences between boys and girls are most pronounced. The American Civil Liberties Union and the National Center for Fair and Open Testing filed a Federal civil rights suit in February charging that the test discriminates against women. The plaintiffs want more girls to get National Merit Scholarships. So do I. But I want to see the girls earn them, in schools that give them a fair chance.

I didn't win a Merit Scholarship either, although if the Fair Test people had their way, I might have. My grades were near perfect. But I didn't take the tough math and science courses. I had different priorities. I started junior high as the only girl on the math team. By high school, I'd long since quit. Instead, I learned to twirl a baton, toss it in the air and catch it while doing a split in the mud or the ice. The problem wasn't the P.S.A.T., but me, and my school.

Things have changed since then, but not as much as one would hope. The American Association of University Women did a major study in 1992 about how schools shortchange girls and concluded that even though girls get better grades (except in math), they get less from school. Teachers pay less attention to girls and give them less encouragement. Two American University researchers, Myra and David Sadker, reached a similar conclusion after 20 years of study. Girls are the invisible students; boys get the bulk of the teachers' time. Boys call out eight times as often as girls do. When the boys call out, they get answers; when the girls do, they're often admonished for speaking out. And that's true whether the teacher is a man or a woman. Even the new history textbooks devote only about 2 percent of their pages to women. What is happening, says Elisabeth Griffith, a historian and headmistress of the Madeira School in McLean, Va., is that "boys learn competence, girls lose it."

If schools shortchange girls, why is it surprising when the tests show that they're doing less well? It isn't just P.S.A.T.'s, where 18,000 boys generally reach the top categories and only 8,000 girls do. While the gap has narrowed, boys also outscore girls on 11 of the 14 College Board Achievement tests, and on the A.C.T. exams and on the S.A.T.'s. It is possible to jimmy selection standards to make sure girls win more scholarships, but equal results don't count for much if those results are forced. Instead of declaring equality, society should be advancing it. The challenge isn't to get more scholarships for baton twirlers but to get more baton twirlers to take up advanced mathematics.

One place that happens is in girls' schools and women's colleges. Sometimes separate isn't equal; it's better. Changing the way teachers teach in coed schools, changing the textbooks to make sure they talk about women as well as men, educating parents about raising daughters—all of these things make sense, since most girls will be educated in coed classrooms. But we've been talking about them for a decade, and the problems of gender bias stubbornly persist. In the meantime, for many girls, single-sex education is working.

In girls' schools, 80 percent of the girls take four years of science and math, compared with the national average of two years in a coed environment. Elizabeth Tidball, a George Washington University researcher, found that graduates of women's colleges did better than female graduates of coed colleges in terms of test scores, graduate school admissions, number of earned doctorates, salaries and personal satisfaction. One-third of the female board members of Fortune 1,000 companies are graduates of women's colleges, even though those colleges contribute less than 4 percent of total graduates. Forty-three percent of the math doctorates and 50 percent of engineering doctorates earned by female liberal-arts college students go to graduates of Barnard, Bryn Mawr, Mount Holyoke, Smith or Wellesley—all women's colleges. Graduates of women's colleges outnumber all other female entries in *Who's Who.*

I stopped twirling my baton when I got to Wellesley. I'd like to say that I knew I needed a women's college after all those years in the mud at football games, but it doesn't always work that way. I went to Wellesley because they gave me a generous scholarship, and because Radcliffe rejected me (the test scores, maybe). I was actually miserable a good deal of the time I was there, particularly during the long winters when the janitor was the only man around. But what I learned was worth it. I spent the better part of four years in a world in which women could do anything, because no one told us we couldn't. I even took some math courses. By senior year, somehow I'd become an accomplished test-taker. When I got to Harvard Law School, where men vastly outnumbered women and sexism was the rule, a professor told me on the first day that women didn't do very well. I laughed and decided to prove he was wrong. That's a Wellesley education.

I'm not proposing that coed public schools be replaced with a network of single-sex academies. But if the problem is that women don't do well in math or science, then single-sex classes, and single-sex schools, may be part of the answer.

The evidence, though scant, is promising. In Ventura, Calif., the public high school has begun offering an all-girls Algebra II course. The girls, one teacher says, think so little of their ability that the teacher spends her time not only teaching math but also building self-confidence, repeatedly telling the girls that they're smart and that they can do it. The Illinois Math and Science Academy in Aurora is experimenting with a girls-only calculus-based physics class for the first semester, with the girls joining the coed class at midyear. In the girls-only class, the students report that they are jumping up to ask and answer questions instead of sitting back, hoping that the teacher doesn't call on them. One student said she was worried about the transition to a coed classroom: "We need to make sure we don't lose our newfound physics freedom." "Physics freedom" for girls—what a wonderful concept.

The biggest obstacles to such classes, or even to all-girls public schools, are erected by lawyers bent on enforcing legal equality. In the 1954 case of Brown v. Board of Education, the Supreme Court declared that "separate but equal" was inherently unequal. That was certainly true in Topeka, Kan., whose school system was challenged. It was true of the black-only law school established to keep blacks out of the University of Texas law school. It is not necessarily true of the Ventura High School math class for girls or the Aurora Academy calculus-based physics class, whose futures are in jeopardy because of the knee-jerk application of Brown.

Classes like those in Ventura County or Aurora, Ill., survive constitutional challenge by formally opening their doors to men, with a wink and a nod to keep them from coming in. Otherwise, the schools could be stripped of Federal support, and even enjoined under the Constitution by Federal court order, because they are "discriminating." Private schools may open their doors only to boys or girls under an exemption from Federal laws mandating "equality." But public schools enjoy no such freedom. The reality is that if you need a Wellesley education in America, you have to pay for it. That's the price of committing to formal equality instead of committing to real opportunity.

Boys may pay the price as well. Some educators in the African-American community believe that all-boys classes may be part of the solution to the dismal failure and dropout rates of African-American boys in school. But the courts prevented the Detroit school district from establishing three public all-boys schools, effectively stopping similar projects planned in other cities. Nonetheless, all-boys classes are being held quietly in as many as two dozen schools around the country, mostly in inner cities.

Such programs may or may not succeed in the long run. Research and careful study are plainly needed. But research and careful study are difficult when classes are held in near secrecy for fear of discovery by lawyers and Government officials intent on shutting them down in the name of equality.

If girls don't want to go to all-girls schools, or if parents don't want to send them, that's their choice. If the experiments with girls-only math classes or boys-only classes should fail, then educators can be trusted to abandon them. But short of that, let the educators and the parents and the students decide, and leave the lawyers and judges out of it.

•

Math's Multiple Choices

By Judith Finlayson

The world has been transformed in the past twenty years. Geared to microchips, floppy disks, and video display terminals, today's society demands a higher degree of mathematical skill than ever before. But, sadly and even dangerously misinformed about the realities of the world, many teenaged girls across the country are repeating their mothers' mistake, a mistake that has propelled the majority of Canadian working women into low-paying, dead-end jobs. In high school, they are dropping out of science and math.

Today, a background in math is required for most high-paying technical jobs in fields such as computer technology and microelectronics, as well as for many apparently unrelated professions such as law, interior design, and urban planning. Some companies require Grade 12 math for all entry-level positions, even for caretaking jobs.

The need for mathematical competence has been heightened not only by the extraordinary technological change of the past two decades, but by social change as well. Women have entered the work force in unprecedented numbers. They can also expect to stay there—from 25 to 45 years, even if they choose to marry and have children as well as a job outside the home. And they should anticipate changing careers at least twice during that time.

As Donna Stewart, educational co-ordinator for WomenSkills, a Vancouver organization devoted to education and research on women's work, warns: "Whole fields of work are shrinking or disappearing entirely. We export enormous amounts of work to countries where labour is cheap, or we give it to machines. One result is that greater levels of competence are required, even for low-level jobs."

It's not surprising that a research report published in 1987 by the Economic Council of Canada stressed the value of flexibility in today's workplace. Not only are better-educated and highly skilled women more likely to benefit from technical change, but the report also concluded that their adjustment may be dependent upon how successfully they enter nontraditional occupations. It is important to note, however, that both higher education and nontraditional work are increasingly linked with competence in math.

Consider, for instance, that a minimum of high-school math is often required for entrance to university courses such as nursing, teaching, and law. It is also mandatory for many social-science courses such as psychology and sociology, as well as for admission to a substantial number of community college courses. The problem is, female students tend to drop math and sciences as they progress through high school. This fact has led educators to conclude that math is an "invisible filter" denying females entry into the growth-related industries of the future.

Math and science avoidance in females is generally acknowledged as a serious issue, but unfortunately there are no national statistics that document the full extent of the problem. Research by the Toronto Board of Education, however, shows that even at the introductory level, the ratio of students in computer science courses is two-thirds male to one-third female. By Grade 13, approximately two-thirds of girls in Toronto schools have dropped out of maths and sciences.

"I'm still seeing the Cinderella myth at work," says Arlene Day, a resource teacher for equality in education with the Manitoba Teachers' Society. "Even though they see their mothers working outside the home because the family needs the money, girls are refusing to believe that the same thing will happen to them. They're still aiming for clerical jobs. Most are not even acquiring the computer skills that are necessary to be successful at office work." And her view is echoed in *What Will Tomorrow Bring?,* a 1985 Canadian Advisory Council on the Status of Women report that concluded, "adolescent girls still see their lives in very traditional and romanticized terms."

Statistics confirm that the majority of women (almost 60 percent) hold clerical and service-sector jobs, which are generally low paid, offer little potential for advancement, and may be in danger of becoming obsolete. Although women have made serious inroads into some male-dominated professions, such as business, medicine, and law, they are still segregated outside the more scientific fields, such as engineering and computer science. According to Statistics Canada, at the university level, the majority of women remain concentrated in the traditional fields of study, such as education, nursing, and the humanities. The pattern also holds true for community colleges, where most women continue to study secretarial science, community and social services, nursing, education, and the arts.

"To some extent, women have succumbed to the myths about women's work," comments Donna Stewart. "They want to be helpers and to work with people. They may be avoiding nontraditional jobs and careers that require a sound basis in math because they haven't seen the human context to these jobs.

Social service agencies need to balance their books. And no one builds bridges alone. You're part of a team."

Women who avoid math may be ignoring more than the human context of working with numbers. Mathematical training has been linked with high salaries and job security in fields that have been targeted for future growth. Engineering technology, a profession that is 92 percent male, is one example of this trend. Two years after graduating from community college, an engineering student can expect to earn $20 000 a year. Perhaps more importantly, engineering technologists who reach the senior level will likely make more than $30 000 and, if they rise in management, they can earn up to $50 000 annually.

Compare these salaries to those in a female-dominated field. Ninety-nine percent of secretaries are female. Not only is their average salary just $14 100 two years after graduation from community college, but according to a 1983 Labour Canada report, even those who reach senior levels earn on average under $20 000.

This kind of wage discrepancy alarms educators who see girls avoiding math. "Nowadays, a math and science background is necessary for most of the higher-paying jobs," says Linda McClelland, a science teacher at Crescent Heights High School in Calgary. "And girls are losing out on these credentials at the same time that more and more women are entering the work force. In addition, there is a rising number of women supporting families on their own who really need to earn a decent wage."

Tasoula Berggren, an instructor of calculus and linear algebra at Simon Fraser University in Burnaby, British Columbia, points to at least 82 careers for which math education is a prerequisite. Last November, she organized what she hopes will become an annual conference, Women Do Math, for girls in Grades 9 and 10 and their parents. Four students from each of 85 Vancouver schools were invited. "I thought we would get 100 people," Berggren recalls, "and 300 registered, with many more schools asking to bring more students."

Berggren designed the conference not only to introduce girls to women professionals but to provide an introduction to basic mathematical concepts. "Once they see the application of calculus—how a formula can give them the volume of a lake—they find it exciting. They say, 'This is great, I'm enjoying math!'"

She stresses the necessity of constant parental encouragement, something that Myra Novogrodsky, co-ordinator of women's labour studies at the Toronto Board of Education, observes does not come naturally. She is conducting a new program designed to make parents of Grade 7 and 8 girls aware of the importance of math and science education to their daughters' futures.

"I usually begin the workshops with a true-or-false quiz designed to test awareness," she says. "I've discovered that a lot of people haven't thought much about the implications of social change. They still think that most girls will live in a nuclear family and be secondary wage earners, if they work outside the home at all."

One result of this misconception is that many parents have lower career expectations for their daughters than for their sons. Their attitude is reinforced by negative role modelling, which can include apparently innocuous statements such as "Women don't have a head for figures" or "Her mother can't balance a chequebook." These stereotypes can seriously undermine the confidence of girls who may have an interest in technical subjects or nontraditional work.

"By Grade 10, I knew I was mechanically oriented, but people said that physics was too hard for me and I believed them," recalls Heather Bears, who is currently studying electronics technology at Red River Community College in Winnipeg. As a result, after graduating from high school, she spent two unsatisfactory years in the work force doing odd clerical or child-care jobs. Career counselling finally revealed her scientific aptitude and motivated her to return to high school as an adult student. Not only did she make up her physics courses, but she earned straight A's.

Today, as a second-year electronics student, she still feels the negative effects of gender roles. "When I entered the course there were only two other girls and approximately 100 guys. There was a real sense that we were bucking the system and it was scary. At its most basic, I'm only five-foot-two and most of the male students are in the six-foot range."

Although Bears admits that it is difficult being a pioneer—"some teachers pick on us and others favour us"—the satisfaction of doing what she finds fulfilling is worth the price. "If I had one piece of advice for girls in high school, it would be, 'Don't be afraid to enter a man's world.' I believed people who said I couldn't do it because I was a girl, and that's what held me back."

Mary Elizabeth Morris, a math teacher at Castle Frank High School in Toronto, believes that the "my mother/my self syndrome" can also influence a girl's career expectations. "A woman who does low-level work could undermine her daughter's success because she might not convey the sense that work can be a rewarding experience," she says. "If her mother is a poor role model in terms of job satisfaction, a girl may cling to the Cinderella myth because she doesn't see work outside the home as desirable."

Studies such as *What Will Tomorrow Bring?* show that professional mothers tend to be positive role models for their daughters. But mothers who don't work outside the home can also encourage their daughters to develop an interest in traditionally male domains by organizing scientifically oriented excursions, such as a visit to a science museum, or by doing traditionally masculine tasks.

"We live on a farm, so my mother is a real handyman," says Robin Chant, a Grade 12 student at MacGregor Collegiate Institute in MacGregor, Manitoba, who excels at maths and sciences. "I think one of the reasons I do well in math is because, like her, I enjoy figuring things out."

Chant was the only girl in her physics class last year and there is only one other girl in this year's math class, compared to nine boys. "Most of my girl-friends have dropped math because they think it's too hard," she says. "They all want traditional jobs as secretaries and day-care workers. They plan to get married and have kids. I'm different because I really want to have a career."

Myra Novogrodsky believes that if mothers are to help their daughters overcome their negative outlook toward math, they must become aware of and overcome their own negative feelings. If parents "suffered" through math class themselves, they may convey their anxiety and inadvertently undermine their children's performance. Equally important are the role models that girls receive outside the home.

"It's hard for girls to accept the message that they can have high career aspirations and study maths and sciences if they don't see any other women doing it," says Linda McClelland. "We need more female math and science teachers as role models, as well as more women in nontraditional careers."

All the women math and science teachers interviewed for this article strongly agreed. Moreover, those who kept statistics on the ratio of males to females in their class reported that the fact that a woman was teaching the subjects had a positive effect on girls.

"In the past there was usually only one female student in senior-level physics," recalls Shelagh Pryke, who teaches physics classes at Kwalikum Secondary School in Qualicum Beach, B.C. "Now as many as 42 percent of my students are girls, and I know the fact that I'm a woman who is married with a family has played a role in this change. The girls see that it's socially acceptable to be a woman who is interested in science."

Lydia Picucha, a math and science teacher at Mount Elizabeth Junior and Senior Secondary School in Kitimat, B.C., shares this point of view. "I've been teaching here for seven years and I know my female students relate to the idea of a woman who enjoys her work and takes her career seriously. As a result, most of my female students—about 70 percent—have continued with science into Grade 11, when girls normally start dropping out."

The lack of female teachers as role models is complicated by the way maths and sciences are taught in schools. Mathematics, for example, may alienate girls because it is typically taught in a masculine style. John Clark, co-ordinator of mathematics at the Toronto Board of Education, says, "Math is usually presented as a search for the right answer rather than as a process of enquiry. Some sociologists believe that females have a more collaborative style. They want to work by consensus and talk with other people."

Whether or not there is any inherent difference between the male and female aptitude for mathematics remains a hotly debated issue. However, there is no doubt that the way girls are socialized undermines whatever natural ability they might have. For example, the kinds of throwing, jumping, and mechanically oriented play that boys engage in actually prepare them for an understanding of maths and sciences.

Consider the game of baseball. Most boys catch balls better than most girls simply because by constantly playing ball sports that they have learned how to estimate where the ball will land and, therefore, how to position their hands. What is less obvious is that this skill requires an understanding of the relationships between distance, force, and velocity that serves them well once they begin to study physics.

At the Institute of Child Study, a school that operates in conjunction with the University of Toronto's Faculty of Education, teacher Robin Ethier confirms that there is a division of play along gender lines by the time the children arrive at kindergarten. "The boys choose blocks and sand to build larger spaces, whereas the girls prefer small paper projects," she says. "The few girls who prefer large motor-skill projects really stand out. They are identified as tomboys."

Even so, Anne Cassidy, the Grade 5 teacher at the school, says she is not aware of a gender difference in her students' approach to maths and sciences. To some extent, she believes the school's emphasis on intuitive and personalized learning has helped minimize the difference. Classes are small and teachers strongly encourage children to learn through their own activities. For example, to teach the laws of averages, she might ask her class to count up the pennies all seven grades collected for UNICEF over Hallowe'en. When she asks her students to work out approximately how many each grade collected, they soon realize that to get an average they must divide the total number of pennies by the number of classes. In the end, they discover the mathematical formula all on their own.

This kind of hands-on learning validates the children's own observations about the world. It also reinforces their sense of themselves as autonomous problem solvers, a skill linked with success in math. Parents can play an important role in helping their children develop this problem-solving ability by transforming daily activities into informal lessons in maths and sciences. Children should be encouraged to play mathematically oriented games such as backgammon and chess. Cooking is an excellent activity for teaching fractions as well as the principles of chemistry. Similarly, carpentry teaches measurement and spatial concepts, and comparing sizes and prices at the supermarket can turn even shopping into a learning experience.

"People make the mistake of trying to introduce new math concepts with paper and pencil," according to Dr. Ada Schermann, principal of the Institute of Child Study. "Start with a game or a fun activity such as cooking, gardening, or playing a mathematically based card game like 21. Then children don't think they're being taught, and the learning comes naturally."

Girls' poor problem-solving abilities have been linked to the fact that they are not usually encouraged to assert themselves as individuals. So perhaps it's not surprising that they begin to retreat from maths and sciences during their teenage years. During this period their willingness to consider a nontraditional career also wanes.

It must be the responsibility of parents and teachers to erase the myth that an interest in math makes a girl "different" or "unfeminine." From preschool to high school, maths and sciences should be as natural and nonthreatening subjects of study as English or history. Without a solid grounding in these subjects, the doors of opportunity will slam shut for yet another generation of young women—and, unfortunately, unemployment figures are the numbers *everyone* understands.

•

When Bright Girls Decide That Math Is "a Waste of Time"

By Susan Jacoby

Susannah, a 16-year-old who has always been an A student in every subject from algebra to English, recently informed her parents that she intended to drop physics and calculus in her senior year of high school and replace them with a drama seminar and a work-study program. She expects a major in art or history in college, she explained, and "any more science or math will just be a waste of my time."

Her parents were neither concerned by nor opposed to her decision. "Fine, dear," they said. Their daughter is, after all, an outstanding student. What does it matter if, at age 16, she has taken a step that may limit her understanding of both machines and the natural world for the rest of her life?

This kind of decision, in which girls turn away from studies that would give them a sure footing in the world of science and technology, is a self-inflicted female disability that is, regrettably, almost as common today as it was when I was in high school. If Susannah had announced that she had decided to stop taking English in her senior year, her mother and father would have been horrified. I also think they would have been a good deal less sanguine about her decision if she were a boy.

In saying that scientific and mathematical ignorance is a self-inflicted female wound, I do not, obviously, mean that cultural expectations play no role in the process. But the world does not conspire to deprive modern women of access to science as it did in the 1930s, when Rosalyn S. Yalow, the Nobel Prize-winning physicist, graduated from Hunter College and was advised to go to work as a secretary because no graduate school would admit her to its physics department. The current generation of adolescent girls—and their parents, bred on old expectations about women's interests—are active conspirators in limiting their own intellectual development.

It is true that the proportion of young women in science-related graduate and professional schools, most notably medical schools, has increased significantly in the past decade. It is also true that so few women were studying advanced science and mathematics before the early 1970s that the percentage increase in female enrollment does not yet translate into large numbers of women actually working in science.

The real problem is that so many girls eliminate themselves from any serious possibility of studying science as a result of decisions made during the vulnerable period of mid-adolescence, when they are most likely to be influenced—on both conscious and subconscious levels—by the traditional belief that math and science are "masculine" subjects.

During the teen-age years the well-documented phenomenon of "math anxiety" strikes girls who never had any problem handling numbers during earlier schooling. Some men, too, experience this syndrome—a form of panic, akin to a phobia, at any task involving numbers—but women constitute the overwhelming majority of sufferers. The onset of acute math anxiety during the teen-age years is, as Stalin was fond of saying, "not by accident."

In adolescence girls begin to fear that they will be unattractive to boys if they are typed as "brains." Science and math epitomize unfeminine braininess in a way that, say, foreign languages do not. High-school girls who pursue an advanced interest in science and math (unless they are students at special institutions like the Bronx High School of Science where everyone is a brain) usually find that they are greatly outnumbered by boys in their classes. They are, therefore, intruding on male turf at a time when their sexual confidence, as well as that of the boys, is most fragile.

A 1981 assessment of female achievement in mathematics, based on research conducted under a National Institute for Education grant, found significant differences in the mathematical achievements of 9th and 12th graders. At age 13 girls were equal to or slightly better than boys in tests involving algebra, problem solving and spatial ability; four years later the boys had outstripped the girls.

It is not mysterious that some very bright high-school girls suddenly decide that math is "too hard" and "a waste of time." In my experience, self-sabotage of mathematical and scientific ability is often a conscious process. I remember deliberately pretending to be puzzled by geometry problems in my sophomore year in high school. A male teacher called me in after class and said, in a baffled tone, "I don't see how you can be having so much trouble when you got straight A's last year in my algebra class."

The decision to avoid advanced biology, chemistry, physics and calculus in high school automatically restricts academic and professional choices that ought to be wide open to anyone beginning college. At all coeducational universities women are overwhelmingly concentrated in the fine arts, social sciences and traditionally female departments like education. Courses leading to degrees in science- and technology-related fields are filled mainly by men.

In my generation, the practical consequences of mathematical and scientific illiteracy are visible in the large number of special programs to help professional women overcome the anxiety they feel when they are promoted into jobs that require them to handle statistics.

The consequences of this syndrome should not, however, be viewed in narrowly professional terms. Competence in science and math does not mean one is going to become a scientist or mathematician any more than competence in writing English means one is going to become a professional writer. Scientific and mathematical illiteracy—which has been cited in several recent critiques by panels studying American education from kindergarten through college—produces an incalculably impoverished vision of human experience.

Scientific illiteracy is not, of course, the exclusive province of women. In certain intellectual circles it has become fashionable to proclaim a willed, aggressive ignorance about science and technology. Some female writers specialize in ominous, uninformed diatribes against genetic research as a plot to remove control of childbearing from women, while some well-known men of letters proudly announce that they understand absolutely nothing about computers, or, for that matter, about electricity. This lack of understanding is nothing in which women or men ought to take pride.

Failure to comprehend either computers or chromosomes leads to a terrible sense of helplessness, because the profound impact of science on everyday life is evident even to those who insist they don't, won't, can't understand why the changes are taking place. At this stage of history women are more prone to such feelings of helplessness than men because the culture judges their ignorance less harshly and because women themselves acquiesce in that indulgence.

Since there is ample evidence of such feelings in adolescence, it is up to parents to see that their daughters do not accede to the old stereotypes about "masculine" and "feminine" knowledge. Unless we want our daughters to share our intellectual handicaps, we had better tell them no, they can't stop taking mathematics and sciences at the ripe old age of 16.

•

Math Myths Have Got to Go, Forum Told

By Jennifer Lewington

Math education in Ontario must become more relevant, rigorous and fun, to shatter the myth "that it's okay not to be good at it," delegates to a conference on the subject were told yesterday.

The forum, organized by the Ministry of Education and Training after Ontario's poor showing on the first-ever national mathematics test last year, called for change in math content, teaching methods and testing.

The one-day event drew about 400 math teachers, parents, students, trustees and representatives of business who offered scores of recommendations. These include measures to:

- Clarify provincial math standards and reduce repetition in the curriculum;
- Diversify teaching strategies to make math more relevant and appealing to students than at present;
- Raise the math education requirements for elementary school teachers;
- Involve parents in the math education of their children.

"The system is not as strong as its parts," forum co-chairman Wayne Samuelson told delegates at the close of the session. He said there is "a need for building connections between students and teachers, between school and the community, between the education system and society."

Next week, Education Minister David Cooke is expected to respond to the recommendations—even before the Royal Commission on Learning tables its report on education reforms later this year.

The Ontario forum signals a growing national interest in the improvement of math education, said Roger Palmer, a senior Alberta education official who helped develop the national math test sponsored by the provinces last year.

"It's part of a general movement across the country," he said of the Ontario meeting.

For example, the four western provinces and two territories are members of a consortium developing a math curriculum that sets clear, more specific outcomes. Elsewhere, the Maritime provinces have embarked on their own project to share in the development of curriculum.

In a speech to the Ontario forum yesterday, York University math professor Patricia Rogers said some myths about math must be shattered to ensure lasting reform.

In her view, too many people believe math is bound by strict rules—those usually set by the teacher. Another false view, she contends, is that math is open only to those with innate ability, making it easier for students and their parents to give up on the subject.

Finally, she said, too many people believe "it's okay" if they are inept at mathematics.

"We don't mind being called readers. If we can't read and write it's a matter of personal shame. People who can't do mathematics to a certain level are proud of it."

Like others at the meeting, she called for teacher education reforms. For example, she suggests that all student teachers take a mandatory mathematics course in preparation for teaching elementary school. The course should be specially designed to teach math concepts to those without a strong math background.

At York, she teaches such a program, but it is not a requirement for all students.

In Ontario, students currently do not have to take math after Grade 10. In other provinces the subject is required through Grade 11.

In Quebec, which outperformed other provinces on the national math test, senior elementary teachers are required to have some subject expertise in math.

•

Analysis

1. Why does Dean include the anecdote about Rosalyn Yalow taken from the Jacoby article? Does she use it in a different way than Jacoby?

2. How relevant do you think the information in the two American articles is to the Canadian experience? Why do you think Dean chose to use American data?

3. Why do you think Dean chose not to endorse fully Estrich's conclusions concerning single-sex schools with reference to "math anxiety"? In answering this question, look at how Estrich has structured her article. It contains much personal anecdote which she uses in place of objective data. Why do you think she did this?

4. Two articles refer to Myra Novogrodsky as an expert. Who is she? How does Dean conflate the information about Novogrodsky in her research paper?

5. What are the four main problems Dean identifies that give rise to and perpetuate "math anxiety"? What are her sources for each of the problems?

6. Dean makes use of paraphrase, summary, and quotation. Find an example of each in her paper and trace it back to its source.

7. The issue of gender bias underlies the symptom of "math anxiety." Which of the sources led Dean to the realization of this fact?

8. How viable are the solutions Dean presents in terms of the problems?

9. What patterns of organization can you identify in Dean's research paper? How are these patterns developed from those of her sources?

10. How clear is Dean's own point of view? At what points in her research paper does she clearly take a stand of her own?

Appendix A

Editorial Checklist

Structure

1. Is there a clear thesis statement written in correct parallel form?
2. Does each paragraph have a topic sentence that contains *one* idea and that relates to the *key ideas* expressed in the thesis statement?
3. Do the supporting details in the paragraphs develop the single ideas expressed in the topic sentences?
4. Does each paragraph have unity and coherence? (See Unit Three.)
5. Are transition words used correctly? (See Unit Three.)
6. Is there a proper introduction and conclusion? (See Units Three and Four.)

Sentences

1. Does each sentence have a subject and a verb? Are the tenses used in the sentences correct and consistent?
2. Are there any fragments, run-ons?
3. Is word order—**syntax**—correct and readable?
4. Do verbs agree with subjects?
5. Do pronouns agree with antecedents? (Note: watch out for use of *their* when referring to a single subject.)
6. Are words in the sentence appropriate to the idea in the sentence?
7. Is sentence length appropriate?
8. Are there any dangling modifiers? Incomplete dependent clauses? Misuse of *which* or *that*? Do all clauses have correct verb forms?
9. Are there any shifts in person (from first to second)? Is the second person *you* overused?

Words

1. Are all verbs correctly spelled (with the appropriate *s* or *ed*)?

2. Are apostrophes used correctly for possessives and contractions? (Be careful with the *its/it's* confusion.)
3. Is there any jargon or unclear use of terms? Is there incorrect usage of words, or inappropriate "big" words?
4. Are there any errors in "mismatched" words (e.g., *there* vs. *their* vs. *they're,* or *then* vs. *than*)?
5. Are all nouns and adjectives correctly spelled? Are adverbs used correctly? (Be careful with the *real/really* confusion.)

Punctuation

1. Does every complete sentence end with a period or semicolon?
2. Are commas used to separate list items, introductory dependent clauses, short phrases, interjections?
3. Is the semicolon confused with the comma?
4. Is the colon used correctly to introduce a series? Make sure the colon is *not* used after any form of the verb *to be.*
5. Is capitalization complete? Are first words of sentences in capitals? Are all proper nouns?
6. Are quotation marks placed correctly? (See Unit Six for use of quotations in research papers.)
7. Are questions clearly marked with question marks?

Presentation

1. If there is a title page, is it accurate? Is the teacher's name spelled correctly? Are the numbers for sections and courses correct?
2. Are pages numbered clearly and consecutively?
3. In a research paper, is the use of the MLA or APA style correct and consistent?
4. If an essay or research paper is keyed or typed, are there any errors in the typing?
5. Is the essay or research paper double-spaced?
6. If an essay is handwritten, is it clear of mark-outs, white-out ink smudges, cross-outs? Is the handwriting readable?
7. If an essay is hand-printed, is it in upper- and lower-case letters?

Appendix B

Additional Readings

What Your Body Language Says About You

By Gerald Astor

"Your lips say, 'No, no, no,' but your eyes say, 'Yes, yes, yes'" is a line from an old popular song. It may sound somewhat phony, but the author was hinting at that kind of nonverbal communication known as body language. It can reflect a person's views more accurately than any words coming from his or her mouth.

Body language covers the infinite range of facial and body movements, including the myriad ways to smile, to walk, to manipulate your eyes, to move your hands and arms. We draw messages from body language, whether it's the "no" that a shake of the head conveys, the "I'm not interested" that a turning away of the head can suggest, or the "Hey, I'm bad" statement Richard Pryor and Gene Wilder expected their swaggers to make in *Stir Crazy.* Sometimes, the messages are conveyed through deliberate, conscious gestures; other times, our bodies talk without our even knowing. But conscious or not, our body language helps us portray a wide range of feelings, including boredom, amusement, impatience, fatigue, concentration, interest, puzzlement, and embarrassment.

Some of our body-language expressions are common idioms. To most people, for example, the thumb and forefinger forming a circle means "Everything's okay." A fist with the thumb pointing up is "Good luck" or "All systems go." Desmond Morris, a behavioral scientist and the author of *The Naked Ape* (McGraw-Hill), was among those who studied the interpretations of twenty specific gestures by people in Europe, North Africa, and the Middle East. He found similarities in understanding despite the geographic and cultural differences. (The most universally recognized signal was the thumb at the tip of the nose with the fingers spread!)

Body language becomes more complicated when we try to translate the movements, postures, and facial expressions that a person has little or no control over—the actions that spring from the dark well within us, our unconscious. These bits of body language are often subtle, may contradict our words, and frequently involve a series of actions.

The eyes are one of the most revealing instruments of body language. Keith, seventeen, from Montclair, New Jersey, learned the hard way about one message the eyes can convey. "I had a teacher who graded heavily on classroom discussion," Keith says. "He seemed to have a weird ability to know just when I didn't have the answers. I couldn't figure out how he could be so sharp. Then it dawned on me. Whenever I didn't know the answer, I would avoid looking at him. When I did know what to say, I always stared straight back at him. From that moment on, I taught myself to look him in the eye, whether I knew the work or not. That trick has saved me a lot of grief."

Many people, including some policemen, believe eye contact is a good test of honesty. If someone can't look you dead in the eye, then he or she is not playing straight, they insist. After many experiments, however, a number of experts have concluded that good liars can fake eye contact. (If you still believe that a chap staring straight into your baby blues will never lie to you, then someday, I'd like to interest you in a share of the Grand Canyon.)

Eye contact, though not a sure sign of honesty, is a clear way to show interest in another person. When a person looks at you and continues to do so, you know his attention is focused on you. When he turns his head away, his mind is probably elsewhere: you are no longer "numero uno." But there are exceptions. A shy person may have trouble making and maintaining eye contact, no matter how interested he is in the other person. And certain nationalities, such as the British and the Germans, are much less oriented to eyeball-to-eyeball encounters than, say, the French and the Arabs.

When the eyes act in concert with other parts of the face, communication becomes increasingly explicit. In a study in which psychologists A. Thayer and W. Schiff showed a series of facial diagrams to a panel of people, there was very strong agreement on the messages (the results of their study were published in the *American Journal of Psychology* in 1969). Pleasure widens the eyes and is usually accompanied by a smile. Thus, poker players who are dealt a good hand must learn to control their body language and develop a "poker face." The "drop dead" or "if looks could kill" expression is produced by wrinkling the eyebrows, narrowing the eyes, and turning down the corners of the mouth. Surprise sends the eyebrows skyward and widens the gaze. Despair hoods the eyes, makes the mouth droop, and often causes the entire body to slump.

Like the eyes, the smile is remarkably varied. The genuinely happy smile flashes both upper and lower teeth and is accompanied by open eyes and relaxed brows. In the sheepish smile—you've spilled your soda pop and that nice fellow offers his help—the corners of the mouth are turned up, the eyebrows lifted. The fiendish smile consists of a wide grin and a scrunching of the eyebrows.

Hand movements are another area where there is common understanding of the action. Shake your fist, and everyone realizes that you're angry. Rub your palms together, and you're probably anticipating something good. Rub your palms and the backs of your hands, and you're probably just cold. Point, and you are signaling a direction. Point a finger at someone, and you're making an accusation.

Sometimes a person brings a hand up to his mouth while talking. That gesture could be an effort to stop others from hearing or an unconscious admission of doubt or that there's something being concealed. A hand at the throat may indicate some uncertainty about the words being spoken.

Politicians frequently use hand movements to hold the attention of an audience. Former President Gerald Ford, regarded as a less than spellbinding orator, was once counseled by advisers to add a number of gestures to punctuate a speech. He did so—but apparently unsuccessfully. A poll of those who listened revealed that one third agreed with Ford, one third disagreed, and one third were so distracted by his gesticulations that they didn't know what he had said. Artificial movements are the bad grammar of body language and confuse listeners (which is why some politicians and actors rely on experts to coach them in effective nonverbal communication).

One of the most clearly recognized expressions of body language is the handshake. (It is believed that originally a handshake was a way of showing a person that one came unarmed.) We draw information from the quality of the squeeze. A flabby grip suggests weakness or a lack of interest. Too much pressure signals a desire to dominate.

The position of the entire body is also important when interpreting nonverbal communication. "When I meet someone sitting with his legs or ankles crossed tightly and his arms folded over his chest, I feel that he's closed off from me and uninterested," says sixteen-year-old Julie, a Brooklyn high school senior. She has correctly interpreted a posture that translators of body language classify as "closed." If an individual feels relaxed, giving, and receptive, he's usually in an "open position": His arms are unclasped, and his legs apart.

Closed positions tend to discourage intruders. And as Marianne La France and Clara Mayo, the authors of *Moving Bodies* (Wadsworth) note, anyone in this posture is also far less likely to be convincing in a discussion; listeners may feel he's not revealing as much as he should. It's important, though, to keep in mind that whether or not a person assumes a closed or open position may have a lot to do with upbringing. Women, for example, because of the female tradition of wearing skirts, have customarily been taught to assume a "ladylike" position and keep their legs together (though that may be changing with the growing acceptance of women wearing pants).

Of course, there are other communicative postures besides the closed and open positions. For example, resting the chin upon the hand—the posture of Rodin's sculpture "The Thinker"—is an accepted sign of cogitation. But, says

Ellen, an eighteen-year-old from New York, "When a person rests his cheek on his hand, it can mean, 'I'm uninterested.'"

Posture—indeed, all of body language—is wrapped up in a person's self-image. People uncomfortable with their bodies may adopt a round-shouldered slouch and wear baggy clothes. People who are content with their self-image are more likely to stand straight and wear form-fitting apparel.

Body language can also serve as a kind of dialogue between two people. For example, if two people sit on a couch with their arms and legs in similar positions, it usually means they're in agreement. A man and a woman on the same couch who have adopted widely different ways of sitting and who are not looking at one another are probably out of touch with each other. A male and female sitting on a couch, facing each other, are announcing closeness. If one leans forward, that one is trying to get even closer. If the other is not interested in more involvement, he or she may lean back.

But once again, cultural differences play a role. Wendy, a high school junior from Scarsdale whose parents are Korean and who spent her first years of life in Korea, says, "I don't like showing signs of closeness in public. I feel uncomfortable greeting people at a party with a hug or kiss. I wasn't brought up that way." Those unaware of the cultural differences might mistakenly read her body language as a sign of aloofness or coldness.

Other mistakes are common when trying to translate body language. Says Kathy, a seventeen-year-old from New York, "When someone just spreads himself out, I can't tell whether he's terribly relaxed or just a slob." When an adolescent slouches in front of an adult, it may be a rebellious statement (parents are always demanding that one stand up straight), or it may be that the person is very much at ease.

But although you can never fully understand another's body language—or fully control your own—you can be aware that nonverbal cues are as important to communication as words. Increase your knowledge of body language, and you'll be a little less confused in a world of many different messages.

•

In the Market for a Mate? Shop Around

By H.J. Barrie

If you are going on 60 and it is five years since your wife died, and you are tired of living alone, or if you would like a little romance in your life, or if you just want someone to play Scrabble with on Sunday night, forget the singles bars, church basements, agony column and Fred Astaire's dancing classes. Think supermarkets.

There is no other place where you can study the fair sex in its natural habitat so closely and few places where you can so easily strike up a conversation without causing offence. A great tide of women flows through the aisles all day long, and with very little trouble, you can find out a lot about a prospective partner before you even try to strike up an acquaintance. For any lonely male who would like to take advantage of this suggestion, here are a few tips.

The day of the week is important. You will be looking for a woman with time on her hands, and you won't find her pushing through the crowds on the weekends. Her presence on Monday may mean that she is incapable of catering for more than a few days at a time and does not know that the vegetables will not be very fresh. Tuesday is a very good day.

You are not hoping for a raving beauty; you just want someone with a face and figure you can live with, and you may have to wait some time. Buy a paper and find a seat at the entrance where people pick up their shopping carts. When a likely prospect comes through the swinging doors, look for an easy move, a woman who has a quarter handy and does not have to spend two minutes rummaging through an untidy bag. Watch to see if she gets hysterical when she puts in her quarter and the carts remain jammed together, but remember that many good women wait for male aid when there is any sort of a mechanical problem, so you should respond accordingly.

Now you follow her discreetly down the aisles. You will soon find out if she lives alone. If she buys a seven-pound bag of potatoes, you will know that she either has company at home or is oblivious to the smell of rotting potatoes in the cupboard under the sink. Look for someone who buys a handful of French beans, two Spanish onions, two avocados and an aubergine. If she buys lobok, nappa or escarole, she is probably well travelled and maybe an inventive cook or a good conversationalist. Buying raspberries and asparagus in December will indicate a woman expensive to feed, and this will be confirmed by asking for 150 grams of rainbow trout without asking the price.

Watch her at the cheese counter. Extra old cheddar is good; spiced cheeses are bad. In every aisle you will find out more about her character and tastes. If she buys potatoes in a tin, go back to the entrance and try again. Do not follow her down the aisle reserved for women's concerns. It is none of your business, and you can always take a peek into her basket at the checkout counter. She may have a daughter at college.

The meat section is important. If she buys two big filet mignon steaks, her Sunday evenings are probably spoken for. Oxtails are good; a big family pack of chicken wings is bad. Does she go up and down the aisles methodically or does she reach the yogurt and then have to dash back to the peanut butter?

Bread is important, not for any theoretical reasons but to determine how much your tastes lie in common. Does she buy a French stick or dark rye? Too much unground cereal is a warning sign, big bags of chips a no-no.

Watch her as she passes the paperback rack. If she slips a bodice-ripper into her cart, it is not a good sign unless you have similar proclivities.

When she approaches the checkout counter, watch to see if she is sufficiently alert to choose the one with the most efficient cashier. Now is the time to make up your mind. Do not wait until you discover whether she can find the opening in the plastic bags. It will be too late then.

Do not expect perfection. Such a thing is not possible. Just add up the pros and cons and come to a decision. It is always reversible. If you give yourself the go-ahead, arrange a slight collision and after the apology say, "We seem to have similar tastes." One look at your cart will send her the message, and if she is looking for someone to play Scrabble with, the conversation may continue.

If you get an unmistakeable brushoff, go back to the entrance for another try, replacing on the shelves as you go the handful of French beans, two Spanish onions, five potatoes and the big pack of chicken wings.

•

Lingophobia ... Anxiety of Choice

By Arthur Black

Do you have trouble with languages—other than the one we're using right now, I mean? Lingophobia seems to be the anxiety of choice these days. I hear people muttering about the French on the back of the cereal box. I run across other folks gnashing their dentures over the unreadability of "Japanified" assembly instructions that come with their "so-easy-a-child-could-put-it-together" barbecues.

Well, pas de probleme, ami. I'm here to convince you that you are a linguistic whiz. Bilingual? You're multilingual—polylingual even. Before you leave this page I'll have you nattering in Japanese, Mandarin, Ojibway, Malaysian, Iroquoiian, German, and Spanish. Best of all, I won't be teaching you—you already know this stuff.

Let's start by examining the status quo. I don't want to feed your ego but the fact is you're no ignoramus. Without going into the pros and cons, conducting a referendum, or issuing an ultimatum, it's safe to say that you have already mastered a substantial chunk of foreign language you may never have studied in school.

You understood that last paragraph, didn't you? It contained eight unadulterated Latin words—which is but a fraction of the Latin words you use every day. Each time you enter an "arena" or a "stadium," try to shoot under "par" on the golf course, read "propaganda" about a "moratorium" or shake your head about the number of "major" and "minor" penalties called in a match that featured one team "versus" another ... you might as well be having a chat with Cicero.

You speak French too—and not just the obvious imports like chaise lounge, filet mignon, and bouquet but also words like envelope, hotel, and prairie.

You speak Greek of course (everything from asbestos to zoology) and Dutch (cookies, coleslaw, waffles). You know German (sauerkraut, noodles, pretzels, hamburgers). You have a little Swedish (smorgasbord), a good deal of Indian patter (papoose, toboggan, moccasin, wigwam, raccoon)—why you even have a smattering of Arabic (zero, algebra, assassin). Why, it's enough to make a guy run amok (Malaysian) or even go berserk (Old Norse).

Anyway, I think you get my point. If you're bad at language, then Wayne Gretzky wears tube skates. You're a regular walking Tower of Babel, chum. But here's a couple of tips that will make your command of languages even more impressive.

Some foreign linguistic trivia first: Know what the Hawaiians call an itsy-bitsy reef-dwelling fish about as long as your thumb?

They call him (or her) "humohumokunokuapuaa."

Know what those same Hawaiians call another fish—a boxcar-sized denizen of the deep that's big enough to swallow your surfboard sideways?

They call him "O."

Foreign linguistic trivia, subsection: traffic signs. Did I mention that your command of Jamaican patois would leave Harry Belafonte gaping in amazement? Of course it would. What would you realize if you were driving into Kingston and saw a road sign warning: "No uovatek naar pass"—that it was against the law to overtake or pass, naturally. Say, you've really got a gift for this sort of thing, haven't you?

But enough bantering. I promised you some helpful language tips and it's time to deliver. Here's one: In Spanish there is an endlessly useful phrase that wins friends, melts hearts, and may even get the other hombre to buy the next round of Fundador. The phrase means "That's right" or "You've got it!" People—Spanish or otherwise—love to be told that they're brilliant. In Spanish the phrase is: "Eso si qeue es!" But forget that. All you have to remember is what you wear between your shoes and your bare bunions—socks—and spell it out. S-O-C-K-S.

Perfectamente.

Japanese? A snap. Want to say "You're welcome"? It's "dooitashimaskite." You'll get by if you say "Don't touch my moustache"—real fast. Similarly you should remember that when you say "hi" in Japanese you are really saying "yes" (hai); when you want to say "Good Morning" just think of the state of Ohio (okayo)—and remember too that the word "Mother" in Japanese is "ha-ha."

That shouldn't be hard to remember—just think of your mother-in-law.

Ooops. My Olivetti is registering Plus Nine on the Richter Scale—I forgot the Old Coot was staying with us. Have to run. For my life. Sayonara, muchachos.

•

Angry Young Men:
Is Violence a Shortcut to Respect for Men with No future?

By Barbara Ehrenreich

Recall the roar of commentary that followed the murderous 1989 assault on a 28-year-old woman jogging in Central Park. Every detail of the assailants' lives was sifted for sociological significance: Were they poor? How poor? Students or dropouts? From families with two parents or one?

Yet weeks before the East Harlem "posse" attacked a jogger, suburbanites in nearby Long Island were shaken by two murders that were, if anything, even more inexplicably vicious than the assault in Central Park. In early March the body of 13-year-old Kelly Tinyes was found in the basement of a house just down the block from her own. She had been stabbed, strangled, and hit with a blunt instrument before being mutilated with a bayonet. A few weeks later 14-year-old Jessica Manners was discovered along the side of a road in East Setauket, strangled to death, apparently with her own bra, and possibly sexually assaulted.

Suspects have been apprehended. Their high school friends, parents, and relatives have been interviewed. Their homes and cars have been searched, their photos published. We know who they hung out with and what they did in their spare time. But on the scale of large social meanings, these crimes don't rate. No one is demanding that we understand—or condemn—the white communities that nourished the killers. No one is debating the roots of violence in the land of malls and tract homes. In the city, apparently, crime is construed as something "socioeconomic." Out here it's merely "sick."

But East Setauket is not really all that far from East Harlem. If something is festering in the ghetto, something very similar is gnawing away in middle-income suburbs. A "way of life," as the cliché goes, is coming to an end, and in its place a mean streak is opening up and swallowing everything in its path. Economists talk about "deindustrialization" and "class polarization." I think of it as the problem of marginal men: They are black and white, Catholic and Pentecostal, rap fans and admirers of techno-pop. What they have in common is that they are going nowhere—nowhere legal, that is.

Consider the suspects in the Long Island murders. Twenty-one-year-old Robert Golub, in whose basement Kelly Tinyes was killed, is described in *Newsday* as an "unemployed body builder." When his high school friends went off to college, he stayed behind in his parents' home in Valley Stream. For a while he earned a living driving a truck for a cosmetics firm, but he lost that job, in part because of his driving record: His license had been suspended 12 times since 1985. At the time of the murder, Golub had been out of work for several months, constructing a life around his weight-lifting routine and his dream of becoming an entrepreneur.

Christopher Loliscio, the suspect in the Manners Case, is 19 and, like Golub, lives with his parents. He has been in trouble before, charged with third-degree assault and "menacing" in an altercation that took place on the campus of the State University campus at Stony Brook. Loliscio does not attend college himself. He is employed as a landscaper.

The suburbs are full of young white men like Golub and Loliscio. If they had been born 20 years earlier, they might have found steady work in decent-paying union jobs, married early, joined the volunteer fire department, and devoted their leisure time to lawn maintenance. But the good blue-collar jobs are getting sparser, thanks to "deindustrialization." Much of what's left is likely to be marginal, low-paid work. Nationwide, the earnings of young white men dropped 18 percent between 1973 and 1986, making those at the low end of the wage scale less than desirable marriage prospects.

Landscaping, for example—a glamorous term for raking and mowing—pays four to five dollars an hour; truck driving for a small firm is in the same range; not enough to pay for a college education, a house, or even a midsize wedding reception at the VFW hall.

And even those modest prerequisites of life in the sub-yuppie class have become, in some sense, "not enough." On Long Island the culture that once sustained men in blue-collar occupations is crumbling as more affluent settlers move in, filling the vacant lots with their new $750,000 homes. In my town, for example, the last five years saw the bowling alley close and the blue-collar bar turn into a pricey dining spot. Even the volunteer fire department is having trouble recruiting. The prestigious thing to join is a $500-a-year racquetball club; there's just not much respect anymore for putting out fires.

So the marginal man lives between two worlds—one that he aspires to and one that is dying—neither of which he can afford. Take "Rick," the 22-year-old son of family friends. His father is a machinist in an aerospace plant that hasn't hired anyone above the floor-sweeping level for years now. Not that Rick has ever shown any interest in his father's trade. For one thing, he takes too much pride in his appearance to put on the dark green, company-supplied work clothes his father has worn for the past 20 years. Rick has his own kind of uniform: pleated slacks, high-tops, Italian knit cardigans, and a $300 leather jacket, accessorized with a gold chain and earring stud.

To his parents, Rick is a hardworking boy for whom things just don't seem to work out. Right now he has a gig doing valet parking at a country club. The tips are good, and he loves racing around the lot in Porsches and Lamborghinis of the stockbroker members. But the linchpin of his economic strategy is living at home, with his parents and sisters, in the same room he's occupied since third grade. This arrangement is less than ideal for his social life. Besides, Rick is a long way from being able to afford even a cramped, three-bedroom house like his family home; given the choice, he'd rather have a new Camaro anyway.

So Rick's girlfriends tend to move on rapidly, looking for men who might someday have a chance in the real estate market.

If this were the '70s, Rick might have dropped out; he might have taken up marijuana, the Grateful Dead, and vague visions of a better world. But like so many of his contemporaries in the '90s, Rick isn't rebellious. He has no problem with the "system," which, in his mind, embraces every conceivable hustle, legal or illegal. He can't imagine demanding better jobs or a living wage when there's easy money to be made elsewhere. Two years ago he made a tidy bundle dealing coke in a local dance club, bought a $20,000 car, and smashed it up. Now he spends his evenings working as a bouncer in an illegal gambling joint—his parents still think he's out "dancing"—and is proud of the handgun he's got stowed in his glove compartment.

Someday Rick will use that gun, and I'll probably be the first to say—like Robert Golub's friends—"but he isn't the kind of person who would hurt anyone." Except that even now I can sense the danger in him. He's smart enough to know he's only a cut-rate copy of the upscale young men in GQ ads and MTV commercials whom he is trying to emulate. Viewed from Wall Street or Southampton, he's a peon, a member of the invisible underclass that parks cars, waits on tables, and is satisfied with a $5 tip and an occasional remark about the weather.

He's also proud. And there's nowhere for him to put that pride except into the politics of gesture: the macho stance, the 75-mph takeoff down the expressway, and eventually, maybe, the drawn gun. Jobs are the liberal solution; conservatives would throw in "traditional values." But what the marginal men—from Valley Stream to Bedford-Stuyvesant—need most of all is *respect.* If they can't find that in work, or in a working-class lifestyle that is no longer honored, they'll extract it from someone weaker—a girlfriend, a random jogger, a neighbor, perhaps just any girl. They'll find a victim.

•

Don't You Think It's Time to Start Thinking?

By Northrop Frye

A student often leaves high school today without any sense of language as a structure.

He may also have the idea that reading and writing are elementary skills that he mastered in childhood, never having grasped the fact that there are differences in levels of reading and writing as there are in mathematics between short division and integral calculus.

Yet, in spite of his limited verbal skills, he firmly believes that he can think, that he has ideas, and that if he is just given the opportunity to express them he will be all right. Of course, when you look at what he's written you find it doesn't make any sense. When you tell him this he is devastated.

Part of his confusion here stems from the fact that we use the word "think" in so many bad, punning ways. Remember James Thurber's Walter Mitty who was always dreaming great dreams of glory. When his wife asked him what he was doing he would say, "Has it ever occurred to you that I might be thinking?"

But, of course, he wasn't thinking at all. Because we use it for everything our minds do, worrying, remembering, day-dreaming, we imagine that thinking is something that can be achieved without any training. But again it's a matter of practice. How well we can think depends on how much of it we have already done. Most students need to be taught, very carefully and patiently, that there is no such thing as an inarticulate idea waiting to have the right words wrapped around it.

They have to learn that ideas do not exist until they have been incorporated into words. Until that point you don't know whether you are pregnant or just have gas on the stomach.

The operation of thinking is the practice of articulating ideas until they are in the right words. And we can't think at random either. We can only add one more idea to the body of something we have already thought about. Most of us spend very little time doing this, and that is why there are so few people whom we regard as having any power to articulate at all. When such a person appears in public life, like Mr. Trudeau, we tend to regard him as possessing a gigantic intellect.

A society like ours doesn't have very much interest in literacy. It is compulsory to read and write because society must have docile and obedient citizens. We are taught to read so that we can obey the traffic signs and to cipher so that we can make out our income tax, but development of verbal competency is very much left to the individual.

And when we look at our day-to-day existence we can see that there are strong currents at work against the development of powers of articulateness.

Young adolescents today often betray a curious sense of shame about speaking articulately, of framing a sentence with a period at the end of it.

Part of the reason for this is the powerful anti-intellectual drive which is constantly present in our society. Articulate speech marks you out as an individual, and in some settings this can be rather dangerous because people are often suspicious and frightened of articulateness. So if you say as little as possible and use only stereotyped, ready-made phrases you can hide yourself in the mass.

Then there are various epidemics sweeping over society which use unintelligibility as a weapon to preserve the present power structure. By making things as unintelligible as possible, to as many people as possible, you can hold the present power structure together. Understanding and articulateness lead to its destruction. This is the kind of thing that George Orwell was talking about, not just in *Nineteen Eighty-Four,* but in all his work on language. The kernel of everything reactionary and tyrannical in society is the impoverishment of the means of verbal communication.

The vast majority of things that we hear today are prejudices and clichés, simply verbal formulas that have no thought behind them but are put up as a pretence of thinking. It is not until we realize these things conceal meaning, rather than reveal it, that we can begin to develop our own powers of articulateness.

The teaching of humanities is, therefore, a militant job. Teachers are faced not simply with a mass of misconceptions and unexamined assumptions. They must engage in a fight to help the student confront and reject the verbal formulas and stock responses, to convert passive acceptance into active, constructive power. It is a fight against illiteracy and for the maturation of the mental process, for the development of skills which once acquired will never become obsolete.

•

Back to the Land?
No Way—Big Cities Are Here to Stay

By John Kettle

Although Canada has grown steadily more urban throughout its history, people still think Canadians really want to live in the country.

Canada once was undeniably rural, if not downright wild. Yet ever since the first census we have known that Canadians have been leaving the land and heading for city pleasures.

Recently, demographers believed the trend was reversing: Former city dwellers were thought to be discovering the delights of rural simplicity.

Nothing of the kind occurred.

It is not just that urban life has proved to be more appealing than rural—the biggest cities have grown the fastest, making clear that what Canadians like is city life as full and complex as it can be.

Take just the nine largest cities in Canada: Vancouver, Edmonton, Calgary, Winnipeg, Hamilton, Toronto, Ottawa–Hull, Montreal and Quebec City. In 1931, they had less than one-third of the population. Now they house about half of it.

But there is more to it than that. At a certain point a city advances to a higher status, not just home to a lot of people but a magnet that draws touring players, resident symphony orchestras, art galleries, architecture, great restaurants, and the visitors who would never venture to a big town that was simply big. The city becomes a metropolis.

At least a third of a million people, probably as many as half a million today, are needed to support the kind of metropolitan arts, shops and shows that attract tourists. Once a metropolis gets to that point, it is close to being self-sustaining—famous for being famous. It is visited because it has so many visitors. It also becomes an exciting place to live.

In 1931, only 18 per cent of the population lived in cities with populations of half a million or more. In fact, only Montreal and Toronto were in that giant category. Now all nine top cities have at least half a million people and can plausibly claim to be successful and glittering metropolises rather than just places inhabited by a lot of people.

So what of all the talk in the big metropolises about people driven out of town by high real-estate prices, rising crime rates and pollution?

Well, the truth is that when people say such things, they don't quit Vancouver and move to Prince Rupert, or pull up stakes in Montreal and head for Trois Pistoles. They move just as far as it takes to find less-expensive housing, and certainly not beyond commuting distance. They like to stay in the local phone-call area. They want cable TV and the metropolitan newspaper, the chance to go into town for an afternoon's shopping, or the major-league ball game, or dinner and an evening at the theatre. If they want to be less intensely urban, they certainly don't want to be rural.

The fastest-growing areas of the country are those that ring the main cities. The boundaries of Greater Vancouver and the Montreal Urban Community are not surrounded by fields but by more urbanization. With a population of 3.8 million, the urbanized area that surrounds downtown Toronto (what Statistics Canada defines as the Toronto metropolitan area) stretches farther afield than the political entity of Metropolitan Toronto and much farther than the City of Toronto. It houses 1.5 million more people than Metro, and three million more than the city—where almost all the metropolitan glamour is located. These millions may be people who don't want to live in Toronto, but they don't want to get too far away from it, either.

The Canadian metropolises continue to attract immigrants and the young, and for much the same reason as always. Because these are world-renowned cities. Because they are still where the jobs are. Where young people have the best chance of meeting other young people. Where the fun is, and the rarer and more elegant things to buy, and the more exciting things to do.

The big metropolises—Montreal, Toronto and Vancouver—house the national media, too. The media, reflecting the interests and values of the people they know, produce programming and content that are essentially metropolitan. And this becomes the national norm. How're you going to keep 'em down on the farm after they've seen TV?

With all that going for them, you can expect the nine metropolises to go on spreading. It wouldn't be surprising if in another 20 years they were home to two-thirds of the population. The metropolitan way of life has arrived.

•

A Modest Proposal

For Preventing the Children of Poor People in Ireland from Being a Burden to Their Parents or Country, and for Making Them Beneficial to the Public

By Jonathan Swift

It is a melancholy object to those who walk through this great town or travel in the country, when they see the streets, the roads, and cabin doors, crowded with beggars of the female sex, followed by three, four, or six children, all in rags and importuning every passenger for an alms. These mothers, instead of being able to work for their honest livelihood, are forced to employ all their time in strolling to beg sustenance for their helpless infants, who, as they grow up, either turn thieves for want of work, or leave their dear native country to fight for the Pretender in Spain, or sell themselves to the Barbadoes.

I think it is agreed by all parties that this prodigious number of children in the arms, or on the backs, or at the heels of their mothers, and frequently of their fathers, is in the present deplorable state of the kingdom a very great additional grievance; and therefore whoever could find out a fair, cheap, and easy method of making these children sound, useful members of the commonwealth would deserve so well of the public as to have his statue set up for a preserver of the nation.

But my intention is very far from being confined to provide only for the children of professed beggars; it is of a much greater extent, and shall take in the whole number of infants at a certain age who are born of parents in effect as little able to support them as those who demand our charity in the streets.

As to my own part, having turned my thoughts for many years upon this important subject, and maturely weighed the several schemes of other projectors, I have always found them grossly mistaken in their computation. It is true, a child just dropped from its dam may be supported by her milk for a solar year, with little other nourishment; at most not above the value of two shillings, which the mother may certainly get, or the value in scraps, by her lawful occupation of begging; and it is exactly at one year old that I propose to provide for them in such a manner as instead of being a charge upon their parents or the parish, or wanting food and raiment for the rest of their lives, they shall on the contrary contribute to the feeding, and partly to the clothing, of many thousands.

There is likewise another great advantage in my scheme, that it will prevent those voluntary abortions, and that horrid practice of women murdering their bastard children, alas, too frequent among us, sacrificing the poor innocent babes, I doubt, more to avoid the expense than the shame, which would move tears and pity in the most savage and inhuman breast.

The number of souls in this kingdom being usually reckoned one million and a half, of these I calculate there may be about two hundred thousand couple whose wives are breeders; from which number I subtract thirty thousand couples who are able to maintain their own children, although I apprehend there cannot be so many under the present distresses of the kingdom; but this being granted, there will remain an hundred and seventy thousand breeders. I again subtract fifty thousand for those women who miscarry, or whose children die by accident or disease within the year. There only remain an hundred and twenty thousand children of poor parents annually born. The question therefore is, how this number shall be reared and provided for, which, as I have already said, under the present situation of affairs, is utterly impossible by all the methods hitherto proposed. For we can neither employ them in handicraft or agriculture; we neither build houses (I mean in the country) nor cultivate land. They can very seldom pick up a livelihood by stealing till they arrive at six years old, except where they are of towardly parts; although I confess they learn the rudiments much earlier, during which time they can however be looked upon only as probationers, as I have been informed by a principal gentlemen in the county of Cavan, who protested to me that he never knew above one or two instances under the age of six, even in a part of the kingdom so renowned for the quickest proficiency in that art.

I am assured by our merchants that a boy or girl before twelve years old is no salable commodity; and even when they come to this age they will not yield above three pounds, or three pounds and half a crown at most on the Exchange; which cannot turn to account either to the parents or the kingdom, the charge of nutriment and rags having been at least four times that value.

I shall now therefore humbly propose my own thoughts, which I hope will not be liable to the least objection.

I have been assured by a very knowing American of my acquaintance in London, that a young healthy child well nursed is at a year old a most delicious, nourishing, and wholesome food, whether stewed, roasted, baked or boiled; and I make no doubt that it will equally serve in a fricassee or a ragout.

I do therefore humbly offer it to public consideration that of the hundred and twenty thousand children, already computed, twenty thousand may be reserved for breed, whereof only one fourth part to be males, which is more than we allow to sheep, black cattle, or swine; and my reason is that these children are seldom the fruits of marriage, a circumstance not much regarded by our savages, therefore one male will be sufficient to serve four females. That the remaining hundred thousand may at a year old be offered in sale to the persons of quality and fortune through the kingdom, always advising the mother to let them suck plentifully in the last month, so as to render them plump and fat for a good table. A child will make two dishes at an entertainment for friends; and when the family dines alone, the fore or hind quarter will make a reasonable dish, and seasoned with a little pepper or salt will be very good boiled on the fourth day, especially in winter.

I have reckoned upon a medium that a child just born will weigh twelve pounds, and in a solar year if tolerably nursed increaseth to twenty-eight pounds.

I grant this food will be somewhat dear, and therefore very proper for landlords, who, as they have already devoured most of the parents, seem to have the best title to the children.

Infant's flesh will be in season throughout the year, but more plentiful in March, and a little before and after. For we are told by a grave author, an eminent French physician, that fish being a prolific diet, there are more children born in Roman Catholic countries about nine months after Lent than at any other season: therefore, reckoning a year after Lent, the markets will be more glutted than usual, because the number of popish infants is at least three to one in this kingdom; and therefore it will have one other collateral advantage, by lessening the number of Papists among us.

I have already computed the charge of nursing a beggar's child (in which list I reckon all cottagers, labourers, and four fifths of the farmers) to be about two shillings per annum, rags included: and I believe no gentleman would repine to give ten shillings for the carcass of a good fat child, which, as I have said, will make four dishes of excellent nutritive meat, when he hath only some particular friend or his own family to dine with him. Thus the squire will learn to be a good landlord, and grow popular among the tenants; the mother will have eight shillings net profit, and be fit for work till she produces another child.

Those who are more thrifty (as I must confess the times require) may flay the carcass; the skin of which artificially dressed will make admirable gloves for ladies, and summer boots for fine gentlemen.

As to our city of Dublin, shambles may be appointed for this purpose in the most convenient parts of it, and butchers we may be assured will not be wanting; although I rather recommend buying the children alive, and dressing them hot from the knife as we do roasting pigs.

A very worthy person, a true lover of his country, and whose virtues I highly esteem, was lately pleased in discoursing on this matter to offer a refinement upon my scheme. He said that many gentlemen of this kingdom, having of late destroyed their deer, he conceived that the want of venison might be well supplied by the bodies of young lads and maidens, not exceeding fourteen years of age nor under twelve, so great a number of both sexes in every county being now ready to starve for want of work and service; and these to be disposed of by their parents, if alive, or otherwise by their nearest relations. But with due deference to so excellent a friend and so deserving a patriot, I cannot be altogether in his sentiments; for as to the males, my American acquaintance assured me from frequent experience that their flesh was generally tough and lean, like that of our schoolboys, by continual exercise, and their taste disagreeable; and to fatten them would not answer the charge. Then as to the females, it would, I think with humble submission, be a loss to the public, because they soon would become breeders themselves: and besides, it is not improbable that some scrupulous people might be apt to censure such a practice (although indeed very unjustly) as a little bordering upon cruelty; which, I confess, hath always been with me the strongest objection against any project, how well soever intended.

But in order to justify my friend, he confessed that this expedient was put into his head by the famous Psalmanazar, a native of the island Formosa, who came from thence to London above twenty years ago, and in conversation told my friend that in his country when any young person happened to be put to death, the executioner sold the carcass to persons of quality as a prime dainty; and that in his time the body of a plump girl of fifteen, who was crucified for an attempt to poison the emperor, was sold to his Imperial Majesty's prime minister of state, and other great mandarins of the court, in joints from the gibbet, at four hundred crowns. Neither indeed can I deny that if the same use were made of several plump young girls in this town, who without one single groat to their fortunes cannot stir abroad without a chair, and appear at the playhouse and assemblies in foreign fineries which they never will pay for, the kingdom would not be the worse.

Some persons of a desponding spirit are in great concern about that vast number of poor people who are aged, diseased, or maimed, and I have been desired to employ my thoughts what course may be taken to ease the nation of so grievous an encumbrance. But I am not in the least pain upon that matter, because it is very well known that they are every day dying and rotting by cold and famine, and filth and vermin, as fast as can be reasonably expected. And as to the younger labourers, they are now in almost as hopeful a condition. They cannot get work, and consequently pine away from want of nourishment to a degree that if at any time they are accidentally hired to common labour, they have not strength to perform it; and thus the country and themselves are happily delivered from the evils to come.

I have too long digressed, and therefore shall return to my subject. I think the advantages by the proposal which I have made are obvious and many, as well as of the highest importance.

For first, as I have already observed, it would greatly lessen the number of Papists, with whom we are yearly overrun, being the principal breeders of the nation as well as our most dangerous enemies; and who stay at home on purpose to deliver the kingdom to the Pretender, hoping to take their advantage by the absence of so many good Protestants, who have chosen rather to leave their country than to stay at home and pay tithes against their conscience to an Episcopal curate.

Secondly, the poorer tenants will have something valuable of their own, which by law may be made liable to distress, and help to pay their landlord's rent, their corn and cattle being already seized and money a thing unknown.

Thirdly, whereas the maintenance of an hundred thousand children, from two years old and upwards, cannot be computed at less than ten shillings a piece per annum, the nation's stock will be thereby increased fifty thousand pounds per annum, besides the profit of a new dish introduced to the tables of all gentlemen of fortune in the kingdom who have any refinement in taste. And the money will circulate among ourselves, the goods being entirely of our own growth and manufacture.

Fourthly, the constant breeders, besides the gain of eight shillings sterling per annum by the sale of their children, will be rid of the charge of maintaining them after the first year.

Fifthly, the food would likewise bring great custom to taverns, where the vitners will certainly be so prudent as to procure the best receipts for dressing it to perfection, and consequently have their houses frequented by all the fine gentlemen, who justly value themselves upon their knowledge in good eating; and a skillful cook, who understands how to oblige his guests, will contrive to make it as expensive as they please.

Sixthly, this would be a great inducement to marriage, which all wise nations have either encouraged by rewards or enforced by laws and penalties. It would increase the care and tenderness of mothers toward their children, when they were sure of a settlement for life to the poor babes, provided in some sort by the public, to their annual profit instead of expense. We should see an honest emulation among the married women, which of them could bring the fattest child to the market. Men would become as fond of their wives during the time of their pregnancy as they are now of their mares in foal, their cows in calf, or sows when they are ready to farrow; nor offer to beat or kick them (as is too frequent a practice) for fear of a miscarriage.

Many other advantages might be enumerated. For instance, the addition of some thousand carcasses in our exportation of barreled beef, the propagation of swine's flesh, and improvement in the art of making good bacon, so much wanted among us by the great destruction of pigs, too frequent at our tables, which are no way comparable in taste or magnificence to a well-grown, fat yearling child, which roasted whole will make a considerable figure at a lord mayor's feast or any other public entertainment. But this and many others I omit, being studious of brevity.

Supposing that one thousand families in this city would be constant customers for infants' flesh, besides others who might have it at merry meetings, particularly weddings and christenings, I compute that Dublin would take off annually about twenty thousand carcasses, and the rest of the kingdom (where probably they will be sold somewhat cheaper) the remaining eighty thousand.

I can think of no one objection that will possibly be raised against this proposal, unless it should be urged that the number of people will be thereby much lessened in the kingdom. This I freely own, and it was indeed one principal design in offering it to the world. I desire the reader will observe, that I calculate my remedy for this one individual kingdom of Ireland and for no other that ever was, is, or I think ever can be upon earth. Therefore let no man talk to me of other expedients: of taxing our absentees at five shillings a pound: of using neither clothes nor household furniture except what is of our own growth and manufacture: of utterly rejecting the materials and instruments that promote foreign luxury: of curing the expensiveness of pride, vanity, idleness, and gaming in our women: of introducing a vein of parsimony, prudence, and temperance: of learning to love our country, in the want of which we differ even from Laplanders and the inhabitants of Topinamboo: of quitting our animosities and factions, nor acting any longer like the Jews, who were murdering one another at the very moment their city was taken: of being a little cautious not to sell our country and conscience for nothing: of teaching landlords to have at least one degree of mercy toward their tenants: lastly, of putting a spirit of honesty, industry, and skill into our shopkeepers; who, if a resolution could be now taken to buy only our native goods, would immediately unite to cheat and exact upon us in the price, the measure and the goodness, nor could ever yet be brought to make one fair proposal of just dealing, though often and earnestly invited to it.

Therefore I repeat, let no man talk to me of these and the like expedients, till he hath at least some glimpse of hope that there will ever be some hearty and sincere attempt to put them in practice.

But as to myself, having been wearied out for many years with offering vain, idle, visionary thoughts, and at length utterly despairing of success, I fortunately fell upon this proposal, which, as it is wholly new, so it hath something solid and real, of no expense and little trouble, full in our own power, and whereby we can incur no danger in disobliging England. For this kind of commodity will not bear exportation, the flesh being of too tender a consistence to admit a long continuance in salt, although perhaps I could name a country which would be glad to eat up our whole nation without it.

After all, I am not so violently bent upon my own opinion as to reject any offer proposed by wise men, which shall be found equally innocent, cheap, easy, and effectual. But before something of that kind shall be advanced in contradiction to my scheme, and offering a better, I desire the author or authors will be pleased maturely to consider two points. First, as things now stand, how they will be able to find food and raiment for an hundred thousand useless mouths and backs. And secondly, there being a round million of creatures in human figure throughout this kingdom, whose sole subsistence put into a common stock would leave them in debt two millions of pounds sterling, adding those who are beggars by profession to the bulk of farmers, cottagers, and labourers, with their wives and children who are beggars in effect; I desire those politicians who dislike my overture, and may perhaps be so bold to attempt an answer, that they will first ask the parents of these mortals whether they would not at this day think it a great happiness to have been sold for food at a year old in the manner I prescribe, and thereby have avoided such a perpetual scene of misfortunes as they have since gone through by the oppression of landlords, the impossibility of paying rent without money or trade, the want of common sustenance, with neither house nor clothes to cover them from the inclemencies of the weather, and the most inevitable prospect of entailing the like or greater miseries upon their breed forever.

I profess, in the sincerity of my heart, that I have not the least personal interest in endeavouring to promote this necessary work, having no other motive than the public good of my country, by advancing our trade, providing for infants, relieving the poor, and giving some pleasure to the rich. I have no children by which I can propose to get a single penny; the youngest being nine years old, and my wife past childbearing.

•

Hand Over Hand

By Margaret Visser

The human body is less symmetrical than it looks. Internally, our organs are not divided neatly down the middle—the heart, for example, being both inclined and on the left—and externally our hands are almost invariably quite unequal, although they apparently mirror each other. About ninety per cent of people are right-handed; the other ten per cent have a strong preference for the left. This is one of our differences from animals, among whom fifty per cent prefer the right front leg, fifty per cent prefer the left, and ambidextrous behaviour is far more common than in human beings.

Body images are among the most powerful metaphors we have; "culture" seizes upon the body and uses it to express moral ideas, social structures, prejudices, preferences, fears, and ideals. Often the metaphor squeezes the facts into its own mould: the "heart" of anything is its middle, even though our hearts are definitely off-centre. We have always emphasized the difference in efficiency between our two hands; we have then meditated on the weakness of the left, and used it to confirm our worst suspicions.

The right hand, in almost every language and culture on earth, means permanence, reliability ("a right-hand man"), power, truth, and rectitude. Dexterity, acceptability, immediacy, and correctness are "right-handed" in English; "sinister" means "left," a word that itself derives from Anglo-Saxon *lyft*: "weak" or "worthless." *Droit* in French is "straight" and also "just," while someone *gauche* ("gawky" in English) is maladroit. An Italian who is *mancino* is left-handed—or treacherous. In many cultures dealings with the dead are carried out with the left hand, since its connotations are with the dark, the inept, the polluted, the obstinately unknowable. Leftness is commonly used to express whatever is outside the official life of the group.

Women have tended everywhere to be classified as "left." The feeling behind this is that they are irrational, lower, dark, marginal, fluid, cold, deceitful, and generally sinister. Men (on the other hand) are high, dry, straightforward, lucid, bright—and right.

On the continent of Europe, couples when marrying give each other rings, a custom that is spreading as equality strengthens between the sexes. Among post-Reformation Anglo-Saxons, only the woman has traditionally worn the ring, on the fourth finger of the left or "female" hand. The "ring" or "gold" finger was believed to have a direct arterial connection with the left-leaning, passionate, irrational, but—one hoped—faithful heart.

Left-handed people have always been pressured by the majority to conform. Even when not forced by anxious parents and misguided educators to use the less capable hand, they have had for example to shake hands with the right because other people do it, or to use tools constructed for right-handers. More men than women are in fact left-handed; in the ancient world they had worse difficulties than we, because it mattered desperately in battle that your shield arm covered your heart, while the other did the fighting.

In many societies where eating is done with the hands, the left hand is disqualified as profane, and kept for polluting and unpleasant tasks deemed beneath the dignity of the right. Roman diners put left hands out of commission by leaning on their left elbows as they reclined at meals, and eating with the right; a left-hander attempting to use his more capable hand would find himself lying down the wrong way round.

Modern science has shown us that the right hand has usually been governed by the *left* side of the brain all along—and vice versa. Speech, even in most left-handers, is a function mainly of the left brain. The right half of the brain has become the subject recently of much attention and speculation: it is as large, as complex, as the left half, but we are far less certain what it does, apart from its evident governance over perceptions of space, including the ability to recognize faces.

"Left" and "right" have lost some of their force as metaphors, as the strength ebbs from the prejudice against women which they used to express. But left- and right-handedness have acquired a powerful new fascination: they are now recognized as clues, the full significance of which remains mysterious, to the workings of the human brain.

•

Copyright Acknowledgments

The authors are grateful to the following students for permission to reprint their essays: Cecile Dean ("Math Anxiety: The Real Social Disease"), Jeff Haas ("The Common Stone"), Marcelo Olenewa ("Effective Driving"), Mayra Perea ("Canadian and American: Is There a Difference?"), and Sandra Stewart ("*Aladdin* and *Beauty and the Beast*").

The authors also gratefully acknowledge the following for permission to reprint previously published material:

John Allemang. "Bedtime Stories," from *The Globe and Mail*, 7 February 1991. Reprinted by permission.

Maya Angelou. "The Fight," from *I Know Why Caged Birds Sing*.

Gerald Astor. "What Your Body Language Says About You," from *Seventeen® Magazine*, 1981. Reprinted by permission of the author.

Margaret Atwood. "The Great Communicator," from *The Globe and Mail*, 24 January 1991, p. C1. Reprinted by permission.

Russell Baker. "The Plot Against People," from *The New York Times*, 18 June 1968. Copyright © 1968 by The New York Times Company. Reprinted by permission.

H.J. Barrie. "In the Market for a Mate? Shop Around," from *The Globe and Mail*, 21 March 1994. Reprinted by permission of the author.

Neil Bissoondath. "I'm Not Racist But ...," from *Between Worlds* (Penguin Books, 1989).

Arthur Black. "Lingophobia ... Anxiety of Choice," from *The Globe and Mail*.

Rachel Carson. "A Fable for Tomorrow," from *Silent Spring*, by Rachel Carson. Copyright © 1962 by Rachel L. Carson, renewed 1990 by Roger Christie. Reprinted by permission of Houghton Mifflin Co. All rights reserved.

Barry Chodirker. "What We Write Reveals How We Think," from *Canadian Secretary* 12, no. 3 (September 1987). Reprinted by permission.

Barbara Ehrenreich. "Angry Young Men: Is Violence a Shortcut to Repect for Young Men with No Future?" from *The Globe and Mail*.

Joseph Epstein. "The Virtues of Ambition," from *Ambition: The Secret Passion*, by Joseph Epstein. Copyright © 1980 by Joseph Epstein. Reprinted by permission of Georges Borchardt, Inc., for the author.

Susan Estrich. "Separate Is Better," from *The New York Times Magazine*, 22 May 1994. Copyright © 1994 by The New York Times Company. Reprinted by permission.

Judith Finlayson. "Math's Multiple Choices," from *Homemaker's Magazine,* 22 May 1994. Reprinted by permission.

Northrop Frye. "Don't You Think It's Time to Start Thinking?" from *The Toronto Star,* 25 January 1986. Reprinted by permission of the Estate of Northrop Frye.

Catherine George. "Curtain Up," from *The Toronto Star,* 7 September 1991. Reprinted with permission – The Toronto Star Syndicate.

Bob Green. Lines adapted from "Unwritten Laws Which Rule Our Lives."

Susan Jacoby. "When Bright Girls Decide That Math Is 'a Waste of Time.'" Copyright © 1983 by Susan Jacoby. Reprinted by permission of Georges Borchardt, Inc., for the author.

Terry E. Johnson. "Slang: Language That's Out of Date," from *The Toronto Star,* 23 March 1985.

John Kettle. "Back to the Land? No Way—Big Cities Are Here to Stay," originally published in the Trends column, Fifth Column, *The Globe and Mail,* 16 September 1992. Reprinted by permission of the author.

Michele Landsberg. "Let's Just Shamble Back to the Cave for Some Bone Gnawing," from *The Globe and Mail,* 11 April 1987. Reprinted by permission.

Margaret Laurence. "The Shack," from *Heart of a Stranger* (1976), by Margaret Laurence. Used by permission of the Canadian Publishers, McClelland & Stewart, Toronto.

Barbara Lawrence. "Four-Letter Words Can Hurt You," from *The New York Times,* 27 October 1973. Copyright © 1973 by The New York Times Company. Reprinted by permission.

Jennifer Lewington. "Maths a Plus, Schoolgirls Assured," from *The Globe and Mail,* 8 February 1992, and "Math Myths Have Got to Go, Forum Told," from *The Globe and Mail,* 7 May 1994. Both reprinted by permission.

J. Anthony Lukas. "Pinball," from "The Inner Game of Pinball," from *The Atlantic Monthly,* 1979.

Edward McCourt. "The Little Things," from *The Yukon and the Northwest* (Macmillan, 1969).

Malcolm X. "Prison Studies," from *The Autobiography of Malcolm X,* by Malcolm X, with the assistance of Alex Haley. Copyright © 1964 by Alex Haley and Malcolm X and copyright © 1965 by Alex Haley and Betty Shabazz. Reprinted by permission of Random House, Inc.

Gary W. Pinder. "Clone Farms: Let's Bring a Capital Idea to 'Life,' " from *The Globe and Mail,* 9 December 1993.

J.B. Priestley. "Wrong Ism," from *Essays of Five Decades* (A.D. Peters and Co. Ltd., 1968). Reprinted by permission of the Peters Fraser & Dunlop Group Ltd.

James C. Rettie. "'But a Watch in the Night': A Scientific Fable," from *Forever the Land,* by Russell and Kate Lord, eds. Copyright 1950 by Harper & Brothers, renewed copyright © 1978 by Russell and Kate Lord. Reprinted by permission of HarperCollins Publishers, Inc.

Lionel Ruby. "What Kind of Language Are You Using?" from *The Art of Making Sense,* by Lionel Ruby and Robert E. Yarber. Copyright 1954, © 1968 by Lionel Ruby. Copyright © 1974 by Harper & Row, Publishers, Inc. Reprinted by permission of HarperCollins Publishers, Inc.

Bertrand Russell. "What I Have Lived For," from *The Autobiography of Bertrand Russell.* Copyright © The Bertrand Russell House. Reprinted by permission of the publisher, George Allen and Unwin, Ltd.

Leslie C. Smith. "Haberdashery: Blue Jeans Born to Last," from *The Globe and Mail,* 12 March 1992. Reprinted by permission.

Alexander Solzhenitsyn. "The Bonfire and the Ants," from *Stories and Prose Poems* (Farrar Giroux Inc.).

Bob Swift. "On Reading Trash," from the *Miami Herald,* 1985.

Judy Syfers. "I Want a Wife," reprinted by permission of *Ms. Magazine,* copyright © 1970.

Judith Viorst. "Friends, Good Friends—and Such Good Friends," copyright © 1977 by Judith Viorst. Originally appeared in *Redbook.* Reprinted with permission.

Margaret Visser. "Hand Over Hand," from *Saturday Night,* May 1990. Reprinted by permission.

Kurt Vonnegut. "How to Write with Style," reprinted by permission of International Paper.

Tom Wolfe, "Columbus and the Moon," reprinted from *The New York Times,* 29 July 1979. Copyright © 1979 by The New York Times Company. Reprinted by permission.

Index

To the owner of this book

We hope that you have enjoyed *Reading Writing: Essay Strategies for Canadian Students,* and we would like to know as much about your experiences with this text as you would care to offer. Only through your comments and those of others can we learn how to make this a better text for future readers.

School _____ Your instructor's name _____

Course _____ Was the text required? _____ Recommended? _____

1. What did you like the most about *Reading Writing?*

_____

_____

_____

2. How useful was this text for your course?

_____

_____

_____

3. Do you have any recommendations for ways to improve the next edition of this text?

_____

_____

_____

4. In the space below or in a separate letter, please write any other comments you have about the book. (For example, please feel free to comment on reading level, writing style, terminology, design features, and learning aids.)

_____

_____

_____

_____

Optional

Your name _____ Date _____

May Nelson Canada quote you, either in promotion for *Reading Writing* or in future publishing ventures?

Yes _____ No _____

Thanks!

FOLD HERE

MAIL ⮞ POSTE

Canada Post Corporation / Société canadienne des postes

Postage paid
if mailed in Canada

Port payé
si posté au Canada

**Business
Reply**

**Réponse
d'affaires**

0107077099   01

TAPE SHUT

TAPE SHUT

Nelson

0107077099-M1K5G4-BR01

Nelson Canada
College Editorial Department
1120 Birchmount Rd.
Scarborough, ON M1K 9Z9

PLEASE TAPE SHUT. DO NOT STAPLE.